PRAISE FOR *SHAPING SOCIAL JUSTICE LEADERSHIP*

"*Shaping Social Justice Leadership: Insights of Women Educators Worldwide* is a powerful text dominated by multiple voices that speak up and speak back to the challenges women educators face in their everyday lives. It is impossible to read this text and not share the joys, sorrows, successes, and anxieties embedded in the narratives. This text is a renewed call for social justice leadership—leadership that matters."
  —Tanya Fitzgerald, professor of Educational Leadership and Management, La Trobe University, Melbourne, Australia

"Socially just leadership as everyday practice is at the heart of these twenty-three narratives of women researchers and leaders in *Shaping Social Justice Leadership: Insights of Women Educators Worldwide*. These stories from fourteen countries illustrate how cultural context intersects with gender, race, ethnicity, and class to frame personal leadership possibilities, while exemplifying how social justice values can be embedded in everyday actions and relationships. This text, the work of the Women Leading Education network, takes up the cause of trans-national feminism, with all its differences, to necessarily focus again on the uses and abuses of power, promote human rights, and condemn violence and discrimination against women and girls. Educational leadership, enacted with a moral purpose, remains central. It is a text that provides hope as well as ways of leading for more equitable social, economic and political change within a globalized context of intensified insecurity."
  —Jill Blackmore, professor and director, Deakin University Centre for Research in Educational Futures and Innovation, Melbourne, Australia

"Drawn from the voices and experiences of female leaders across different cultures, *Shaping Social Justice Leadership* is a must read for anyone interested in leadership and education for social justice. Hearing the personal stories of resilient, courageous women provides opportunity for all of us to reflect on past experiences as well as renew the energy and commitment necessary to overcome injustice in both personal and global settings. Read it and you will be inspired!"
  —Patricia Neudecker, superintendent, Oconomowoc Area School District, Wisconsin; president of the American Association of School Administrators, 2011–2012

"*Shaping Social Justice Leadership: Insights of Women Educators Worldwide* is the story of the struggle, motivation, and will to achieve of every woman in the world. The stories and insights presented relate not only to the challenges of Afghan women, but to all women. While women have a long way to go, the words of Lyman, Strachan, and Lazaridou will inspire readers about a world where all can have access to justice."

—Samira Hamidi, Afghanistan Country Director, Afghan Women's Network, Kabul, Afghanistan

"*Shaping Social Justice Leadership* breaks new ground in studies on education and social justice by bringing together an unprecedented conceptual richness and innovation combined with real-life narrations on the practice of leadership by leading women drawn from across continents and countries. The fact that these stories of leadership are drawn from a deliberate cross-national sample of education leaders breaks the ethnocentrism so evident in the major books and journal articles on leaders, leadership and social justice emanating from the West. But these are not 'mere stories'; each narrative is deeply grounded within theory and data that emerge naturally from the life-experiences of those who lead in difficult contexts and, quite often, against the grain of an androcentrism afflicting scholarship and practice on education leadership that remains susceptible to corporate models of how to lead. The book's additional value lies in its valuing of complexity; gone are those simplistic and formulaic accounts of 'ten steps to leadership' or 'leadership in thirty minutes.' You are drawn as reader into the many layers of leadership, its contradictions and contestations, its emotions and politics, its spirituality and the resilience of its women practitioners."

—Jonathan Jansen, rector and vice-chancellor of the University of the Free State, Bloemfontein, South Africa

SHAPING SOCIAL JUSTICE LEADERSHIP

INSIGHTS OF WOMEN EDUCATORS WORLDWIDE

*Linda L. Lyman, Jane Strachan,
and Angeliki Lazaridou*

Published in partnership with the
American Association of School Administrators

ROWMAN & LITTLEFIELD EDUCATION

A division of
ROWMAN & LITTLEFIELD PUBLISHERS, INC.
Lanham • New York • Toronto • Plymouth, UK

Published in partnership with the American Association of School Administrators

Published by Rowman & Littlefield Education
A division of Rowman & Littlefield Publishers, Inc.
A wholly owned subsidary of The Rowman & Littlefield Publishing Group, Inc.
4501 Forbes Boulevard, Suite 200, Lanham, Maryland 20706
www.rowman.com

10 Thornbury Road, Plymouth PL6 7PP, United Kingdom

British Library Cataloguing in Publication Information Available

Library of Congress Cataloging-in-Publication Data

Lyman, Linda L.
  Shaping social justice leadership : insights of women educators worldwide / Linda L. Lyman, Jane Strachan, and Angeliki Lazaridou.
      p. cm.
  Includes bibliographical references and index.
  ISBN 978-1-61048-563-0 (cloth : alk. paper)—ISBN 978-1-61048-564-7 (pbk. : alk. paper)—ISBN 978-1-61048-565-4 (electronic)
  1. Women educators—Cross-cultural studies. 2. Educational leadership—Social aspects—Cross-cultural studies. 3. Social justice—Cross-cultural studies. I. Strachan, Jane. II. Lazaridou, Angeliki, 1969- III. Title.
  LB2837.L96 2012
  371.20082—dc23

                                                    2012005177

Printed in the United States of America

We dedicate this book to women leaders everywhere,
and to all women who aspire to lead.
May these stories from women
leaders on five continents
inspire courageous
actions.

—L.L.L., J.S., and A.L.

I dedicate this book to my husband, Joe, a steady and unfailing force in my life, and my son Alexander, the brightest star of my life, and the reason for dreaming and striving for a better world.

—A.L.

I dedicate this book to my sons Matthew and Simon Thomson. I am very proud of you both.

—J.S.

With love and gratitude I dedicate this book to my phenomenal family—my husband Dave Weiman, who shares my passion for social justice; my daughter Elaine Gale and son-in-law Roc Lowry; grandsons Jack, Charlie, and Thomas Gale, sons of daughter-in-law Kristine and my son David Gale; grandsons Tyler and Carter Gale, sons of daughter-in-law Beth Bear and my son Steve Gale.

—L.L.L.

CONTENTS

LIST OF TABLES

FOREWORD

Shaping Social Justice Leadership: Insights of Women Educators Worldwide begins with the question "How have the lived experiences of women educational leaders influenced their lives and professional/leadership decisions?" Make no mistake, this book has more in common with Kate Millet, Betty Friedan, Germaine Greer, and Carol Gilligan than with traditional educational leadership researchers, past or present. The authors, Linda Lyman from the United States, Jane Strachan from New Zealand, and Angeliki Lazaridou from Greece, have created a book in which successful school, school district, and university leaders teach social justice by exposing and academically exploring the most personal of personally lived realities. The personal narratives in the book are not narratives in the traditional educational leadership research tradition of reflective/narrative inquiry. What they have done is to marry feminist theories to narrative methods, and the result is a new methodological genre for studying social justice. The book takes the reader from the individual and the personal to the international/global/collective (and that explicitly includes men/educators) on the metaphorical journey.

As a university professor of educational leadership, I am not used to reading personal details of women's lives revealed page after page. But that's what you and I are being asked—no, invited—to read in this book. Here are twenty-three women from fourteen countries, all of whom society would call successful educational leaders. But the details of their journeys have not been like anything you or I could imagine. Nothing is made up or hidden behind abstract concepts. Their experiences are all very real for these Women Leading Education Across the Continents (WLE). And if that is so, then how many other countless women educational leaders have also had to work through pain, anger, violence, and struggle? As a man, I can't even imagine. So, for me, calling this book a *classic* or a *gift* is to say that I don't have the right words to capture what you find here.

Be prepared for the unexpected, for powerful ideas and powerful women to come alive, in sadness and joy; and, for all of us who have come to social justice as a central educational construct, their words tell us that our social justice work is right in front of our faces. I end not with my own words, but rather with their words from the final chapter: "Just as there are silent 'no applause' separations between movements in symphonies, there are times in our lives when we cannot hear the music, do not know if we are being heard. We need each other. Consider this book your invitation to join in creating new possibilities."

Ira Bogotch, Professor of Educational Leadership,
Florida Atlantic University

FOREWORD

Education has a vital part to play in all societies. It is both the channel through which values, customs, and culture are passed from one generation to the next and the most potent means for bringing about change. As educators, the women whose voices are heard in this book are involved in both, that is, in passing on what seems to them best in their heritage and in bringing about change for social justice.

The authors of the book have woven together the narratives of twenty-three women leaders and educators. These narratives look back at the formative experiences which have made the women who they are, with the values they have chosen to inherit, and look forward to the changes that they seek to bring about through their own work and through the examples they set. The book has been authored by three of the women whose stories also appear within it. They have taken the raw material of the twenty-three stories, each one of which is idiosyncratic in content and style, and formed an integrated whole of the book, which makes fascinating and absorbing reading. Although there are similar and overlapping features in each of the original stories, the authors have analyzed the themes that emerged and chosen to highlight one particular theme for each contributor, allowing her words to illuminate that theme.

The twenty-three women are part of a larger group: Women Leading Education, which was first brought together in 2007 through the leadership of Helen Sobehart, whose narrative is also included in the book and whose reflections bring the book to a close in the Afterword. Fuller information about the group and about the twenty-three who contributed to this book is included in chapter 1, but it is important to note the range of countries and continents that are represented in this book (see table 1.1).

Unlike most books on educational leadership, this volume therefore represents the experiences and views from many different countries, fourteen in all. Most literature on educational leadership takes at best an Anglophone stance, that is, drawn mainly from the United States or the United Kingdom and to some extent from Australia and New Zealand. There are some honorable exceptions, which seek to represent the practice of educational leadership and the application of theory to a wider field (see, for example, Harber and Davies 1997; Foskett and Lumby 2003). However, there is a dearth of literature in the field of educational leadership that draws on the experience of those outside the Anglophone world. A major part of this book's importance is that it offers the viewpoints of individuals both from the dominant English speaking countries and from elsewhere: Brazil, Greece, Jamaica, South Africa, Ghana, Tanzania, Uganda, Pakistan, Thailand, and Hong Kong. The book therefore offers a valuable breadth of cultural experiences, but the uniqueness of the book lies elsewhere. It comes from the fact that the voices are those of women leaders who bring to their work the insights of those who are "outsiders" as far as leadership is concerned.

There is a widespread assumption that leaders "should be" male (Schein 2007), and this expectation appears to hold good across continents and age groups and to a large extent is shared by both men and women. Assumptions that men are natural leaders create inbuilt barriers to women who aspire to leadership positions. Although the barriers are surmountable and are becoming more permeable, particularly in Western societies, there are still very firm expectations about the place of males and females in the stories presented in this volume. In social settings, we commonly make assumptions about people which are based on categorizations of gender, ethnicity, and so on, which in turn draw on stereotypes (for a fuller discussion, see Lumby with Coleman, 2007). Gender stereotypes are particularly resilient, casting the male as generally assertive, strong, decisive, and able to see the "big picture" and the female as supportive, nurturing, and good at detail. Overcoming gender or other stereotypes is difficult, and women experience that difficulty particularly when aspiring to leadership positions and when carrying out a leadership role where they are likely to be more prone to criticism than a male equivalent. For example, Still (2006) refers to the femininity/competence double bind by which a woman leader is either judged as too "feminine" and therefore unsuited for leadership or, if she adopts a "masculine," tough style of leadership, seen as not feminine and therefore criticized as strange and betraying her sex. Gender stereotypes are particularly strong, but negative stereotypes tend to be attached to anyone who is not in the dominant group, for example, ethnic minorities, those in a lower class, or those belonging to a religion which is not the norm in their country. All the women recognized that there were difficulties in being women leaders. However, this book is not simply about women and leadership; it is about leadership for social justice. The formative experiences of the women have given them insight as "outsiders." Discriminatory issues identified in relation to gender and leadership are largely the same as those that apply to any "outsider" who aspires to leadership. The stories of the women in this book bear testament to the impact of stereotypes, with many of them experiencing the impact of class and/or ethnicity as well as gender stereotyping.

Despite having to face some form of discrimination based on stereotypes, the voices of the women in this book are positive and strong. It is typical of their stories that they can look back and pinpoint an event or events that opened their eyes to make them understand about privilege and discrimination in society. It is also typical that they have learned from their experiences and used them to work for social justice, refusing to accept the status quo and using their own agency and determination to change circumstances for themselves and others. Social justice is the focus of the book and is therefore discussed throughout, but here I would define it in its simplest form of human rights, giving everyone equality no matter what their race, gender, or any other quality. However, this definition does raise the question of what sort of equality? Are we are seeking equality of opportunity or equality of outcome? Some years ago I received a letter from a Chinese woman scholar recounting her experiences:

> Women and men are like two athletes running on the same track. But the men run free while the women balance children in one hand and kitchenware in the other. And even if the encumbered women run as fast as the men, people then criticize them for not running gracefully. (Fu Jun, personal correspondence, 1995)

Where individuals are disadvantaged at the start of a race, pure equality of opportunity is not necessarily going to mean that they have an equal chance of winning a prize when other contestants have never experienced disadvantage and "run free." For equality of outcome, those who are disadvantaged may need additional support or special circumstances. In the case of those who are "outsiders" as potential leaders, this might mean having access to specialized training, focused mentoring, or affirmative action, as happened in Australia with the "femocrats" (Blackmore 1999) and is to some extent encompassed in South African legislation to put right the wrongs of apartheid (Grobler et al. 2006). The stories in this book illustrate women working for equality of outcomes, each striving in her own way to bring about change for social justice.

The book takes us through the challenges that the twenty-three women have faced, dealing with prejudice and overthrowing cultural expectations about the place of women. In this they act as role models and as pioneers of change. There is a strong focus on the values of social justice that motivate the women and on the ways in which they practice the leadership and scholarship which is authentic to them. The chapter which presents the qualities that the women have exhibited focuses on courage, perseverance, and speaking out, bringing our attention toward the outcomes of social justice. The aspect of opening up pathways for others is the particular focus of chapter 7 of the book, which concerns taking action for social justice, including political work, active mentoring, and, importantly, as scholars and writers using their public voice to bring about change for more equality of outcomes. The women have found their own pathways and in so doing have opened and continue to open opportunities for others. A note of warning is that the community of women scholars who have provided the impetus for this book is aging, with the majority of the contributors being over fifty years of age. It is therefore important that they work individually and as a group to recruit and mentor younger members to continue to work for social justice.

The book is not attempting to generalize about women and leadership, nor to say that social justice as an outcome of leadership is the province of women. The stories of the women who have emerged as leaders despite their "outsider" status help to illuminate problems and ways of addressing problems for all those who experience injustice and discrimination and focus the reader on the importance of values in leadership and of striving for social justice. This is particularly appropriate at a time when huge economic and environmental problems form the context in which we ask questions about the role of education in human society.

Marianne Coleman, Emeritus Reader, University of London

ACKNOWLEDGMENTS

This book was composed from contributions of many persons who helped in countless ways. Our first acknowledgment goes to the women who submitted their personal and professional narratives, for without their stories this book would not exist. Equally important has been the support, creativity, and leadership of Dr. Helen Sobehart. Planting the seed for this book, Helen said to Linda Lyman at the 2009 AASA conference after their workshop presentation, "I think there is a book in here." Not only is Helen the founding chair of the Women Leading Education Across the Continents (WLE) group, but her legacy continues in this book and other *possibilities* that have come to fruition because of her gifts as a leader.

Linda offers special thanks to reviewers of chapter drafts, who provided valuable feedback throughout the writing process: Dr. Kathleen Hickey, Dr. Jacqueline Oram-Sterling, Bridget Delaney Feldman, Douglas MacGowan, Dr. Elizabeth Reilly, Dr. Joe Fris, and Dr. Elaine Gale, her daughter. She is grateful for Illinois State University (ISU) doctoral students—research assistant Bridget Delaney Feldman, who found relevant literature, and Samantha Schopp, who integrated and formatted the references. Thanks also go to Dr. Patricia Klass (EAF department chair) and Dean Deborah Curtis for supporting Linda's attendance at the WLE international conferences.

Inspiration came from Linda's retired former colleague Dr. Dianne Ashby and from the practice of the Illinois Women Administrators to annually honor women's stories at the Dare to Be Great conference. Friends offered much needed encouragement—Linda J. Ging, Ann Grove, Dr. Nancy Sherman, Diane Brown, Dr. Margo Tennis, Sherrie Campbell, and her sister Dr. Margo Thompson. Finally, Linda acknowledges the unfailing support of her husband Dave Weiman, whose innumerable loving actions included hours of listening, proofing every page, and always bringing "a song of love and a rose in the winter time."

Jane would like to acknowledge and thank her wonderful women friends and colleagues who over the years have supported her social justice work in so many ways.

Angeliki wishes to acknowledge her husband, Dr. Joe Fris, for his unrelenting support during the times of writing, and also for his insights, ideas, and thoughts to make the chapters better. His editorial advice, in particular, was instrumental for the improvement of the chapters. She also extends a heartfelt acknowledgment to her colleague and dear friend, Linda Lyman, for inviting her to be a part of the writing team and for providing this opportunity to revel in the beauty and marvel of the world of personal stories.

Finally, collectively we are also grateful to several individuals from Rowman & Littlefield Education for encouragement and support received throughout the process. Tom Koerner, vice president and editorial director, and Kristina Mann, former acquisitions editor, gave us wise counsel during the proposal development process. AASA's Kitty Porterfield also provided encouragement and support during the proposal development process. We extend thanks also to Mary McMenamin, an RLE assistant editor, who skillfully facilitated the manuscript submission process and offered creativity and sound advice.

1

EXPLORING MEANING THROUGH PERSONAL NARRATIVES

It is our inward journey that leads us through time—forward or back, seldom in a straight line, most often spiraling. Each of us is moving, changing, with respect to others. As we discover, we remember, remembering we discover; and most intensely do we experience this when our separate journeys converge.

—Eudora Welty, *One Writer's Beginning*

We begin with questions leading to layers of meaning in the book. How have the lived experiences of women educational leaders influenced their lives and professional/leadership decisions? How do they view the meaning of their experiences? What meaning do their experiences hold for educational leadership as a field? How do their individual and collective commitments define social justice leadership? How have their separate journeys converged? We explore these and other layers of meaning in this book based on personal narratives from twenty-three women educators representing fourteen countries. All persons featured, including the authors, are members of an international research group that began in 2007 called Women Leading Education Across the Continents (WLE).

Whatever our country, WLE members have found much to learn from leadership experiences of women in other countries. Many educators embrace as a growing reality that in today's global community education is simultaneously a local and global experience. In the context of shaping social justice leadership, why explore meaning through personal narratives? Clearly expressed in all of the narratives was that life experiences created an awakening to gender and other social justice issues. Commitment to social justice leadership begins when the meanings of social injustice arise from lived experience.

Personal narratives offer a record of awakenings and stimulate reflection. In the words of Witherell and Noddings (1991), "Stories and narrative . . . provide meaning and belonging in our lives. They attach us to others and to our own histories by providing a tapestry rich with threads of time, place, characters, and even advice on what we might do with our lives" (1). Through the passages of our personal and professional journeys we continue to evolve. Our challenges or passages become our pathways as each of us "leads the spirit of social justice to where it needs to be" (Sobehart 2009, 220). The challenge of creating a book from these life history narratives was "to condense and draw meaning from them within and across" the participants (Huberman 1995, 128).

Organized into thematic chapters, the book offers women's experiences in their own words, as well as insights gleaned from the narratives, followed by selected scholarship. Coleman (2005) argues that giving voice to women and minorities "will lead to greater social justice in the vital field of education and an enrichment of the practice and theory of educational leadership" (18). In that spirit, we share personal narratives of our life experiences as educators committed to social justice leadership.

PURPOSE OF THE BOOK

The purpose of the book is to show what social justice leadership looks like and accomplishes in the lives, actions, and communities of women educational leaders worldwide. To do so we examine facets of social justice leadership illustrated in the lived experiences portrayed in the twenty-three narratives. The stories illuminate how women educators are shaping social justice leadership. We offer no generalizations about "all women" in any country. Each leader and context are unique, and essentializing is unwise (Lyman, Ashby, and Tripses 2005; McKenzie et al. 2008; Young 2003). Nevertheless, the narratives convey meaningful insights to any reader—female or male—confronting the challenges of social justice leadership.

In telling the stories we offer each other "situated knowledge" (Lave and Wenger, 1991), what has been true for us. We hope readers will experience how "narrative ways of knowing function collectively to affirm the values of multiplicity and connection" (Helle 1991, 49). The stories illustrate both diversity and the ways lives are connected. Coleman (2005) suggests that women and social justice issues are inherently linked because "half the population is female, and in most societies the differences in the ways that women and men are perceived work to the advantage of the male" (3). We call on educators—women and men—to devote renewed efforts to social justice issues, such as increasing opportunities for leadership roles for women, securing equal educational opportunities for girls, and eliminating policies and practices that unfairly limit the learning and lives of marginalized individuals and groups. Working together and learning from each other, we shape social justice leadership.

In this introductory chapter we present brief discussions of selected scholarship focused on defining social justice leadership, women's leadership in education, and the power of story and narrative. We present the historical background of the Women Leading Education Across the Continents (WLE) international research group and review the origin of the book. Tables display demographic information about the featured leaders and their careers. The conclusion unfolds an overview of the chapters as a preview of the book.

DEFINING SOCIAL JUSTICE LEADERSHIP: SELECTED SCHOLARSHIP

Whether in countries at the top or bottom of a variety of indicators of prosperity—such as GDP (gross domestic product), GNI (gross national income), or HDI (human development index)—research reveals patterns of gender-based discrimination that mean women have significantly less access to education, limited opportunities to participate in leadership roles, and lack of professional mobility and development (Coleman 2005; Magee 2001; Strachan et al. 2010). Issues of social justice for women and girls exist in both highly and less developed countries. Historically, according to Larson and Murtadha (2002), in the 1980s increases in the number of women professors in preparation programs in the United States "stimulated greater interest in issues of equity and gender within the field" of educational leadership (138). A dearth of information exists, however, about women in leadership, particularly in countries regarded as "developing." Women scholars have been central to the research about social justice leadership that began to emerge at the end of the twentieth century in Western countries (Anyon 2005; Delpit 1995). Continuing that trend, this book contributes to the discourse about social justice leadership, including how it is defined.

Definitions are important because our understanding of complex concepts influences our actions (Lakoff and Johnson 1980; Lyman and Gardner 2008; Rost 1993; Senge 1990). Social justice is a focus of scholars and practitioners. In addition to issues of gender, the women leaders featured in this book are interested in the social justice issues of class, race, ethnicity, inclusion of different abilities, sexual orientation, religion, language learners, and other diversities that relate to marginalization in schools and society through exclusionary processes or attitudes.

Larson and Murtadha (2002) write that "today, scholars are increasingly concerned with articulating the connections between their theoretical understandings of leadership for social justice and the everyday practices of school leaders" (126). In terms of the discourse about social justice leadership, in particular how it can be defined, the authors of this book contend that ultimately we define social justice leadership through our actions. We agree with Bogotch (2002), that "there can be no fixed or predictable meanings of social justice prior to actually engaging in educational leadership practices" (153).

Social justice can be defined from a variety of approaches. An example of a commonsense nonacademic definition is a statement from the *Annual Report of the Aboriginal and Torres Strait Islander Social Justice Commission*:

> Social justice is what faces you in the morning. It is awakening in a house with an adequate water supply, cooking facilities and sanitation. It is the ability to nourish your children and send them to a school where their education not only equips them for employment but reinforces their knowledge and understanding of their cultural inheritance. It is the prospect of genuine employment and good health: a life of choices and opportunity, free from discrimination. (Dodson 1993)

Goldfarb and Grinberg (2002) use more academic language, defining social justice in terms of human rights and fairness. They believe that social justice work is about changing the system through "the exercise of altering these [institutional and organizational] arrangements by actively engaging in reclaiming, appropriating, sustaining, and advancing inherent human rights of equity, equality, and fairness in social, economic, educational, and personal dimensions" (162). Marshall and Ward (2004) take a legal approach, maintaining that "social justice means ensuring that laws for individual rights are observed so that access to educational services is available . . . social justice can mean finding ways to 'fix' those with inequitable access" (534).

Other definitions focus on achievement of social justice specifically in education. For example, Theoharis (2007) grounds his definition of social justice in the daily realities of school leadership, of what principals can do to advance social justice through "their advocacy, leadership practice, and vision" (223). He offers a definition that "centers on addressing and eliminating marginalization in schools" (223). In a proposal for educating leaders for social justice, US scholars McKenzie, Christman, Hernandez, Fierro, Capper, Dantley, Gonzalez, Cambron-McCabe, and Scheurich (2008) argue for a nonessentialized definition, but also for one that "links social justice with three goals: raising academic achievement, developing a critical consciousness, and inclusive practices" (116). They emphasize that there is no universal understanding of social justice leadership among scholars.

A Non-Western View

The goals McKenzie et alii (2008) advocate are in contrast with the Tongan conceptions of social justice and leadership presented by Fua (2007). He stresses that Western conceptions of social justice often reflect the ideas of

John Rawls. Fua writes that "according to Rawls (1971) social justice is based on Western ideology, beliefs and value systems that support ideologies of human rights, equality and democracy as believed by most English-speaking Western societies" (673). Fua argues that "social justice is a concept that is already embedded within each South Pacific knowledge system in various degrees and form" (674).

From Fua's (2007) perspective, social justice leadership is not defined as working for the rights of individuals but is based on the Tongan conceptualization of social justice called *Faka'apa'apa*, translated to mean "respect." "*Faka'apa'apa* operates from a collective perspective where the good of the collective is valued over the individual. *Faka'apa'apa* begins with an individual giving, sharing, considering and listening to the other; it is fundamentally about honouring and protecting the dignity of the other" (677). According to Fua,

> Tongan conceptualization of social justice is based on *Faka'apa'apa* as it is displayed through *Va* or relationships. Such a relationship is based on rank, status and consequently on equity rather than equality as in comparison to social justice as defined by Rawls (1971). Further to this, social justice in the Tongan conceptualization is relationship-based and therefore focuses more on the collective good over the individual. (679)

A leader in the Tongan context is evaluated, then, not on technical skills of leadership but more on behaviors that display *Faka'apa'apa* by building relationships. In the Tongan context, "social justice (based on *Faka'apa'apa*) and leadership (based on *Va*) are intertwined, fundamental and essential to ensuring effective leadership" (681).

Definition through Actions

The diversity of the cultures and social justice work of the women leaders who submitted narratives for this book incline us to support the concept that social justice leadership is best defined through actions. Strachan (2005) connects social justice with feminist leadership when she articulates that no matter what definition a person holds of feminist leadership she would expect to see the following actions: "working for social justice and equity, empowering others, establishing a caring environment (the ethic of care), sharing power (giving away control and working alongside others), being outspoken and challenging injustices, promoting anti-violence and using consensual decision-making processes" (49).

We are influenced by Rapp's (2002) conceptualization of the importance of actions: "Perhaps the greatest challenge for educators committed to social justice, then, is to remember that our actions can inform our theories as much as our theories inform our actions" (241). We concur with Bogotch (2002), that "the concepts of social justice and educational leadership provide for socially constructed agreements to emerge around specific problems, solutions, and courses of action. By connecting social justice to educational leadership, we can *direct* these possibilities toward creating new and just communities" (154). We believe that the approach of defining social justice through actions demystifies the term and may lead others to include social justice in their leadership work.

Complexity arises because countries differ and exhibit the whole range of prosperity indicators—such as, for example, the GDP (gross domestic product), GNI (gross national income), and HDI (human development index), which measures three dimensions: life expectancy, education index, and standard of living. Defining social justice is also complex because of differences in knowledge systems, culture, and leadership approaches. Skrla, McKenzie, and Scheurich (2007) state that "work focused explicitly on the intersections of these two areas of scholarship—social justice and international educational leadership—however, has been extremely scarce" (784). They conclude, "Thus, much remains unknown, even at this beginning stage, about how leadership for social justice might operate in other international settings that have histories and culture vastly different from these" (786).

WOMEN'S LEADERSHIP IN EDUCATION: SELECTED SCHOLARSHIP

The knowledge base on women's leadership in education is a relatively recent development. According to Shakeshaft (1999), the research on women's leadership that emerged in the United States in the 1970s was a response to the androcentric research dominating the field of educational leadership at that time. The earliest citation in Shakeshaft's (1999) six-stage historical categorization of the literature on women's leadership is Smith's (1979) *Ella Flagg Young: Portrait of a Leader*. Informed by the work of Lawrence-Lightfoot and Davis (1997), we carry that spirit of portraiture into this book.

For the most part the literature on women's leadership has come from developed countries; however, the oppression of women is an accepted pattern of behavior exhibited most often in developing countries with strong gendered cultures (Coleman 2005; Magee 2001; Nussbaum 2004; Strachan et al. 2010). The Western literature is relevant, but "research is needed that is undertaken in diverse cultural contexts" (Strachan et al. 2010, 66). This book is in part an answer to that need. As Shakeshaft (1999) states,

> Trying to document the number of women in school administration worldwide is even more difficult; administrative titles and jobs are not comparable across

countries and few countries keep accurate records by sex of administrative office holders. Thus there is no one study that gives a global snapshot of the number of women in school administration. (100)

The scholarship about women's leadership is still primarily Western. As Strachan et alii (2010) articulate, however, "The body of research on women in educational leadership in the developing world is small but growing" (66). Included in that growing international literature is Sobehart's (2009) *Women Leading Education Across the Continents*, an edited compilation of papers presented by scholars at the 2007 WLE Rome conference. The only other book that addresses women and school leadership from an international perspective (Reynolds 2002) is neither as current nor as comprehensive, only including chapters written by women from five English-speaking countries.

Four groundbreaking scholars in the study of women's leadership are WLE members whose stories are contained in the book, beginning with Charol Shakeshaft, who in 1987 published *Women in Educational Administration*, now in its fifth printing. With this book, research on women's leadership became academically respectable. The book is typically cited in reviews of the women's leadership literature. Women's leadership and associated topics continue to be included in Shakeshaft's research agenda.

Jane Strachan, New Zealand, has published research on women's leadership since 1993. Beginning in 1998, her writing includes advocacy for feminist leadership, and recent publications report on her work in Vanuatu and the Solomon Islands. Her teaching and research interests are focused on educational leadership, social justice, gender, women, policy development, and Pacific education.

Marianne Coleman, United Kingdom, began scholarship on women's leadership with a chapter she was invited to write in a 1994 book coedited by two of her colleagues. At the last moment it was decided there should be a chapter on women, and since she was the only woman on the team she was asked to write it. Writing the chapter launched her interest in women's leadership, and she has been researching gender and leadership ever since. For example, she completed two national surveys of headteachers (principals) of high schools in England, reporting on the first survey in *Women as Headteachers: Striking the Balance* (2002).

Finally, Margaret Grogan, United States/Australia, is a prolific scholar who has contributed to knowledge about women superintendents. In 1996, she published her first book, *Voices of Women Aspiring to the Superintendency*, based on her 1994 dissertation research. Then she coauthored in 2000, with Mary Gardiner and Ernestine Enomoto, a book titled *Coloring Outside the Lines: Mentoring Women into Educational Leadership*, a significant contribution to the scholarship on mentoring.

Margaret's latest book, coauthored with Charol Shakeshaft, is *Women and Educational Leadership* (2011). Based on a review of recurring themes in the literature on women's leadership, they name five approaches that characterize the ways women lead: "*leadership for learning, leadership for social justice, relational leadership, spiritual leadership,* and *balanced leadership*" (2). In the book they argue that a cognitive shift has occurred "away from conceiving of organizational leadership as residing primarily in an individual" (3). Reconceptualizing, they offer the view that "diverse collective leadership" is an emerging leadership practice that builds on approaches common to women's leadership and represents a new way (41).

THE POWER OF STORY AND NARRATIVE: SELECTED SCHOLARSHIP

We believe the book will inspire readers to action through powerful narratives that stimulate personal reflection. The stories communicate the authenticity and integrity that matter to leadership. "Whether direct or indirect, leaders fashion stories—principally stories of identity. It is important that a leader be a good storyteller, but equally crucial that the leader embody that story in his or her life" (Gardner 1995, ix). As Polkinghorne (1988) states unequivocally, "People conceive of themselves in terms of stories" (105).

Biklen, Marshall, and Pollard (2008) explain that narratives of *women's lives* are said to "make sense to many readers because these words refer to certain experiences that feminism has theorized within power relations" (465). Calling personal narratives a form of writing that second-wave feminism nurtured, they continue, "Many feminists used this form of analysis and writing to make visible those aspects of social life that were missing from public texts and to underscore how the personal is political" (452).

From his work with life histories, Huberman (1995) understood that "whole segments of life events, at least when reconstituted by an outsider, appeared almost accidental. Such a line of inquiry would then imply that only in retrospect does this career path, this event, this choice appear to be logical or inevitable" (134). Reflection on life history narratives of other people can provide "aha" moments about our own lives.

Narratives also have metaphorical power. These narratives are no exception. Much of the power of a reflective narrative or story can be in its use of metaphorical language. In *Metaphors We Live By*, scholars Lakoff and Johnson (1980) describe the power of metaphor to shape people's lives, explaining that "metaphor is typically viewed as characteristic of language alone, a matter of words rather than thought and action" (3). They argue, however, that metaphor is ubiquitous in our language and that our "concepts structure what we perceive, how we get around in the world, and how we relate to other people" (3).

Metaphors and Meaning

Making an important link, Lakoff and Johnson (1980) suggest that our language is a source of important evidence for what that conceptual system is like, concluding that "we act according to the way we conceive of things" (5). Searching for meaning, we are naturally drawn to the power of metaphor, either chosen consciously or embedded unconsciously in our own words or in poetry or cultural proverbs that speak to us. The metaphors that draw us contribute to our actions.

Several examples illustrate the variety and power of metaphoric language in the WLE narratives. With one exception of a narrative written in Greek and translated, the stories were written in English, the first language of thirteen of the women leaders who submitted stories. A maxim that recurred in different wordings in several narratives was the understanding that "information is power," expressed emphatically as "information really is power," and also as "knowledge is power." This juxtaposition of power with information suggests both a barrier and an approach to power for women, who when kept out of the upper circles of leadership can be cut off from valuable information.

Moving to more specific metaphors, one woman called her life story a "storied patchwork" and a "crazy quilt." She explained, "Nothing matches. Not even the threads that hold it together. It's as if the Divine Seamstress grabbed whatever materials were on hand at the moment." Literature on women leaders documents that most women do not have a career plan and that their career paths do not match the patterns typical for men. Echoing that thought, an African WLE leader quoted what she identified as an Asian proverb—"There are many paths to the top of the mountain but the view is always the same."

A Chinese traditional belief shared by another woman captures a belief pervasive in many other cultures, that "a girl without knowledge could be a virtue." A Greek woman told the story of the arched stone bridge at Arta, well known because according to the legend the wife of the head workman was sacrificed in its first arch so that the bridge would stay strong. Speaking of surviving a sacrifice of self, another woman's narrative included a poem ending with these words—"I decided it was time to . . . figure out how not to get caught dead."

Finally, one woman likened her quest for equality as a fisherwoman to experiences of discrimination in her academic career. She wrote "For me, fishing could be about doing my time," explaining in descriptive details how "each time I begin a fishing trip I feel marginalized. . . . I no longer hear the trickle of the stream because I am listening out for snide comments belittling my talents and superfluous snippets of unsolicited advice."

The Journey Metaphor

Recurring explicitly in fourteen of the narratives was the journey metaphor, undoubtedly in part because the invitation was to submit the story of your personal and/or professional journey. One woman titled her narrative "Intertwining Journeys," and elaborated this image for how her personal and professional journeys combined in complex ways. Another created the title "My Journey to Ithaca," writing a personal tale with echoes of Homer's *Odyssey*. It is a story of departure, struggle, overcoming trials, and eventually a return home to Greece and dreams come true.

One woman's narrative featured an extensive reflection on a labyrinth, an example of a form found many places in the world. In her narrative, titled "Pondering Power—Line or Labyrinth," she describes walking an actual labyrinth. Reflecting on that experience, the metaphor captures the entanglement of leadership and power in her journey. Finally, a woman expressed sadness about her beloved grandmother traveling "to the Ancestors' Land" unexpectedly. The phrase *Ancestors' Land* serves as a metaphoric reminder of our debt to past generations and of the reality that journeys end.

Because the narratives submitted are descriptions of life journeys, they are by definition metaphorical, whatever the language used. As Bateson (1989) explains, "Each of us constructs a life that is her own central metaphor for thinking about the world. But of course these lives do not look like parables or allegories. Mostly, they look like ongoing improvisations" (241). Each narrative in this book offers a glimpse of another way to think about one's own world. Additional words from Bateson (1989) reinforce the importance of sharing our stories. She articulates how "for all of us, continuing development depends on nurture and guidance long after the years of formal education, just as it depends on seeing others ahead on the road with whom it is possible to identify" (55). Reflecting on experiences in the book's narratives can stimulate reflections on personal experience in a way that clarifies the meaning, purpose, and future direction of one's leadership.

HISTORICAL BACKGROUND OF THE BOOK

This book is the product of the international research group Women Leading Education Across the Continents (WLE), whose members first came together as a group of invited scholars in 2007 at a conference in Rome on the Duquesne University Italian campus. The WLE group is the first ongoing international research group focused on the important topic of women's leadership in education. Members, including several men as well as women, now number around seventy persons from twenty-four different countries.

WLE Conferences

The first conference in 2007 was convened and hosted by the founding chair, Dr. Helen C. Sobehart, assisted by Melanie Simile as conference manager. At the time, Helen was serving as associate provost/academic vice president of Duquesne University in Pittsburgh, Pennsylvania. She was uniquely positioned to be the WLE founding chair, serving as chair of the University Council for Educational Administration (UCEA) Women's Special Interest Group (SIG). A former superintendent, she was also a longtime member of the American Association of School Administrators (AASA), a second organization with an interest in creating a forum for discussion and understanding of the underrepresentation of women in the highest levels of educational leadership across the globe, as well as the social and educational impact of that leadership gap. UCEA and AASA have continued to be ongoing conference sponsors. Dr. Michelle Young, executive director of UCEA, and Dr. Sharon Adams-Taylor, associate executive director of AASA, served as conference cohosts.

The first conference theme, "Women Leading Education Across the Continents: Sharing the Spirit, Fanning the Flame," was inspired by words of Hildegard of Bingen, a twelfth-century nun and mystic. She wrote, "The woman was in the flame, but not consumed by it. Rather, it came from her." These words offer support to women committed to *fanning the flame* of social justice leadership. Attending the first conference were thirty-seven scholars from countries around the world, representing every continent. The purposes of the conference were "to develop and share research-based papers which highlight the situation of women in basic and higher education leadership in major regions of the world, and second, to arrive at consensus around a common international research agenda and related work" (Sobehart 2009, 1). We shared research papers about our common interests in the status of women in leadership in basic and higher education, issues of equity affecting leadership opportunities for women, and securing equality of educational opportunities for girls in our countries. We also established several research groups. One group focused on beginning a global database; another group initiated the Sharing Our Stories project that led to this book.

The second conference was held at the University of Augsburg in Augsburg, Germany, in September 2009, with thirty-six attending. The theme was "Gender and Education: Toward New Strategies of Leadership and Power." The conference host was Dr. Hildegard Macha, professor and chair of Education and Adult Education at the University of Augsburg, assisted by Dr. Claudia

Fahrenwald, Dr. Quirin Bauer, and Melanie Simile. New members joined the group and, again, papers were presented. The database project (Demographics and Gender Audit) continued, a Survey/Interview Strategies group undertook piloting of an instrument, and Narrative Illumination was formalized as a group and charged with turning the Sharing Our Stories project into a book.

In 2010, Dr. Charol Shakeshaft, professor and chairperson of the Department of Educational Leadership at Virginia Commonwealth University, assumed leadership as the second WLE chair. A third conference was held in September 2011 in Volos, Greece, with thirty-six attending. The conference was hosted by Dr. Angeliki Lazaridou, lecturer and co-coordinator of the educational administration graduate program at the University of Thessaly in Volos. She was assisted by Dr. Whitney Sherman Newcomb, Kerry Robinson, and Apostolia Beka. The goal of this conference was to continue a research-based global conversation about the status of women in educational leadership. Again many new people attended and took part in the sharing of research papers. A fourth conference will be held in 2013.

WLE Projects and Goals

WLE intends to serve as a gender watch group, questioning and monitoring what is happening with gender equity globally. WLE is committed to continuing the biannual international conferences and ongoing collaboration. The Women Leading Education Across the Continents website (http://women-leading-education.com/) contains detailed information about research groups and goals as well as past conferences. An overall goal is to document the status of diverse women in educational leadership across continents. In 2007 the group began compiling a global database that could be updated and disseminated to document where women are in the education continuum, as students, workers, and as educators at all levels. This work continues.

A tangible accomplishment of WLE has been collective scholarship. The first publication, titled *Women Leading Education Across the Continents* (Sobehart 2009), contains papers presented at the 2007 conference. The second book, *Gender and Education–Towards New Strategies of Leadership and Power* (Macha, Fahrenwald, and Bauer 2011), provides the content from the second conference in 2009 at the University of Augsburg. A third publication is this book, *Shaping Social Justice Leadership*, a collaborative effort with stories shared from twenty-three members and written by an international trio of authors.

Origin of the Book

The coauthors of this book were members of the Sharing Our Stories research group initiated at the 2007 conference. The group's original intention was not to write a book, but rather to provide a forum for sharing our stories internally so that we could know one another better. In that spirit, we invited each conference participant "to submit the story of her personal and/or professional journey in whatever format and with whatever emphasis made sense and was comfortable for the individual." That invitation was issued through the listserv on November 5, 2007. The book project was officially launched at the 2009 conference after a keynote presentation by Linda Lyman based on themes in the twelve narratives then collected. With stories continuing to be submitted through the summer of 2010, we received a total of twenty-three personal narratives. They were shared on the WLE listserv as they arrived.

The narratives submitted for the book varied in length from 1,300 to 8,900 words. Most were written as informal reflections, but several were in formal academic style with references. One was written as a letter to a daughter. Several contained poetry. One person wrote in the third person, giving herself a fictitious name. Some were constructed as chronological autobiographies, but others were life histories with particular gender slants. Several could be called stream of consciousness pieces. Yet others can be classified as autoethnographies. The openness and nonspecific wording of the invitation to submit the narratives contributed to the richness of the data but increased the complexity of the thematic analysis.

Using NVivo 8 qualitative data analysis software to code the themes in the narratives, we identified commitment to social justice leadership as the overarching theme in all the narratives. Our stories elaborate how we have lived out the commitments to social justice that brought us to the WLE group. Further data analysis processes identified the recurring themes that are developed in the book chapters. A total of fifty-five NVivo coded data files were created. In the process of writing the chapters, we developed additional subthemes from ongoing analysis of these files.

THE FEATURED LEADERS

The WLE members featured have successfully confronted the worldwide cultural expectation that men, not women, will be the leaders. Even so, most struggle with balancing the needs and expectations of family and career. We describe the challenges that individual women faced as well as the leadership values, strengths, and skills that enabled them to build impressive careers. We portray them as skillful authentic leaders. We illustrate how they became committed to leadership for social justice and describe the outcomes of those commitments worldwide. We share their insights.

Basic Demographic Information

The twenty-three women leaders featured in the book are from different regions of the world, including countries representing the whole range of indicators of prosperity. They represent fourteen countries as well as a variety of professional positions. Many have faced discrimination, confronted cultural barriers to women leading, and experienced marginalization as women seeking and serving in leadership roles. Four of the leaders featured are from Africa (Ghana, South Africa, Tanzania, and Uganda), four are from Europe (United Kingdom and Greece), two are from the southwestern Pacific (New Zealand), three are from Asia (Hong Kong-China, Pakistan, and Thailand), one is from South America (Brazil), one is from the Caribbean (Jamaica), and eight are from North America (United States) including one with dual U.S./Australian citizenship.

Of the group, twenty-two have earned doctorates, and one is enrolled in a PhD program. A total of seven are the first members of their families to graduate from a university, and five others are the first female members of their families to graduate from a university. Three are the first in their families to earn graduate degrees. Twenty of those featured are mothers, with numbers of children parented ranging from one to six.

Table 1.1 presents basic demographic information about each leader: her country, university granting PhD, current professional position, and age. Reviewing the information about current professional positions, three women are retired. One person is a central office PK–12 administrator, and another is a journalist who does consulting and professional development work with teachers. A third is an academic project manager for a leadership development program. The other seventeen are at universities. Twelve are in faculty positions with titles ranging from lecturer to professor; five are in primarily administrative positions with titles ranging from consultant to director to department chair to dean. Another is a project manager (academic). Almost all hold or have held positions in higher education. They range in age from mid-thirties to late sixties, with one woman in her early seventies. Ten, the largest number, are in their fifties, with six in their sixties.

For full understanding in reviewing and comparing the position titles of the women in different countries, consider that titles in higher education mean different things in different systems. This adds a complexity to interpreting the tables. For example, in the United States the rank system for tenure-track faculty members typically has three levels, beginning with assistant professor, followed by associate professor, and ending with professor as the highest rank. In Greece, however, the four-level system begins with an initial tenure track lecturer position, followed by assistant professor, associate professor, professor, and the upon-retirement professor emeritus. Only persons at the professor or professor emeritus ranks are entitled to be addressed with the title "professor." A lecturer in Greece is equivalent to an assistant professor in the United States.

In New Zealand yet another variation is in place. A lecturer is approximately equivalent to an assistant professor, and then a senior lecturer is approximately equivalent to an associate professor. The third level is associate professor and/or reader, and the final level is professor. In most Commonwealth countries, "professor" is a title for only the most senior academics, with others known as lecturers, senior lecturers, and readers. Faculty titles of WLE participants include lecturer, senior lecturer, assistant professor, associate professor, professor, and emeritus reader. Administrative positions that have been "held" by the WLE participants include university president, dean, deputy dean, assistant dean, department president, department chair, co-coordinator, and director.

Demographics of Career Experiences

Demographic information about the career experiences of the featured leaders is also important. Career experiences individually and collectively represent many years of service to the causes we value. Table 1.2 displays an overview of career experiences, including teaching and administrative positions in PK–12 or basic education (includes preschool, primary/elementary, and secondary levels) and teaching and administrative positions in higher education, as well as other positions they have held.

As displayed in table 1.2, twenty-one persons began their careers in classrooms as teachers of PK–12 students. The PK–12 teaching careers of the participants ranged from one to twenty-four years. Earlier in their careers, thirteen taught at the secondary level, with one combining elementary and secondary experience, while three had elementary experience only, and one noted middle level only. Additionally, one had a combination of middle and elementary experience, one described PK–12 and special education, one noted elementary special education. Nearly a third of the group taught for ten years or more, with twenty-four years being the longest time spent in the classroom. Both building-level and/or central office PK–12 administrative experiences were reported by fourteen of the participants. Of the total, at this time only one has not held a full-time university faculty position, and only six have not held university administrative positions.

Also included in table 1.2 are positions other than teaching or administration reported by fifteen of the participants. This is undoubtedly only a partial list of other work experiences. For some these are first jobs, or positions held during time out from the participants' careers in education, or part-time positions. Examples include being a civil servant, secretarial work, radio and television work, consulting, and various church roles. These other positions are not

Table 1.1. Overview with Country, University Granting PhD, Current Position, and Age Range for Featured WLE Leaders

Name	Country	University Granting PhD	Current Professional Position	Age
1. Anastasia Athanasoula-Reppa	Greece	Panteion University, Athens, Greece	Retired, formerly Professor and President of Department of Pedagogical Studies, ASPETE, Athens, Greece	Mid 50s
2. Sister Hellen Bandiho	Tanzania	Duquesne University, Pittsburgh, PA, USA	Director of Postgraduate Studies, Research and Consultancy and Senior Lecturer at St. Augustine University of Tanzania	Mid 50s
3. Panpim Cheaupalakit	Thailand	Illinois State University, Normal, IL, USA	Senior Lecturer at International College for Sustainability Studies, and Department of Educational Administration, Srinakharinwirot University, Bangkok, Thailand	Early 50s
4. Marianne Coleman	United Kingdom	Leicester University, Leicester, England, UK	Retired, Emeritus Reader and formerly Assistant Dean of Research at Institute of Education, University of London, London, England	Mid 60s
5. Margaret Grogan	United States/ Australia	Washington State University, Pullman, WA, USA	Professor and Dean of School of Educational Studies, Claremont Graduate University, Claremont, CA, USA	Mid 50s
6. Esther Sui-chu Ho	Hong Kong-China	University of British Columbia, Vancouver, Canada	Professor and Director of Hong Kong Centre for International Student Assessment at Chinese University of Hong Kong	Late 40s
7. Alice Merab Kagoda	Uganda	University of Alberta, Edmonton, Canada	Associate Professor, formerly Deputy Dean of the School of Education at Makarere University, Kampala, Uganda	Mid 50s
8. Angeliki Lazaridou	Greece	University of Alberta, Edmonton, Canada	Lecturer and Co-Coordinator of Educational Administration graduate program at the University of Thessaly, Volos, Greece	Early 40s
9. Pamela Lenz	United States	Duquesne University, Pittsburgh, PA, USA	Director of Curriculum, Instruction, and Assessment, Iroquois School District; Adjunct lecturer in Educational Leadership at Gannon University, PA, USA	Mid 50s
10. Linda L. Lyman	United States	University of Nebraska, Lincoln, NE, USA	Professor, Department of Educational Administration and Foundations, College of Education, Illinois State University, Normal, IL, USA	Early 70s
11. Rachel McNae	New Zealand	University of Waikato, Hamilton, New Zealand	Senior Lecturer in Faculty of Education, Department of Professional Studies in Education, University of Waikato, Hamilton, New Zealand	Mid 30s

Name	Country	Institution	Position	Age
12. Rosangela Malachias	Brazil	University of São Paulo (USP), Brazil	Journalist; Researcher at Center of Research and Interdisciplinary Studies about Brazilian Black People from USP, Owner of Consultancy Office—Media, Ethnicity, Communication and Education	Late 40s
13. Katherine Cumings Mansfield	United States	University of Texas at Austin, USA	Assistant Professor, Virginia Commonwealth University, Richmond, VA, USA	Late 40s
14. Jacqueline Oram-Sterling	Jamaica	Illinois State University, Normal, IL, USA	Senior Lecturer in History, Sociology, and Social Studies Methodology and Programme Officer for the Graduate School, The Mico University College, Kingston, Jamaica	Mid 40s
15. Diane Reed	United States	University of Rochester, NY, USA	Associate Professor, Co-Director Educational Leadership Program at St. John Fisher College, Rochester, NY, USA	Mid 60s
16. Elizabeth C. Reilly	United States	University of San Francisco, CA, USA	Professor of Educational Leadership and Administration, School of Education, Marymount University, Los Angeles, CA, USA	Mid 50s
17. Vanita Richard	South Africa	University of Johannesburg, South Africa	Senior Project Manager (Academic), Matthew Goniwe School of Leadership and Governance, Johannesburg, South Africa	Late 50s
18. Saeeda Shah	Pakistan	University of Nottingham, Nottingham, England, UK	Senior Lecturer, School of Education, University of Leicester, Leicester, England, UK	Late 50s
19. Charol Shakeshaft	United States	Texas A and M University, College Station, TX, USA	Professor and Chairperson, Department of Educational Leadership, Virginia Commonwealth University, Richmond, VA, USA	Early 60s
20. Helen C. Sobehart	United States	Doctor of Arts, Carnegie-Mellon University, Pittsburgh, PA, USA	Graduate Education Consultant, Point Park University, Pittsburgh, PA; former President of Cardinal Stritch University, Milwaukee; and former Pennsylvania superintendent	Mid 60s
21. Jill Sperandio	United Kingdom/ United States	University of Chicago, Chicago, IL, USA	Associate Professor in International School Leadership program, Lehigh University, Bethlehem, PA, USA	Early 60s
22. Jane Strachan	New Zealand	University of Waikato, Hamilton, New Zealand	Retired, formerly Associate Professor in Faculty of Education, Department of Professional Studies in Education at University of Waikato, Hamilton, New Zealand	Mid 60s
23. Joyce Wilson-Tagoe	Ghana	PhD student in Educational Leadership, Univ. of Educ. Kumasi Campus, Ghana	Lecturer, Centre for Teacher Development and Action Research, I.E.D.E. University of Education, Winneba, Ghana	Mid 50s

Table 1.2. Overview of Career Path Experiences of WLE Featured Leaders in Teaching, Administration, and Other Positions

Name	PK–12 Teaching	PK–12 Admin	Higher Ed Faculty	Higher Ed Admin	Other Positions
1. Anastasia Athanasoula-Reppa	Secondary		X	X	Ministry of Industry
2. Sister Hellen Bandiho	Elementary		X	X	
3. Panpim Cheaupalakit			X	X	
4. Marianne Coleman	Secondary		X	X	Secretary
5. Margaret Grogan	Secondary	X	X	X	Radio/TV work
6. Esther Sui-chu Ho	Secondary		X	X	
7. Alice Merab Kagoda	Secondary	X	X	X	Diocesan Mothers/ Women's Worker
8. Angeliki Lazaridou	Kindergarten		X	X	Consulting for multi-national corporation
9. Pamela Lenz	Elementary	X	Adjunct Lecturer		
10. Linda L. Lyman	Secondary	Regional Coordinator Educational Service Unit	X		Admin. Asst. to Fine Arts and Gifted Coordinator in Nebraska Department of Education
11. Rachel McNae	Secondary	X	X		Trustee for two not-for-profit Community Education Trusts
12. Rosangela Malachias	Provided Professional Development for Teachers			University grant project researcher	Researcher, Journalist, Communications consultant
13. Katherine Cumings Mansfield	PK–12 and Special Education	Curriculum Development; Professional Development for Teachers	X	Project Manager	Minister for Adult Ed. (Protestant Church); Education Support for Pediatric Services (University of Nebraska Medical Center)

# Name	Level				
14. Jacqueline Oram-Sterling	Secondary	X	X	X	
15. Diane Reed	Elementary & Middle	X	X	X	Consulting
16. Elizabeth C. Reilly	Secondary	X	X	X	Radio Announcer, State Professional Development Trainer, Educ. Consultant
17. Vanita Richard	Secondary		X	X	Life Skills Facilitator, Department of Education
18. Saeeda Shah	Secondary	X	X	X	
19. Charol Shakeshaft	Middle	X	X	X	
20. Helen C. Sobehart	Elementary Special Education	X	X	X	Executive Director of ASSET, Inc. (Achieving Success in Science through Excellence in Teaching)
21. Jill Sperandio	Secondary	X	X	X	Activities director for seniors' home
22. Jane Strachan	Secondary	X	X	X	Advisor to the Director of Women's Affairs, Republic of Vanuatu
23. Joyce Wilson-Tagoe	Elementary/ Secondary		X		
Totals	21	14	22	17	15

easily categorized and help illustrate the theme of the multiplicity of career paths we have experienced.

OVERVIEW OF CHAPTER THEMES

In each chapter, featured narratives of selected leaders are used to develop a major theme. We share the stories, identify practical insights, and highlight relevant scholarship. We acknowledge that although each leader is featured in only one chapter, each could certainly have been featured in more than one. We take an interdisciplinary approach, comparing and interpreting the experiences of featured leaders within the context of practical wisdom and existing scholarly literature.

Chapter 2, "Passages into Pathways," explores challenging passages in accessing education and pursuing a career. Narratives of five diverse women from four different countries illustrate the influences of place, age relative to the women's movement, and socioeconomic status. Commonalities exist in stories of women who confront the worldwide cultural expectation that men, not women, will be leaders. Common themes are embracing difference, balancing expectations, finding the way, weaving the threads, and pursuing excellence. The featured leaders are: Angeliki Lazaridou, Greece; Esther Sui-chu Ho, Hong Kong-China; Linda L. Lyman, United States; Katherine Cumings Mansfield, United States; and Jacqueline Oram-Sterling, Jamaica.

Chapter 3, "Imperatives," features how personal awakening to gender and other social justice issues can become an imperative to action. Motivation for social justice leadership can include critical personal incidents, educational experiences, workplace discrimination, religious convictions, and experiences of marginalization or violence, to name a few. Three imperatives are specifically explored: living with the intersectionality of gender, class, and race-based discrimination; surviving personal violence; and benefiting from transformative education. The featured leaders are: Rosangela Malachias, Brazil; Charol Shakeshaft, United States; and Saeeda Shah, Pakistan.

Chapter 4, "Values Create a Larger Circle," highlights values inherent in the moral purpose of social justice leadership. Values are the foundation for extending humanitarianism, expanding circles of concern, and developing cosmopolitan consciousness. Social justice work may look different depending on where a country falls on the range of economic indicators, but the values motivating leaders are similar. Women tend to live and lead from their values. Different theories about values are presented to anchor understanding and stimulate reflection. The featured leaders are: Elizabeth C. Reilly, United States; Alice Merab Kagoda, Uganda; and Marianne Coleman, United Kingdom.

Chapter 5, "Skillful Authentic Leadership," begins with a discussion of the meaning of authenticity in leadership. Skills associated with themes of growing into authenticity, leading with phronesis (practical wisdom), and leading for eudaimonia (well-being) are described in presentation and analysis of the stories. The chapter includes insights for leadership practice both implied and directly stated in the narratives. The featured leaders are: Sister Hellen Bandiho, Tanzania; Pamela Lenz, United States; and Rachel McNae, New Zealand.

Chapter 6, "Resilience," explores components of resilience and associated insights. Courage and persistence are required for social justice work, which is by its nature unfinished and risky. Speaking out is required to challenge the status quo. The chapter shares how three leaders work in vastly different cultures to contribute to advancing social justice causes. The featured leaders are: Diane Reed, United States; Panpim Cheaupalakit, Thailand; and Joyce Wilson-Tagoe, Ghana.

Chapter 7, "Multiple Paths toward Advancing Social Justice Outcomes," suggests that each leader has found the path that is uniquely hers, that feels right. Although career paths differed, analysis of the narratives identified three pathways of social justice work in the world: activism, mentoring, and scholarship. Although the pathways interact, for most of the women one path or another predominated. These pathways and their outcomes are discussed and illustrated in the chapter. The featured leaders are: Vanita Richard, South Africa; Jill Sperandio, United Kingdom/United States; and Margaret Grogan, Australia/United States.

Chapter 8, "Actions Define Social Justice Leadership," illustrates how actions focused on making a difference become a force for good and define social justice leadership. Serendipity or chance as a factor in women's careers, the mixed blessings of power, and the need for self-care are considered. The stories highlight three action themes: doing feminism, engaging in political activism, and using power to make a difference. The emphasis in the chapter is on how actions are always the real story and the realization of our motivation and values. The featured leaders are: Jane Strachan, New Zealand; Anastasia Athanasoula-Reppa, Greece; and Helen C. Sobehart, United States.

Chapter 9, "An Invitation," begins with the idea that social justice leadership is by definition an unfinished journey, however social justice is defined. Major practical insights from each chapter are summarized. A focus on untold stories is a reminder that every story has layers of meaning. Unique contributions the book makes to understanding social justice leadership are reviewed. Finally, readers are invited to shape social justice leadership by joining all who are about the work of change to create new possibilities for a more just world.

UNIQUENESS OF THE BOOK

The uniqueness of the book includes its international scope and the power of personal narratives to both inform and inspire. The variety of continents, countries, personal backgrounds, professional positions, and ages of the women who contributed narratives gives the book comprehensiveness and credibility. Knowledge is power, and this book offers understandings that have the power to transform. Using details from the featured narratives to advance common themes, in the chapters we utilize the power of story to stimulate reflection and inspire readers to leadership that advances social justice.

We agree with these words from Joanne Cooper (1991) about how sharing stories can enrich leadership: "As chroniclers of our own stories, we write to create ourselves, to give voice to our experiences, to learn who we are and who we have been. . . . These stories, these myriad voices, then serve to instruct and transform society, to add to the collective voice we call culture" (111). By hearing other stories and through understanding other cultures, we are better able as educators to lead skillfully and authentically, to contribute purposefully, and to make a world of difference.

Voicing the concerns and causes of our lives, we contribute to transforming lives, education, and ultimately societies through purposeful sharing of aggregated wisdom. We call on educators—women and men—to devote renewed efforts to social justice issues, such as increasing opportunities for leadership roles for women, securing equal educational opportunities for girls, and eliminating policies and practices that unfairly limit the learning and lives of marginalized individuals and groups. Working together and learning from each other, we shape social justice leadership.

2

PASSAGES INTO PATHWAYS

Composing a life involves a continual reimagining of the future and reinterpretation of the past to give meaning to the present, remembering best those events that prefigured what followed, forgetting those that proved to have no meaning within the narrative.

—Mary Catherine Bateson, *Composing a Life*

Born in different countries, WLE members have traveled varied pathways. Clearly expressed in all of the narratives was that life experiences created an awakening to gender and other social justice issues. In spite of our different origins, many commonalities exist in the challenging educational and career passages we have experienced. A passage can be defined as a challenge or opening by or through which a person may pass, or go from one place to another. The word connotes a journey featuring challenge and growth, such as happens in a period of transition, for example. Sheehy (1995) defines life passages as "those predictable 'crises' or turning points that usher in a new stage, a crucial period of decision between progress and regression" (12).

Another view of passage is as a pilgrimage. It is Elie's (2003) definition of pilgrimage that Van Hoose (2008) eloquently conveys in these words: "A pilgrimage is about leaving the familiar to seek out and be open to the Other, to be an eye-witness to something that has called to you, to see for yourself. We go, we are changed, we come back to tell the story" (7–8). The end result of a passage or pilgrimage can be finding where we belong, a convergence of gifts, or clarification of one's life purpose as our passages become our pathways.

Ultimately the educational and career passages we are willing to take enable us to compose the meaning of our careers and lives. Educational passages facilitate career passages, as growth leads through reimagining to new previously unimagined opportunities. Bateson (1989) writes, "It is no longer possible to follow the paths of previous generations. . . . Our lives not only take new directions; they are subject to repeated redirection" (2). She understands how one thing leads to another.

CHALLENGING PASSAGES: THE STORIES

A woman seeking a meaningful role in the public as well as the private sphere must confront widespread cultural expectations that a woman's place is in the home. Challenging passages sound common chords as we have sought education and careers in developing a harmonious life. The chords occur in no particular order because each life has its own melody line. Each woman had to find her own way, embrace difference, balance expectations, weave the threads, and pursue excellence. These five themes recur as chords in the personal and professional journeys featured in this chapter. The featured leaders for each theme explored are: (1) Embracing Difference—Angeliki Lazaridou, Greece; (2) Balancing Expectations—Esther Sui-chu Ho, Hong Kong-China; (3) Finding the Way—Linda L. Lyman, United States; (4) Weaving the Threads—Katherine Cumings Mansfield, United States; and (5) Pursuing Excellence—Jacqueline Oram-Sterling, Jamaica.

Embracing Difference

Embracing difference in a woman's life takes many forms and can include education, marriage, and careers. Especially in more traditional countries, where women's roles are seen to be primarily domestic, embracing difference means confronting those norms and making other choices. Harmonies include dissonance.

Angeliki Lazaridou

Dr. Angeliki Lazaridou was born in Athens, Greece, at the beginning of the seventies. She described herself as "the first-born child of a mature working class couple." She and her brother, born three years later, "grew up in a very attentive and loving environment with plenty of room for play and a lot of freedom to develop our unique characters." Angeliki titled her narrative "My Journey to Ithaca." Ithaca serves as a many-layered metaphor in her version of the classic tale of "leaving home" for adventure and the tough passages of returning home. Instead of entering the sea of early matrimony, she ventured across the ocean to Canada for graduate school.

In 2002, Angeliki returned to Greece with a PhD in educational administration and leadership from the University of Alberta after eight years in Edmonton, Canada. Getting reestablished in Athens took a while, with Angeliki working successfully in various teaching positions at colleges in Athens and as a consultant in a multinational cooperation. She met WLE member Anastasia Athanasoula-Reppa during teaching at the Athens School of Pedagogical and Technical Education (ASPETE). Anastasia "became my mentor and initiator into the Greek academic scene," she wrote.

Following two years as a full-time faculty member at the University of Nicosia in Cyprus, since 2008 Angeliki has been lecturer and co-coordinator of the educational administration program at the University of Thessaly in Volos, Greece. The program is one of only two accredited graduate programs in educational administration in the country. She has edited a book on contemporary issues in educational administration and policy (Lazaridou 2004) and published numerous peer-reviewed journal articles. Her teaching and research interests focus on leadership, with an emphasis on issues in the principalship, ethics and values, gender, and complexity theories.

Angeliki's only goal in life during her early carefree preschool years "was to compete in children's games, for example skip rope and hopscotch." School began as an interruption on "the first day my mother took me to kindergarten. I vividly remember that day, as I was sitting quietly at my little desk, observing the strange new environment I found myself in, and getting annoyed with those children who were crying and calling out for their mothers."

Elementary school was better because "there was a much bigger yard for my favorite games and more children to play with." She remembers that "as a student I was good but not excellent, perhaps because I lived more for play and less for reading and doing math." Both of her parents wanted her to perform well in school and monitored her progress. "They were in close contact with the teachers the first few years of my education, more than I wanted them to be." They instilled in her "respect for teachers and knowledge."

Books were never at the top of her priority list, she confessed, "except for one particular volume of the student's encyclopedia that had pictures of peoples and places around the globe. Whenever I pretended to study, I would look at these pictures and mentally travel all the way to Bolivia, Africa, North America and Australia for hours on end."

As her education continued into high school, Angeliki reported, "I may not have been a straight-A student, yet I managed to enter university after succeeding in the national entry exams. At the same time, I got engaged to a math teacher, and was planning to get married as soon as I got my degree." She elaborated,

It was the natural result for a Greek woman who got the basic education and, in exceptional circumstances, a university degree. The first few years of my engagement I didn't seem to mind this plan. I was part of that culture, after all, and was brought up to accept marriage at an early age with the ultimate goal to have a family. In fact, it was customary for mothers of girls at that time to start building up their daughters' dowries very early in their children's lives. The same happened with my mother, who started my dowry when I was just 5 years old!

"The university years were a turning point for me," Angeliki declared. "They opened new horizons and brought opportunities I hadn't dreamed of before." With a mature fiancé five years older than she, her life experiences outside school included travel, camping, skiing, and hiking. "I would never have been allowed to have these experiences on my own, as it wasn't proper at that time for a girl to be going out a lot with friends and experiencing these things." She also enjoyed the classes and the intellectual stimulation of university life, "but at the back of my mind I knew it would come to an end soon."

Angeliki resisted the future that lay before her—"settling down in a small village, living in the same house with his parents, working at the local school, and raising children appeared to be the most impossible thing in the world. . . . After all, I was a city girl. What was I going to do in a small community of less than two thousand people, all of whom were farmers?" Her indifference to the dowry her mother was so carefully assembling foreshadowed that she would embrace a different way.

Angeliki was the first woman in her family to earn a university degree, breaking her five-year engagement soon after graduation. "The break-up caused a huge upheaval in my family. My mother desperately tried to make me reconsider. After all, it was a shame and a social stigma for the family to have an engagement broken." It took her mother "years to come to terms with this decision" and she and her mother "had endless conversations about the subject for years to come."

Instead of marrying, Angeliki continued her education. "The love of knowledge that university studies had awakened in me led me to enroll in a one-year post-degree program at the university to study children with special needs, especially those with hearing problems." As part of the program she visited schools abroad in collaboration with universities in Cyprus and in the United States. "That was the first time I traveled outside the borders of Greece. Images of my childhood swirled in my head as I recalled my favorite book of peoples and places I used to read in elementary school. Finally, my imaginative travels came true!" She wrote, "That year was a catalyst for my future life and career path."

At the end of that year Angeliki was hired to teach kindergarten in a small private school in Athens. "It was the most difficult year of my life," she reported. "By the end of my first teaching year I had more questions than answers and felt truly ill-prepared to continue teaching unless I studied more." Graduate opportunities in Greece were limited, so she had to go abroad. "Chance and contacts led me to Canada for my master's in educational psychology with a specialization in special education," she explained.

Angeliki's decision to continue her education "met with mild objections from my parents. My mother thought that this was completely unnecessary. My father, in accordance with his calm character, remained silent," she wrote. After long, painful discussions, "they finally gave in to my insistence and my determination to follow the path I had chosen and despite their limited resources they partially supported my education for the first few years."

Beginning her master's at the University of Alberta in Edmonton in 1994, Angeliki embraced difference, absorbing "every detail of life inside and outside campus. I wanted to see more, to know more, to feel more. I made new friends, met interesting people from all over the world, tasted new foods, danced new dances and felt like I was born again a new person." Before the degree was complete she had applied to a doctoral program in the area of educational administration and leadership. "My mother's reaction to news of my doctoral studies still echoes in my ears today. 'And who will marry you if you have a PhD?'"

She called her doctoral student years "a mix of happiness and suffering." Finances were difficult and a supervisor proved less than helpful as she struggled with the dissertation and working to support herself. Angeliki wrote, "Those years were a test for my spirit and character. I began, for the first time, to wonder whether what I was doing was really worthwhile—and I came to suspect that perhaps my mother was right after all. I knew I had to persist, but I was running out of energy and money. At last, when I had almost made up my mind that I had to accept the reality of having to return home without my degree, a miracle happened."

She described how a professor "offered to take over as my supervisor and help me finish. He also fought the system that strongly resisted a change of supervision at that late stage in my program. After winning that battle, it was only a short time for me to complete my program successfully and to get my degree." Angeliki describes being changed by the challenging journey.

> After the completion of my degree, I returned home stronger and more mature than before I left. I was richer in experiences and more knowledgeable about myself. I had overcome my former self and had been reborn into a new person. Through those last painful years, I learned the values of patience, determination, perseverance, and forgiveness. I gained new confidence and was eager to prove to the world and myself that the path I had taken in my life was not in vain.

Angeliki's career and personal life started a new phase in September 2007, after the first WLE conference, when she married the Canadian professor (a native of New Zealand) who helped her finish the PhD five years earlier.

Writing her narrative a year later, she described herself "holding in my arms my newborn baby and feeling happier than ever. As I look at his face, I'm reminded of the words of T. S. Eliot: 'Only those who will risk going too far can possibly find out how far one can go.'"

Insights

A total of ten WLE members specifically commented on cultural barriers encountered in their passages to education and careers. For Angeliki, a woman who grew up in a traditional patriarchal culture like Greece, to find the way to a career in academia implies *embracing difference*, going against tradition and cultural norms. As Kaparou and Bush (2007) write, "In Greece, patriarchy ensures that society is based on a male model, where men are at the top and women at a lower level" (229). Cultural realities for Greek women are quite complicated.

Writing for a Greek newspaper, Karaiskaki (2006) comments that "the image of Greek women [is that they are] educated, economically independent, and unafraid of taking their lives in their own hands. However, this image does not account for the multiple roles of women, the dramatic changes they experience through their lives, and the stereotypes which affect them." In embracing higher education, Angeliki Lazaridou was the first female member of her family to become a university graduate.

In the narratives twelve women reported that leaving home was required for education. Some women, particularly those growing up in rural areas, left home for education even before the university years. The university experience altered Angeliki's willingness to accept the life that the prevailing Greek culture laid out for her. Degrees earned in Canada made possible her career as an academic, still in its early stages. Spending eight years as a graduate student in Canada, Angeliki embraced difference and independence. She experienced culture shock when she first returned home to Greek culture and its traditional patterns.

Finding the way to a doctorate and back to Ithaca was not without sacrifice. The melody was not always clear, but Angeliki has composed a meaningful life, fulfilling in her own thoroughly modern way the cultural dreams of marriage and a family symbolized by the dowry her mother assembled. Today a young son is providing new lessons about balancing expectations and time.

Balancing Expectations

Cultural patterns in many countries mean that educational opportunities are reserved for the boys, and offered to girls only as second choice. In most countries cultural expectations reinforce the belief that the woman with a career is still responsible for domestic duties and bringing up the children. Balancing these expectations can be a challenging chord to sustain.

Esther Sui-chu Ho

 Dr. Esther Sui-chu Ho is a professor in the Department of Educational Policy and Administration, and director of the Hong Kong Center for International Student Assessment at the Chinese University of Hong Kong (CUHK). Her research specialties of parental involvement and student assessment have taken her around the world. In 2011, for example, she completed a second Fulbright program in the United States at Johns Hopkins University, Baltimore, Maryland, where she was a visiting scholar at the Center on School, Family and Community Partnerships, focusing her research on youth transition.

Esther's earlier Fulbright program was at Pennsylvania State University. Her scholarship has a social justice focus that comes from her own social background in a working-class family raised by a single mother. She wrote, "I am always concerned about how to support disadvantaged groups (girls and immigrants from lower SES) to get access to quality basic education" (E. H., e-mail message to author, September 22, 2010). Now in her late forties, Esther was the second-born daughter in a family with two boys and two girls, a situation inauspicious for her educational future. She began her narrative, simply titled "Biography," with this sentence: "In traditional Chinese society, girls are usually deprived of the opportunity for school learning."

She described her mother as "a very independent woman" who married when she was thirty-five years old. She lost her husband after ten years, when Esther was only five. From then on her mother worked hard as a domestic helper to earn a basic living for the family, and Esther's grandmother took care of the children. Esther's mother did not have the resources to support all four of them with formal education. With their father gone, one of them needed to quit school to earn money to help support the family. Esther explained,

Of course it could have been that my eldest brother quit school. But the Chinese traditional belief is that a "girl without knowledge could be a virtue." My elder sister was an optimistic and happy girl. It didn't matter to her whether she stayed in school or worked in a factory. Her school grades happened to be not as good as our elder brother, so my elder sister quit. I still remember that she was only eleven years old. Children under fourteen years old were not allowed to work according to the law in the 1970s. Therefore, she needed to borrow an ID card of a fourteen-year-old to get a job from a nearby factory. I understood that I would follow a similar path when I was big enough to pretend to be fourteen. As a girl, I accepted this obligation to support the family.

In fact, all four children did factory work at home to earn some money to support the family, even when in primary school. Esther wrote, "I found that we quite enjoyed the work at home and that actually enhanced our sense of efficacy as we could help the family. We also learned to take responsibility very early in life." With her elder sister giving up school to support the family, Esther understood she was lucky to have the opportunity to complete basic education.

She wrote, "I still remember my mother telling me that I would have to work after the basic education." Esther also understood "that I needed to grip any opportunity to have better academic results so that I could keep learning" (E. H., e-mail message to author, September 22, 2010). She worked hard to excel in school and did well on the public examination required at the end of basic education for all children in Hong Kong in the 1970s. "This public examination was high stakes because only those outstanding performers would be allocated schools with full subsidy."

Esther wrote, "I was lucky that I performed quite well and was allocated a subsidy." Her mother agreed that she could continue her education at the nearby secondary school as long as she could still help with the home-based work for a factory. She also had a job during every summer holiday to earn the fee for the books and learning materials. "My mother reminded me that the family really needed my support after I finished the junior secondary program. However, when I finished junior secondary, my brother decided to drop out and started his work in an office. As the financial burden could be shared by my elder brother, I got the second unexpected opportunity to continue my studies."

When Esther graduated from Kit Sam Secondary School, her top scores on another public examination earned the highly sought-after opportunity to attend the Chinese University of Hong Kong. "In the early 1980s, only 2–3 percent of the students in Hong Kong had the opportunity to be university students." It was an honor for the whole family to have someone enrolled in university, "so my mother accepted gratefully to have the first university student in the family," she explained. Esther continued her study with financial support from the government but also worked as a private tutor to earn additional money.

Esther earned a BS in biology and began teaching. "That was the usual way for working-class students to start their work, since the starting salary as a teacher was quite high and the career was quite stable." Esther wrote, "I loved to talk to my students and tried to help them solve their problems in their learning or daily life. I hoped I could be a positive driving force to the teenagers when they were growing up." But after three years Esther was not content to remain a secondary biology teacher. She decided to study educational administration because the role of the school administrator was more influential in the school as a whole.

Esther married, received an MA in school administration, and had her first child all in the same year. Soon after that, she, her husband, and daughter left Hong Kong for Los Angeles so that he could study for an MA at UCLA. She observed, "It was quite a relaxing experience to be a full-time mother and take care of my elder daughter and my husband. I enjoyed that very much at the beginning. Then cooking, cleaning, cutting coupons, and playing with my daughter became the major tasks of my life." Experiencing discontent after eight months of full-time mothering, Esther wrote, "The content of my conversation with my husband was really dry. I missed my teaching and learning. I missed my previous interesting life. I did not actually know what I wanted by that time but I was quite sure being a full-time mother was not it."

Prior to their departure for the United States, Esther had been accepted as a PhD student at the University of British Columbia, so she traveled with her daughter from California to Vancouver, Canada, to begin her doctoral study. Her mother was then in Vancouver and helped Esther to take care of her daughter so that Esther could finish the course work in two years. Unfortunately, her mother died before Esther could finish her dissertation.

When her husband finished his degree at UCLA, he found a job at the Chinese University of Hong Kong (CUHK). She followed him back to Hong Kong with their daughter and started her career as a research associate at CUHK. When she finished her dissertation on parental involvement, Esther was hired as an assistant professor in the faculty of education in CUHK. She obtained a large grant to conduct an action research project on parental involvement in Hong Kong using her previous research experience in Canada.

A major purpose of the research was to support working-class parents' involvement in their children's education in disadvantaged communities. She wrote, "The research went well and the subsequent workshop training presented to forty primary schools was well received. I became one of the major experts in parental involvement research in Hong Kong." She further integrates her research on parental involvement into her current international study. Because her work was based on one- or two-year contracts, Esther found it enjoyable but "very stressful." She explained, "Our performance had to be reviewed every year in terms of three criteria: teaching well, getting substantial grants, and good international publications. When I had my second daughter, the balance of work and family became even more difficult."

In 2000 Esther received a grant for a major Program for International Student Assessment (PISA) project and set up the center at her university in 2003. She continues to serve as the principal investigator of PISA in Hong Kong. Through PISA she conducts research focused on "the disparity between boys and girls, immigrant and local students, and low SES versus high SES students" (E. H., e-mail message to author, September 22, 2010). Esther has also been a consultant for both the Macau-PISA project and the China-PISA project. The PISA project is led by the Organization for Economic Cooperation and Development (OECD) and assesses learning of fifteen-year-old students in countries all over the world on three subjects: science, reading, and mathematics. The data are used by the cooperating countries to raise student achievement.

In addition to her ongoing major research projects, in 2010 Esther took on the responsibility of supervisor at the Kit Sam Secondary School, the Catholic school from which she had graduated. Kit Sam in Chinese means "purity" and "heart." As the supervisor she is a volunteer; "that means no pay but legally responsible to supervise the school. We have about one thousand female students and seventy teaching staff. I recruited a new principal before I left for the Fulbright."

Esther explained her supervisor task in these words. "I am trying my best to support the new principal to lead and collaborate with the teachers of my school to revitalize the learning atmosphere as well as sustaining the caring norms. It is a new and good learning experience for me—to be down to earth and not just at the university conducting system-level policy analysis. It's challenging but meaningful to serve my own school" (E. H., e-mail message to author, August 26, 2011).

Esther wrote, "Balancing my work and family life is still and always my major concern." She acknowledged in a graceful concluding note, "I enjoy my work—the achievement, the intellectual exchange, and the possible contribution to the students and the field of education. All these accomplishments would have been impossible without the support of my mother and sacrifice of my elder sister."

Insights

Choosing a career in teaching was typical for working class Chinese students. Esther, however, went well beyond that expectation in completing a doctorate, becoming a professor, and making a name for herself as a researcher. According to Xin and Hongyi (2000), "facts have shown that a woman's determination for career attainment cannot be snuffed out" (52). Esther, like many of the WLE members, found the way to an academic career by embracing difference. When going beyond cultural norms for women, each confronted issues of how to balance family with a career.

From the beginning Esther has called balancing expectations of a career and family her major concern. In that she is not alone. Mahtani (2005) conducted interview research with twenty-two Hong Kong women leaders in business and the professions. She writes that "the women leaders generally believe Hong Kong is a good place for women to work. However, a 'glass ceiling' exists because of a fundamental belief in Hong Kong that women—even those in leadership—are the primary caregivers at home" (5). She also observes, "For many women with children, they seem to be constantly 'juggling' work and family life" (27). Time allocation is the biggest issue.

Dual-career families frequently confront balancing expectations issues. To keep the family together, Esther temporarily gave up her own career and went with her young daughter and husband to Los Angeles. She wrote that "the only choice was to support my husband, and postpone or give up my own study." Ultimately she embraced the third alternative—the family being separated while she studied in Canada. Other WLE women have experienced this dilemma when careers call a couple in two directions.

Of the twenty-three WLE women who submitted narratives, twenty are mothers. Several, like Esther, had support from family in caring for children. Some women in their sixties took time out from their careers when their children were young. Some found live-in help to care for their children. The youngest woman, who is in her thirties, has been able to take advantage of high-quality day care, an option that along with paid maternity leaves did not exist at the time when many of the older women in the group had young children.

Esther's academic success is an example of why students from low-income families deserve an equal chance at quality education. One suggestion Chiu and Walker (2007) make for creating greater social justice in Hong Kong schools is to flatten the status hierarchy and reduce student inequality through strategies that yield closer teacher-student relationships (734). Esther believes that factors underpinning the inequality in student achievement in Hong Kong are related to social and academic segregation between schools (Ho 2005). As a practicing supervisor she works to create a harmonious environment by nurturing the learning and caring norms at the secondary school she herself once attended.

Finding the Way

Finding the way through a maze of cultural norms and expectations to a life that fits with an individual woman's uniqueness can be a lifetime journey. If a woman is caught in patterns that no longer fit, then the challenge becomes whether to carry on or to seek a new way.

Linda L. Lyman

Dr. Linda Lyman's "Intertwining Journeys" narrative opened with this sentence: "Four words that describe dimensions of me are *lover, mother, teacher,* and *writer*—listed in alphabetical order." Incorporating her poetry, the narrative illustrates how finding the way interacted with cultural norms for women in the United States midtwentieth century before the second wave of the women's movement. She remembers wanting to be different from the six other girls named "Linda" in her grade-school class.

Linda has been a professor in the Department of Educational Administration and Foundations at Illinois State University (ISU), Normal, Illinois, since 1999. Her university teaching began in 1990, at Bradley University in Peoria, Illinois, after she earned a PhD at the University of Nebraska, Lincoln. Her scholarship addresses leadership, with an emphasis on issues of caring, poverty, social justice, and gender. She served as executive director of Illinois Women Administrators for four years. Linda was named in 2011 as co-honoree of an endowed scholarship, the Patricia H. Klass-Linda L. Lyman Endowed Scholarship, given by an anonymous donor to recognize excellence in teaching.

A Fulbright Scholar award in 2005 took Linda and her husband to Thessaloniki, Greece, for six months to teach about women's leadership in American culture at Aristotle University. She also collaborated with WLE members Angeliki Lazaridou and Anastasia Athanasoula-Reppa to research Greek women principals, presenting a paper at the 2007 WLE conference (Lyman, Lazaridou, and Athanasoula-Reppa 2009).

In 1941 Linda was born in Hutchinson, Kansas, the older daughter of parents who were both teachers when they met. She was two years old when her father, a Navy communications officer, left for duty in Australia during World War II. Linda, her mother, and sister Margo lived with her father's parents until he returned some three years later. He settled into a career as an accountant and office manager, eventually serving a term as mayor of Hutchinson, a town of 35,000 located in the middle of the Kansas wheat fields. Her mother did not return to teaching again until Linda was in ninth grade and her sister in sixth. In doing so she became the only one among the mothers of Linda's friends who worked outside the home, retiring after twenty-five years of teaching.

Active in high-school activities, Linda was elected governor of Kansas Girls State in 1958 and attended the National High School Journalism Institute at Northwestern University that same summer. She twice attended a Kansas

Association for Youth week-long summer leadership camp for girls and was inspired by the closing campfire dedicated to a vision of world peace. Becoming a local and regional president in this school, community, and world service organization was the beginning of Linda's concern for social justice and dream to make a difference. "I wanted to be a diplomat and contribute to world peace, and took that ambition with me in 1959 when I left Kansas for Northwestern University on a scholarship."

In college Linda continued to be a leader in student activities. Recognized for her scholarship, leadership, and service, she was elected president of Mortar Board in her senior year. Majoring in political science and studying Russian, Linda seemed well on her way to composing a future based on a choice women were not perceived to have at that time. Explaining what happened to that dream of being a diplomat, Linda recounted,

> In the middle of my junior year I made the first of many major decisions I have made based on love and romance. I changed my major from political science to English, believing I would go to Nigeria in the Peace Corps with my boyfriend and that English was a more practical major. By the time I graduated from Northwestern in 1963 my boyfriend, who graduated the year before, had gone to Nigeria without me.

Choosing to continue her education, Linda was accepted in a program at Harvard University and earned a master of arts in teaching. After a year of teaching English she made another decision motivated by love and romance, and left Boston for Nebraska. Having fundamentally changed the landscape of her life by moving back to the Midwest, she was blindsided when the romance ended. Regrouping, she planned to leave her teaching position in Omaha for one at the American School in Brussels when a new love appeared. "I married my first husband in 1966, giving up teaching high-school English two years later when we moved to Washington, DC, and decided to start a family. I had not considered teaching as a career—just something I would do until I had children."

Her son David was born in Washington, DC, where the family lived for two years; daughter Elaine was born in Lincoln, Nebraska, where the family lived for one year; and son Steve was born in a small town on the edge of the Nebraska sandhills. Her children were the emotional center of her life. They were thriving, as was her husband's career, but Linda experienced discontent as the years passed.

> I had agreed to the move to this small town even though I had said I would never live in a place smaller than my hometown in Kansas. I remember standing on a corner after looking at the house we eventually bought and saying to my husband, "It will be good for your career, but I will probably die here." Much of life

was good. I loved being a mother. But I knew I had to figure out how "not to get caught dead." I had no idea how long the journey would be or what it would cost.

Reflecting on that time in her life, Linda wrote, "I felt oddly disconnected from my real self." She made multiple efforts to get control of an emerging anger. "I got involved with local politics, ran for the board of education, served, and was elected again to a second term." She took a part-time job as a gifted education and staff development consultant. "I renewed my teaching certificate and began taking extension classes to get an administrative endorsement." A period of unsettling grief engulfed Linda after her six-year-old son's best friend unexpectedly drowned in a country club swimming pool and her marriage was in turmoil.

Choked

Grief had been
distant
remote
a gruesome word
and other world
until that evening
when I opened to the sadness,
felt it rise from some
deep layer
to overpower my control,
contort the shapes
of my face and frame,
have its way with me.

Breathless finally
I lay felled by felt needs,
among them
a frantic needing
not to be
at this spot,
making
this choice,
yet knowing
that choice
no longer existed,
had likewise died,
split open in wasting efforts

in waning attempts
to span the opposing worlds
of no longer
and not yet.

After much counseling and indecision, with the support of her husband, Linda was considering whether to move two hundred miles east to Lincoln with her daughter for a PhD program at the University of Nebraska. When her daughter, who had been making some bad decisions in the small town, said "yes"—that she would come with her and start over again as a junior at a new high school—Linda was faced with a "no-turning-back" point. "Elaine's willingness to journey to a life in a new place enabled me to take the risks involved in this departure from convention. I would not have survived leaving home without any of my children."

"My older son was going into his senior year in high school. I thought he would be fine. My younger son was only 11, but I thought that I would finish the coursework in two years and come back home to complete my dissertation." She remembers saying to him shortly after the move to Lincoln, "I don't know if I am doing the right thing." His quick reply was, "This is so good for you, Mom. I'm really proud of you." Ultimately the marriage did not survive, "although I did live again," Linda related.

"My professional journey to become a professor began in the midst of an anguish-filled personal journey I had not planned to take. Divorce had never been an option." When she entered the doctoral program her goal was to finish, resume her former life, and become a principal. "With my marriage over, that pathway no longer existed. The road led on but I did not know where," she wrote. When people asked Linda what she would do with the degree, her answer was, "I don't have to know that yet." Becoming a professor did not occur to her until the third year of doctoral study, when she worked on her dissertation. "I asked my advisor Dr. Marilyn Grady if she thought I could be a professor. After a characteristic hearty laugh, her quick reply was, 'I wondered how long it was going to take for you to figure out it would be a perfect job for you.'"

Linda's academic job search led her to Bradley University and Peoria, a racially and ethnically diverse smaller metropolitan area with big-city problems. Her commitment to social justice work intensified as she became involved with the community. In 1998 she won a coveted community Partners in Peace award from the Center for Prevention of Abuse for "teaching that encourages educators to bridge boundaries and promote social justice." In 1999 when Linda accepted a position at Illinois State University, forty miles away, she decided to continue to live in Peoria. That "not-leaving-home-again" decision turned out to be absolutely critical in her journey to a new love, an unexpected joy at age sixty. "Dave Weiman and I have managed to draw a larger circle than I could have imagined the day of our wedding in 2001 at the Universalist Unitarian Church of Peoria where we met."

In addition to the six months in Greece, Linda and Dave have traveled widely, including trips to Rome in 2007 and Augsburg in 2009 for WLE conferences. Their mutual interests include embracing and supporting each other's social justice work on a wide range of issues. A joy is visiting grown children and the grandchildren as often as possible. Committed to seeking peace in the world through peace building among the religions, they participated in the Parliament of the World's Religions in 2004 in Barcelona. At the 2009 parliament in Melbourne, Linda conducted a workshop session on journeys of women leaders. Linda concluded her narrative with this observation, "My personal and professional journeys have been not only intertwining, but inseparable. Finding the way began when I left my home in Kansas at age eighteen, not understanding that I would need to leave home many times to become myself."

Insights

Linda's life passages seem marked by characteristics of what Sheehy (1995) calls "the silent generation," those born between 1930 and 1945. Sheehy believes "the lives of this generation were broken by tremendous discontinuity" (31). Linda began college in 1959 before the second wave of the women's movement in the United States. At that time, "not getting married—as soon as possible—was regarded almost as unthinkable" (Collins 2009, 36). Collins articulates cultural beliefs before and after 1960, the time she says "when everything changed." Linda's narrative shows evidence of a life caught between generational shifts in expectations for women.

A job is more easily given up than a career. Female college graduates expected to work only a few years in jobs such as teaching, nursing, or secretarial work. According to Collins (2009), "The belief that marriage meant an end to women's work life provided an all-purpose justification for giving the good opportunities to young men" (21). Ironically, women's low expectations for careers contributed to limited opportunities. Additionally, "By the time they reached the age of 24, over *one half* of Silent Generation males and *70 percent* of the females were married" (Sheehy 1995, 30). Raising children and fulfilling domestic responsibilities were expected from women. Marriage was expected to last and "divorce, though hardly unknown, was regarded dimly" (Collins 2009, 36).

Linda was vulnerable to being sidetracked by romance. Majoring in political science was opening new worlds intellectually, but her vision of a diplomatic job was ahead of the times. According to Coontz (2011), "In 1963, women, who were 51 percent of the population, composed just 2 percent of the U.S. senators and *ambassadors* [emphasis added] and 2.5 percent of the U.S. representatives" (14–15). Linda's untraditional career dream didn't have a chance against the prevailing urgency of college-age women to marry and the belief that middle-class women did not have careers. She was attracted to the Peace Corps, but not enough to join alone. Sheehy explains that "this generation did not come of age angry. Instead, its members developed a highly sensitive social conscience" (32). This generational characteristic may be a source of Linda's commitment to social justice leadership.

Linda's three children were born during the years that the women's movement in the United States was getting under way. She believed that what a man wanted was more important than what she wanted. For example, she dutifully followed where her husband's career took them, moving to a small town in Nebraska and ignoring her own premonitions that the move would not be good for her. At a fundamental level, the anger that emerged in her life as a wife and stay-at-home mom was anger at herself. It is possible for a woman to give too much of herself away and find her "self" lost.

Weaving the Threads

Composing a life requires blending together many seemingly unrelated melody strands from the past and present into an improvisational song. A story woven with threads of memory also creates a valuable patchwork of experiences interlaced with wisdom.

Katherine Cumings Mansfield

In 2011 Dr. Katherine Cumings Mansfield became an assistant professor in the Educational Leadership Department at Virginia Commonwealth University in Richmond, Virginia, having completed her PhD in educational policy and planning at the University of Texas at Austin. She also earned a doctoral portfolio in women's and gender studies. Her practitioner background includes twenty years of teaching and leadership from preschool to college. Her interdisciplinary scholarship focuses on the history and politics of education and the relationship of gender, race, religion, and class on educational and vocational access and achievement. In 2011 Katherine became program chair of the Leadership for Social Justice Special Interest Group (SIG) of AERA.

Katherine titled her narrative "What Is Past Is Prologue," weaving many threads together to tell her story. The poetic opening of her narrative embraces difference in an underlying metaphor:

> I have come to accept that some life stories resemble a vigilantly woven tapestry, each stitch intricately positioned, fibers and threads complementarily dyed, with each individual scene harmonizing into a comprehensive chronicle. Mine, however, seems more akin to a crazy quilt. An eccentric collection of fabric, yarns, textures, styles, and eras. Some sections are sanguine and pretty while others are gloomy and ugly. Nothing matches. Not even the threads that hold it together. It's as if the Divine Seamstress grabbed whatever materials were on hand at the moment.
>
> But it's mine. It's the only thing that I truly own. My Self.

Katherine's story moves from one vignette to another as if each were a patch in a quilt. Growing up during the women's movement, as early as second grade Katherine wanted to be an astronaut. She recalled the specific day that Mrs. Madison told her that girls were not allowed to become astronauts. She argued with her, saying, "My mom says I can do anything I want when I grow up! And I want to be an ASTRONAUT!" Katherine rushed home after school, found her mother doing the dishes, and blurted out what her teacher had said.

She remembers her mother breathing deeply and saying, "Let's sit down a minute." As they sat on lawn chairs in the living room, her mother began: "This is going to be the hardest thing I've ever had to tell you. Mrs. Madison is right. Girls are not allowed to be astronauts. Only boys." She explained that astronauts have to be pilots and "since all pilots are men, all astronauts are men." Katherine still could not believe it. "But you *said* I could be *anything* I *want* when I grow up," she protested. Her mom said, "I know. I was wrong. There are just some things that women are not allowed to do yet. All I can say is: maybe things will be different by the time you are a woman."

Another patch of memory conveys the centrality of Katherine's belief in God and how attending church became important. She wrote, "I do not remember a time that I did not believe in God. I remember praying to a Holy Presence as early as three years of age. There was a lot to pray about. When I was twelve years old, I began going to church on my own. It didn't matter the denomination. I just walked to whatever congregation was closest to wherever we were living at the time."

Each time, she was welcomed. "They invited me to sing with and for them. They said I looked like an angel in my white robes." She remembers musing, "Sometimes I wonder if they ever wondered about me. They could never know that I came home one day after school (again) to find our meager belongings shoved into the wheezing automobile. 'We're moving. Get in.'" The daughter of a single mother, Katherine did not enjoy financial security growing up.

Living in Minnesota with her mother, she had started experimenting with alcohol and pot with her friends. At fourteen, she wrote, "In a moment of clarity, I decided I needed to go to college in order to break this cycle of poverty and wasted potential that I was living. I was not sure how to go about accomplishing this, so I made an appointment with the school counselor to discuss my academic future." Introducing herself to the counselor, Katherine asked, "What do I need to do to go to college?" The counselor laughed and mockingly answered, "Well, you aren't exactly college material."

Katherine wrote, "I felt ashamed of my ragged hand-me-downs and her gape that named me *white trash*. My cheeks were aflame as I realized she must know about the verbal taunts. The punching. The kicking." She replied courageously, "How would you know I'm not college material? You don't even know me." Summing up the encounter, Katherine said, "I left angry but undaunted and brought the matter up again at my third high school." Understanding that her daughter was struggling, Katherine's mother sent her to Iowa to live with relatives and attend what was her third high school.

Katherine continued to explore faith widely, finding "the teachings of Jesus Christ especially fitting. . . . My emergent faith provided the sustenance and belonging I needed to accept myself and reach out to others." She elaborated, "It is during this time I began writing and performing music regularly. I wrote songs and skits for teens in my youth group to perform in the sanctuary. I also started teaching frequently. First Vacation Bible School. Then Sunday school."

Again, Katherine went to the counselor's office in her new high school to try to find out what she had to do to go to college. She wrote, "The counselor was meeting with someone, but the secretary offered to help me. The first question she asked me was what my GPA was. I didn't know what GPA stood for!!! She seemed surprised, but didn't let that get in the way. She said, 'Hmm. Well, let's find out!'" Her GPA was a 2.6, but the secretary said, "This is something you can change. It is not too late'" (K. C. M., e-mail message to author, September 18, 2011). She figured out the grades Katherine would need to earn each semester to raise her GPA to a 3.00. Then she listed the courses Katherine should take and made her promise to study harder and turn in all her homework.

The secretary went a step further and asked Katherine to come and visit her every marking period to check in. Katherine reported,

And I did. I visited her every quarter. And every quarter she would praise me for my good grades and get out that old, giant calculator and figure out what my current cumulative GPA had become. Every quarter, it went up. And she would rejoice with me. One quarter, during my senior year, I got a 4.0 and she literally squealed with excitement, jumped from her chair, and hugged me! Everyone else in this larger office area emerged from their smaller offices and wanted to know what was going on. They all rejoiced with me, too. It was wonderful! (K. C. M., e-mail message to author, September 18, 2011)

This secretary also guided Katherine through the college entrance exams and told her about a scholarship opportunity for future teachers. By the 1990s Katherine was an accomplished educator, and her head was full of names and faces of the many unique children she had worked with as a teacher.

She wrote, "I didn't refer to myself as a 'leader for social justice' or really think too much at all about what I was doing and why. I just knew I loved my work and felt 'at home' teaching and serving children and their families." She was also a leader, a teacher who would bring up the hard issues, such as "why there were more 'free and reduced lunch' students referred for special education and more middle-class students identified as *gifted and talented*." Katherine explained, "It never once occurred to me that I was doing something extraordinary. I worked against the grain of policy and practice to ensure equal opportunity for students. It just seemed like the right thing to do."

During her doctoral program Katherine kept asking questions. A professor and a fellow student told her that it would be inappropriate for her, as a "White woman who has lived a life of privilege," to "conduct research that concerns students or other participants who are Black, Latina, or any other race besides White . . . or who did not grow up wealthy." She wrote, "While this professor and student refer to themselves as *scholars of color*, they also come from two-parent households of highly educated mothers and fathers who, according to them, met their every physical and intellectual need as growing children, adolescents, and adults."

Katherine observed, "My white skin seemed to blind my colleagues to the class privilege they enjoyed, and continue to enjoy as they seem to effortlessly navigate the culture of academe; an alien world whose ways of being and doing remain elusive to me to this day." It took Katherine two years to puzzle through the dilemmas of cross-cultural research and begin her dissertation.

She remains troubled by the vocabulary scholars use to name others. Referring to published research, she asked, "What does it say about us when we define the world in terms of us? What does it indicate about our attitudes and assumptions when we refer to someone as *nonwhite* or a *woman of color?*" Her belief is that "defining the other (whether fellow academicians or the students and families we claim to serve) as that which is the negation of us is unattractive at best and should make us at least moderately uncomfortable."

A few months into Katherine's doctoral studies, her mother was diagnosed with early-onset Alzheimer's. "Concurrently, as her memories became ever more tangled and jumbled, mine increasingly surfaced effortlessly acute and fresh." Many things her mother taught her echoed. For example, "Watch your mouth!" were words her mother often said with a variety of expressions and gestures. "I eventually realized that *watching my mouth* also meant *guarding my intentions and my attitudes*. . . . The memories of her admonishing me as a child to 'watch my mouth' seem especially prescient as I learn to frame my words—and guard my attitudes and assumptions—in my new life training as an academician."

Katherine returned to the storied patchwork metaphor to end her narrative.

I have come to appreciate this life I've been given. This borderless bricolage of embodied scraps entwined with silvery filament into storied patchwork. An imperceptible mantle worn about my shoulders that whispers wisdom while I sleep. I know where I've been. I know where I am. But I do not know where I will be. But the Divine Seamstress knows what She's doing and I submit to Her Creative Spirit.

This story is mine. It's the only thing that I truly own. My Self.

Insights

An insight from Katherine's story is that educators who look beyond the superficial indications of poverty will see children of enormous potential. Particularly in the United States, it is too common for educators to take a deficit view of students, with parents blamed for failures of their children to achieve. Low-income parents are often described as not caring about their children or education (Lyman and Villani 2004; Ryan 1971). Katherine's story displays how strong intrinsic motivation to learn and excel can arise in a person from less-than-ideal family and economic circumstances.

Katherine's story also displays the power of mentors. When her mother sent her away to Iowa for the last two years of high school, Katherine seized the opportunity to grasp for a new reality when a secretary provided the mentoring that sent her on the way to college. Katherine undertook her graduate degrees because of another important mentor. During her undergraduate years, Dr. Judson P. Martin said as she turned in her final exam, "You know, I fully expect you to graduate and go on and get your master's degree. And then, go on and get your PhD and sit where I sit. You can do this. You are a scholar" (K. C. M., e-mail message to author, September 18, 2011). She remembers being stunned at the time.

Although at first she experienced being sent to Iowa as rejection by her mother, eventually Katherine could look back and say, "I know she was right." She also rose above the feeling of shame engendered by poverty as her emerging faith—in metaphorical language, the "Divine Seamstress"—helped her accept herself and begin reaching out to others. She did not let go of any threads completely, understanding that the painful experiences and memories are also a source of who she is as a person and an educator.

Katherine concluded, "My path included terrible pain and rejection and uncertainty. But all these experiences made me who I am today. I am a compassionate, loving educator who refuses to throw people away. I refuse to relegate people to the garbage heap as our scientifically organized society is trying to do" (K. C. M., e-mail message to author, September 18, 2011). Her narrative encourages educators to reach out to those students who just need one person to make a difference, thereby helping them to reweave the tapestries of their lives.

Pursuing Excellence

Pursuing excellence is a recurring theme that resonates with the chords in the previous stories. Embracing difference, balancing expectations, finding the way, and weaving the threads harmonize in a self that is a unique composition. Pursuing excellence describes the essence of the next narrative, but it is also the transformative grace note heard in the story of each woman featured in this chapter.

Jacqueline Oram-Sterling

Dr. Jacqueline Oram-Sterling was supported in her study for a PhD at Illinois State University (ISU) by a LASPAU/ Fulbright scholarship and a fellowship grant from the Margaret McNamara Memorial Fund (MMMF), an initiative of the World Bank. She titled her narrative "Journeys to Finding Me." Graduating in 2009, she won the university's prestigious Clarence W. Sorenson Distinguished Dissertation Award for her work "The Joan Wint Story: Biography of a Principal Whose Leadership for Social Justice Transformed a Rural Jamaican High School."

Jacque's three children attended her dissertation defense, and both of her parents and other family members attended graduation. She taught undergraduate foundations classes at ISU before returning to Jamaica in 2010, where she is a senior lecturer in history, sociology, and social studies methodology and programme officer for the graduate school at The Mico University College in Kingston. Jacque began her narrative with an excerpt of the tribute to her children in her dissertation acknowledgments: "You are my greatest gifts and my biggest cheerleaders. . . . You cheered me up when I could not control the tears, you are the strong ones and I truly appreciate your strength. Thank you for believing in me and supporting me in all my endeavors. The sacrifices were great, but I just want you to know that mommy loves you."

In the narrative Jacque shares details about her family and her early life circumstances in rural Jamaica.

I was born in the small rural district of Park Hall. I am the eldest of eight children, having three sisters and four brothers. One brother died tragically and mysteriously at age sixteen and his death brought great sorrow to my family and changed our lives profoundly. Both my parents are unable to read, and even though my mother attended primary school, she still does not recognize words. My father has always encouraged me and sacrificed everything to give me an education.

He has a small farm and my mother usually sells the produce to support our family. My father's farming has been our only source of income all my life. As a child I did not realize we were poor, because we always had food to eat and kerosene oil for the lamp. I did all my school work using a kerosene lamp. I loved to read and would stay up all night reading—of all things—romantic novels. I would then fall asleep imagining myself as the heroine in these stories. Growing up without electricity or a television in rural Jamaica, books gave meaning to my life.

Sharing specifically about her father, Jacque wrote that he was a major influence in her life growing up. "He was a man's man. He never hugged us then, nor would he tell us he loved us, but we knew he did. He was always inspecting my school shoes to make sure they were still intact, because then we walked miles to school." She continued, "I always tell others that even without a formal education my father is one of the smartest men I know."

One sentence in particular captured Jacque's drive and determination: "I grew up poor, but poverty never deterred my drive to excel." She described what growing up poor meant.

Poverty is widespread in Jamaica and in the 1970s when I was growing up rural children often went barefooted and clothing was usually "hand me downs." We survived without piped water or electricity. Televisions were unheard of. We carried on our heads water drawn from underground springs in the community. Meals were prepared in an outdoor kitchen, using firewood gathered from nearby fields. Almost everyone in my community lived in unpainted small board houses devoid of indoor plumbing or any sort of modern amenities.

"In elementary school, I was not self-conscious about poverty," Jacque remembered. During each school day her mother would meet her halfway between her home and school with lunch. "She would lug the baby and my cooked lunch and we would sit in an open field. This was an orange grove and an area we call the Pen. We would sit daily and I would eat my lunch and run back to school. . . . She did not have the money for me to buy lunch, but I would not go hungry; she brought lunch to me."

These outdoor lunches happened when Jacque went to the local primary school. Then her father transferred her to another school, which was miles away from home but where his youngest sister taught. "She took me under her wings, helping to create a successful foundation in my early education."

Jacque believes that "both her guidance and the new school helped me tremendously."

For Jacque, "Gaining entry into high school was not a straightforward path. In the 1970s the students who were successful in passing the local high-school entrance examinations had their names published in the local newspaper. On that fateful day when the results came out, my name was not in the paper. I did not pass the common entrance exam." Fortunately, however, "there was still the special entrance through a test offered by the local high school. I passed this test by some miracle and was admitted to high school."

High school brought a new awakening. "High school opened my eyes to the opportunities I did not have. My friends lived in nicer houses made of concrete. They were able to go on educational trips, which I did not tell my parents about because I knew they would not be able to afford them. Despite my family's lack of financial resources I excelled in school." When asked what made her academic success possible, Jacque answered, "I realize that it was a strong family support system—including the value my parents placed on education, and my aunts (Nessa and Pearline) who gave me opportunities that my parents could not give me, such as an exposure to books and visits to the city." Giving credit to herself, she wrote, "But above all one has to be intrinsically motivated."

At sixteen, Jacque passed the examinations required for access to higher education and was admitted to Church Teachers College in Mandeville. "Being away from your family for the first time was not easy and in the beginning I tried to quit, thinking college was not for me." Fortunately, a turning point came "when a sociology professor targeted me, saying, 'Jacqueline Oram, you are not a "C" student,' and ranting at me for a long time."

She did not quit. "I made a pledge to myself to show her that I could do it, and at the end of the school year I gained an A in my sociology class." Jacque emphasized, "It was then that I believed I could be anything I wanted to be." She graduated with a diploma in teaching at age nineteen, having majored in social studies and religious education. Her first year of teaching was at the local primary school.

Principal Joan Wint, whose leadership was the subject of Jacque's dissertation, hired her to teach the following year at Denbigh High School in Clarendon Parish. A newly appointed principal, Joan drove to Jacque's house to offer her the job. Jacque was just twenty years old. "I guess she really needed a teacher, so she asked, 'Can you manage big boys?' Never having to manage 'big boys,' but really wanting to leave home, I told her 'yes.'"

Reflecting on her career, Jacque wrote, "As a young teacher in my twenties I had so much self-doubt and kept wondering what Joan Wint saw in me when she started assigning me to positions of responsibility. She kept telling me that I would go very far; then I had no idea what she meant." Joan Wint was the first of a series of significant mentors who have "propelled and encouraged" Jacque. "My mentors cared about both my professional and personal growth and so we crossed professional borders and found real friendship," she wrote.

Jacque used her first paycheck of five hundred Jamaican dollars and one hundred more borrowed from a cousin "to buy my family a television set with cash." She married, and when the youngest of her three children was a year old she decided, with the encouragement of Joan Wint, to go back to the university full-time to pursue a bachelor's degree in history and sociology. She enrolled as a full-time student, received a scholarship from the Ministry of Education, and traveled three hours each way every day from her rural home in May Pen on public transportation to attend classes at the University of the West-Indies.

According to a feature article in the *Jamaica Gleaner*,

> In order to reach classes at eight o'clock in the morning, she left May Pen at five a.m., a pattern that would continue for many years. The mother of three ran a tight schedule. She would run her home by telephone, supervising the activities of her children and the cooking of meals. On reaching home she would help with the housework and do assignments when the children were in bed. (McPherson 2006)

Jacque wrote, "Everyone was amazed that I lived at home, traveled many miles each day, but was still able to maintain good grades. I told them, 'You can do whatever you set your heart upon.'"

Jacque was promoted to head of the Social Studies Department at Denbigh High School, but she wanted to be a college lecturer. Following that dream, in 2001 she took a position with the Mico University College as a lecturer in history, sociology, and social studies methodology. She began a master's degree program in educational leadership through Central Connecticut State University's offshore program held at the Mico University College.

The demanding course of study required a final semester on the home campus in the United States. Jacque wrote, "I had no idea that this stint was preparing me for my doctoral studies, which would require years of separation from my children." She graduated in 2003 as class valedictorian with a 4.00 GPA. At that time, "I told my fellow graduates that for me success was a journey, not a destination. I had no idea what these words would mean for me."

Returning to Jamaica in June 2010, after spending four years in the United States, "has been eye-opening and extremely challenging," Jacque confessed. "I no longer have access to the necessities/luxuries I took for granted in the US. I have no ready access to telephone, Internet, cable television or even a warm shower." Jacque continued, "I also face another life-changing situation—the reality of divorce. I am back home, but without a home. Again the tears have flowed, but not from remorse; these are cleansing tears."

Reflecting on her journey, Jacque wrote, "I left home in part to find me; now I literally have returned home to the country of my birth, but I have also returned to 'Me.' Finding me has been a circular process. . . . At some level I have come full circle." She continued, "Along my life's journeys I have learned many lessons. I have grasped the essence of the meaning of my life—what it means to have dreams and to follow them, how to let go of stifling situations, how not to cower even if one is afraid, but to face your battles head-on."

Jacque's closing words offer insights about the role of those who are privileged. She ended the narrative with a comment on her own privilege and a call to action:

> As a woman living in a third world country, I also realize that I am the voice of my sisters who are often silenced due to poverty, lack of educational opportunities, unemployment and lack of access to technology, as well as those who are trapped in situations of violence. As we women leaders from "across the continents" blend our raised voices, I certainly believe that we echo the ills faced by our sisters whose voices we do not hear, those crying out in the trenches for a better tomorrow for themselves, their children and certainly our society as a whole. Women working together across the continents can bring change—the word is a powerful tool.

Insights

The success of Jacqueline Oram-Sterling as a scholar with an academic appointment could not have been predicted from her position as the oldest girl in a family of eight, headed by parents who could not read in a household centered on farming. Her parents valued education, however, and two aunts who were teachers provided her with books when they discovered her love for reading. Whereas her father wanted his sons to help with the farming work, he wanted his daughters to go to school. Jacque is the only one of her siblings with a university degree, however. Both family support and mentors are important factors in Jacque's success, as they were for other WLE members.

Family support took many forms and was elaborated in fifteen of the narratives. Family members often sacrificed to provide financial support for educational opportunities. Others helped with child care. Family from various income levels emphasized the importance of education. Several reported family support for education in cultures where education for girls was not the norm. Bepko and Krestan (1993) observe from their study about women who lead that "they have a strong sense of purpose. Their lives have often been affected by loss or struggle. They are frequently supported by fathers in their desire for achievement outside the traditional pattern of home and family" (128). The support of her father was important to Jacque, and a father's support was particularly noted by nine others who submitted narratives.

Supportive mentors encouraged Jacque at each step of her educational journey. This was true for other WLE members also. A total of nineteen of the narratives included comments specifically about mentors who were crucial to the individual's success. Mentors were often instrumental in important turning points. A professor who saw Jacque's potential and demanded that she do better work built her self-confidence and made possible both her graduation from teacher's college and her teaching career. Principal Joan Wint encouraged Jacque to leave Denbigh High School and study full-time to earn a university degree. These were both critical turning points.

Jacque's academic success is a reminder that students from all economic levels have the potential to be successful in school, that the drive to excel is not dependent on social class. The intrinsic motivation to succeed, support by family, and cultivation by mentors, were critical factors in the successes of each woman featured in this chapter.

CULTURAL COMPARISONS: SELECTED SCHOLARSHIP

The educational and career passages of each woman featured in this chapter involve confronting and overcoming cultural expectations of a woman's place. Presenting these narratives we have emphasized how each woman experienced her education and how each arrived at her present career position. Each journey has featured challenge and growth. Participants have experienced the complex influences of different geographic places on their personal and professional journeys. Commonalities are greater than one might at first expect. Three aspects of the complexity of place creating commonalities among the stories are the conception in a country of a woman's place in society, her age relative to the women's movement, and her socioeconomic status.

In any cross-cultural comparison of women's personal and professional journeys, conclusions about the role of place are framed with difficulty, in part because of the danger of essentializing. According to Bose and Kim (2009), "women's conditions and needs vary by region, country, or locality in which they live" (2). They also assert,

> Most feminists would concur that whatever progress has been made in the recent past—in freeing women from full-time domestic work, in increasing their visibility and participation in the public sphere, and in addressing a whole gamut of critical women and gender issues—is still far from subverting or transforming the entrenched sexist and unequal power structures and relations that prevail all over the world. (2)

What is perceived as "a woman's place" in a country or society influences her access to education and who she can become, particularly in terms of leadership roles.

Common cultural expectations across the world are that leaders will be men and that a woman's place is in the home. Even though things are changing, deeply embedded in the Greek, Chinese, Jamaican, and American cultures are similar beliefs. Regarding Greece, Kaparou and Bush (2007) observe that "in Greek culture, men still have the main responsibility for meeting the financial needs of the family, while women are responsible for family caring. Most domestic tasks are undertaken by women, notably those related to children. Indeed, women face expectations that they will prioritize family over work" (227).

Wilson (2004) asserts about the United States that "despite the enormous gains we have made in the last twenty-five years, the 'cultural ideal' for a woman remains that of wife and mother" (xii). Characterizing family structure in China, Kim and Bose (2009) state,

> In many Asian countries, marriage is still a social and cultural norm that is expected of all men and women above some "appropriate" age. . . . Family structure remains based on heterosexual marriage, and patriarchal ideology is embedded in various aspects of family, ranging from custom to family law. (70)

Jamaica is considered a matriarchal culture because of the prevalence of female-headed families. However, as Jacque explains, "Throughout Jamaica and the rest of the Caribbean, men are assigned to the public sphere as wage earners and supporters of their families, whereas women are relegated to the private sphere as housewives and caregivers" (Oram-Sterling 2009, 61). Women are still largely excluded from leadership and governance roles.

A common background to our individual experiences has been the global pioneering of the women's movement as illustrated by growing recognition in the 1970s of women's studies as an academic interdisciplinary field; the first World Conference on Women in Mexico City in 1975; creation of the annual celebration of March 8 as International Women's Day; designation of 1975–1985 by the United Nations as the Decade for Women; the recent ongoing United Nations' Millenium Development Goals that include attention to gender equality and women's empowerment; and other efforts of continuing transnational feminism to change the gender power imbalance (Bose and Kim 2009; Mohanty 2003).

Expanding the complex picture, Sperandio (2010) writes that "the context of women in educational leadership is now both local and global. At the local level, societal attitudes toward the education of girls, women's domestic responsibilities and ability to provide leadership contribute to female self-image and ability to envisage careers involving leadership" (716). Continuing development of transnational feminism paralleled the second wave of the women's movement in the United States, which was well under way by the 1970s.

Collins (2009) identifies 1960 as the year everything changed in the United States for women. Betty Friedan's *The Feminine Mystique* was published in 1963, and reactions were at first mixed as women recognized themselves in its pages. Born in 1941, Linda's conflicted decision making with regard to a career and romance represented typical thinking among American women who came of age in the 1950s. Although career options for women were expanding beyond teaching, nursing, and secretarial work, many perceived their choices still to be limited. Born in 1962, Katherine's desire to be an astronaut at age eight illustrated how things changed in the United States with regard to women's thinking about career options as a result of the second wave of the women's movement.

Angeliki, the youngest of the five, seemed to understand instinctively that she needed more than a Greek script on which to pattern her life. Even though born into a traditional Chinese culture, Esther seems to have headed straight for a career, in part as a way to escape from what had been the poverty of her youth. Now in her late forties, she was making her early career decisions during the 1975–1985 UN Decade for Women as the women's movement became increasingly transnational. And in Jamaica, Jacque explains, "Education created new opportunities for women and diminished their dependence on the Jamaican male" (Oram-Sterling 2009, 61). Nevertheless, she continues, "their visibility in the public sphere is still relegated to gendered professions" (66).

A further complexity of place in educational and career passages is the socioeconomic status of a woman's family. According to Mercer, Nichols, and Doyle (1989), a "woman's family of origin and the socioeconomic conditions in which the family was enmeshed were powerful influences on her adult development" (189). Angeliki and Linda grew up in middle-income families, while Esther, Katherine, and Jacque were from lower-income families. The entire spectrum of family economic circumstances—lower to upper—existed for the WLE group members. Nevertheless, education was a priority.

Cost did not provide an insurmountable barrier to education, although getting financing together was often difficult. Scholarships, government subsidies, graduate assistantships, and family contributions were required. Some families covered the entire cost of education. Some women won scholarships, held jobs, and took out loans. In several countries, those who enrolled in undergraduate and then graduate programs won admission through high-stakes exams to state-subsidized programs. Although more women are achieving higher education degrees and leadership opportunities for women have increased, basic cultural beliefs have not fundamentally altered. Each woman in some way interacted in her own developmental journey with two cross-cultural constants, that leaders should be men and that a woman's place is in the home. Differences in their experiences lie in the details of the contexts.

CONCLUDING THOUGHTS

Angeliki Lazaridou grew up Greek, but cultural expectations for early marriage did not keep her from embracing difference and pursuing a newly awakened love of knowledge all the way to a PhD. As a girl, and given her family's impoverished situation in Chinese culture, Esther Sui-chu Ho could not expect education; but when it came, she made the most of each opportunity and now balances expectations in combining her family and academic life. Linda Lyman inhaled the 1950s script for women and lived the *feminine mystique*, but in finding the way to wholeness she excelled professionally and became herself. Katherine Cumings Mansfield grew up during the second wave of the women's movement in the 1970s when belief that "a woman could be anything she wanted" was in the air. Even so, fulfilling her potential involved some unraveling and reweaving of the threads, guided by the hand of the "Divine Seamstress." Jacqueline Oram-Sterling grew up poor, but poverty never deterred her drive to excel academically and every other way.

What does it all mean? The chapter shares stories of women whose challenges have shaped who they are. In the words of poet David Whyte (2001), "To have a *firm persuasion*, to set out boldly in our work, is to make a pilgrimage of our labors, to understand that the consummation of work lies not only in what we have done, but who we have become while accomplishing the task" (5). Reflecting on the life stories shared in this chapter, it becomes increasingly clear that our passages have become our pathways. The passages are the challenges we have met in the process of composing our lives and becoming ourselves. They are the pathways we hope to open for others by sharing our stories.

3

IMPERATIVES

People are raising deeper questions about the nature of power, the abuse of human rights, the human cost of global inequities, and the meaning of a just world order.

—V. Spike Peterson and Anne Sisson Runyan, *Global Gender Issues*

As educational leaders and scholars from around the world, WLE members are asking the deeper questions about gender inequities—the nature of power, the abuse of human rights, the human cost of lack of access to education, and the meaning of a just world order. These questions take a variety of forms. Do women who are powerful leaders recast the meaning of power? How can violence against women, an abuse of human rights, be stopped? What is the human cost of existing global gender inequities in girls' access to education? How can educational leadership be generative, bringing to life a more socially just world order? As we have pondered these urgent questions they have become imperatives, moving us toward social justice leadership.

Each person who came to the Women Leading Education Across the Continents (WLE) conferences in 2007, 2009, and 2011 was invited because of commitment to gender equity as a social justice issue. At the conferences we have shared research about the status of women's leadership in education and girls' access to education in the countries we represented. These and other issues of social justice for women and girls exist in countries whatever their levels of economic development. Global gender issues for women that are linked to social justice leadership include discrimination, violence, poverty, education, invisibility, and the social construction of gender as it impacts a woman's sense of agency and worth (Bose and Kim 2009; Kelly, Bayes, Hawkesworth, and Young 2001; Mohanty 2003; Peterson and Runyon 1999).

Each of the narratives touched in some way on these social justice issues. We have experienced our questions turning into imperatives. For some, a vision of social justice developed early from difficult economic circumstances of their families and in their countries. Still others were called to action by discrimination witnessed or experienced in the educational process. Some committed to furthering social justice as a result of workplace discrimination. Yet others were motivated by observing or enduring violence. Some were moved by values learned from family, faith traditions, and culture. Finally, in every narrative is a story of how education functioned as an imperative, a force giving life the shape of social justice. In this chapter we explore how personal negative experiences of discrimination and violence against women, as well as positive transformative education, have moved us individually and collectively toward commitments to social justice leadership.

COMMITMENT TO SOCIAL JUSTICE: THE STORIES

Sources of imperatives that move a person to social justice leadership are many. Stories of personal commitment to social justice found in the WLE narratives can be framed by three recurring thematic categories. Narratives of three featured leaders illustrate how commitment to social justice unfolds and deepens in a particular life. The thematic categories and leaders featured are: (1) Discrimination–Rosangela Malachias, Brazil; (2) Violence–Charol Shakeshaft, United States; and (3) Education–Saeeda Shah, Pakistan.

Discrimination

In the whole collection of narratives, specific instances of discrimination and marginalization assumed many forms and often resulted from intersections of gender, class, race, and ethnicity (Collins 2000). Depending on the cultural context, gender alone accounted for many episodes of discrimination. Of the twenty-three participating leaders, only one–Sister Dr. Hellen Bandiho (Tanzania)–did not describe personal experiences of discrimination either in accessing education or advancing her career. Sister Hellen was, however, clearly aware of discriminatory practices affecting other women's lives.

Particularly for women, discrimination can be intensified by the intersection of gender, race, and class. According to Acosta-Belen (2009), in Latin America and the Caribbean "social, racial, and gender marginality [are] endured by a substantial majority of their citizens, especially those of indigenous and black racial origin" (151). This accurately describes Brazil, one of the most racially diverse nations on earth. Today only 49.7 percent of Brazilians consider themselves white (Downie and Lloyd 2010). Although the country never formalized racial segregation, unlike the United States and South Africa, Brazil was the last Western country to formally abolish slavery, not doing so until 1888.

Rosangela Malachias

Dr. Rosangela Malachias from São Paulo, Brazil, has rigorously worked to address barriers of discrimination. Her story illustrates multiple and intersecting experiences of discrimination. Determination to transcend the constraints of class and race has impelled Rosangela, a communication consultant and journalist, to over two decades of social justice activism. Her ongoing commitment as a black movement activist is to reduce prejudice and discrimination against black people, with a special sensitivity to issues of discrimination against black women. In 2002 she became the first black woman to receive a PhD in the Department of Communications and Arts at the University of São Paulo. Now in her midforties, she wrote, "I am a journalist who goes to public schools 'to teach' public teachers about diversity, African, and African Brazilian culture."

Rosangela grew up with her mother, father, grandmother, and brother in São Paulo. Her narrative, titled "The Dreams Come True," begins with this story of how she decided to become a journalist:

> I decided to become a journalist when I was a little child and my family influenced my choice. My grandmother, Maria Aparecida, was a public servant who cleaned schools. When I was five years old, she told me: "You don't need to be a servant like me. If you study, you can have a better profession." Some months later, my father, Antonio Malachias, bought our first television. When I watched the news, I asked my mom, Zulmira, "Who was that man who was telling the news" and she said: "He is a journalist." Running to my grandma, I said to her: "I want to be a journalist."

Public universities in Brazil are regarded as superior to the private schools and competition for entrance is high, in part because tuition is free. Selection of students is up to the individual universities, based on a standardized testing process using tests of their own design.

> *Vestibular* is a test open to all students who have completed high school (similar to American GMAT, but the preparation of tests and evaluation of results is up to each college); the students with the best scores qualify to enrollment. . . . In consequence of this system, the vacancies in the most sought after courses (Engineering, Laws, etc.) in public colleges are taken by candidates from the upper and middle class, who can afford to have a good fundamental and secondary education. The poorer usually resort to the private institutions, where competition is lower. (www.vbrazil.com/science/universities)

Rosangela did not qualify for undergraduate admission to the largest public university in her city, the University of São Paulo (USP). Only 2 to 3 percent of students at public universities are black, with a minority of mixed race. The vast majority are white. She began her higher education at the age of seventeen at a private college. Only seventeen years old, she needed her father's help to take out a loan to pay the tuition for the first semester and found a job at a law office. She was the first person in her family to graduate from a university, continuing work at the law office for two more years. In 1985, when she was twenty-three years old, her father found a job for her at *São Paulo Zona Sul Journal*, a south-side regional newspaper for which he was a distributor. The founder of the paper gave her a job as an administrative assistant.

Two years later Rosangela finally became a reporter at that paper—four years after earning a degree qualifying her as a journalist. She wrote, "I was happier working in my major field than in the law office. However, I was upset by my low salary." In 1988 she was invited to give a lecture about "my professional success." The event was a celebration of two historical occasions: the hundred-year anniversary of the abolition of slavery, and the new constitution establishing Brazil as a democratic country.

Rosangela's activism to implement public policies for the inclusion of black people began at that event after she heard a famous and powerful black woman lawyer in her sixties, Orlanda Campos Gentile, lecture about her life and struggle against prejudice and discrimination. Rosangela described this as a turning point. "I awoke to 'a new reality': I was a Black woman too, who received a low salary while my white colleagues received three times more than me." Reviewing her life, she decided to go back to the university to earn a graduate degree. Rosangela applied three times to begin a master's degree at the University of São Paulo before her enrollment was finally approved in 1993.

During the five years of waiting she continued her work as a reporter and became involved in black movement activism. For example, Rosangela and a group she called "her first Black friends" organized the first Black Student Conference at the Law School of University of São Paulo (USP) to debate the constitutional rights and citizenship. She remarked, "During my educational socialization, I hadn't met Black people. This is a Brazilian paradox. Brazil has a population of almost 50 percent African descendants; however, the more you study the fewer black people you find." Finally admitted, she completed her master's degree in Latin American integration in 1996. She focused her studies on black youth, comparing African Brazilians and African Cubans.

In 1997 Rosangela developed an interactive youth project (Juventude Interativa) and became a MacArthur Foundation fellow. In this capacity, from 1997 to 2000, she studied youth and prevention of STD, HIV-AIDS, and drugs. This issue put her inside public schools. Then, in 2001, she was selected as a Ryoichi

Sasakawa fellow (a Japanese institution that supports leadership) and received an invitation to learn the Educomuniçāo ("educommunication") method. As a result of her training and expertise, she started giving lectures about cultural plurality and media for thousands of public teachers.

> During four years, every Saturday, I had meetings with teachers to analyze the media and produce new possibilities of curricula. . . . Unfortunately, schools are also spaces of prejudice, and to end this situation, education and legislation must walk together. However, these issues are associated with hard topics, such as racism, chauvinism, prejudice, violence. I have developed a methodology in which I use media—newspapers, magazines, soap operas, movies—to give teachers alternatives for their curricula. Sometimes, I talk to [anywhere from] 50 to 450 teachers per session, during three or four meetings of four hours. We exchange knowledge about education (from their side) and communication (from my side). . . . What intrigues me about my work is the fascinating chance to unify two big fields of knowledge—communication and education.

After receiving her PhD, Rosangela was an academic consultant from 2003 to 2007 for the Race, Development, and Social Inequality program, a FIPSE-CAPES (Fund for the Improvement of Postsecondary Education) consortium among four universities for exchanging Brazilian undergraduate students and American graduate students. The purpose was "to help them combat institutional racism and receive fellowships to study in the United States for one semester." With that work under way, in 2003 with two other black women Rosangela created the Media and Ethnicity Group (Grupo Midia e Etnia), and in 2004 they organized the First International Conference about Media and Ethnicity, sponsored by the federal government in São Paulo.

In 2006, Rosangela became a UNESCO researcher and with other scholars studied and published about "Access and Retention of Black Students at USP." From 2008 to 2009 she was in the United States at the University of Maryland, College Park as a Hubert H. Humphrey fellow (Fulbright program) in communication, education, and advocacy. When Rosangela returned to São Paulo she took a position as a communication consultant for the Center on Labor Relations and Inequality (CEERT), a large NGO (nongovernmental organization) in São Paulo. For one year in that position she had several projects, including e-learning initiatives around issues of gender, race, management, and public policies.

Now Rosangela maintains simultaneous jobs. The first is working as an independent advisor hired by the Department of Education of São Paulo that is linked to the municipal government. The second is with her own communication consulting firm, which won a governmental competition to train public school teachers in a small city about African Brazilian culture and history and also the history of Africa in basic education. This mandated program is in response to the federal law that changed the Brazilian constitution. Rosangela says she cannot refuse work because her income is needed to help with family expenses.

Since returning to Brazil from the United States in 2009, Rosangela continues to live with her family. "Why? Because I am an ordinary Brazilian Black woman. It means to live with my family, in the same house, to work and share expenses, to share a bathroom too. If we do not do it this way, we cannot live. Black people in Brazil receive low salaries." In a comment about being single she wrote,

> I am not complaining or crying. I am aware and happy about my "blackness," but you need also to understand that I learned to live in family. In contrast, I also learned to be alone and sometimes I thank God for this freedom. Most of the Black women who have high educational levels are single. This is not an option. This is our reality. (R. M., e-mail message to author, July 16, 2009)

Further describing Brazilian reality, she observed, "Brazil is famous for 'racial democracy,' but really Black people are the most poor among White and Asian people. Big companies, universities, do not hire Black people. It is very difficult to see Black people on media too."

A line in Rosangela's narrative reads, "I have had dreams and I am lucky because some of them have been possible." But some other dreams have not yet come true.

> I would like to have married. I have a lot of friends, but I never had a child and I think that God gave me this challenge. In my free time I am a volunteer in a center where I develop activities with young people. They are "my children." I love to study, but was not hired as a professor by University of São Paulo (USP) yet. I tried twice and competed with dozens of people. I won't give up. I love to be Black, but I would like to live in a country (world) where racial equity was real. I also have watched a lot of white teachers become aware about racism and prejudice. They tell me that I opened their eyes and now they have been partners combating racism in the public schools where they work. (R. M., e-mail message to author, July 16, 2009)

With a master's, a doctorate, and her own communication consulting office, Rosangela wrote, "Education is our only chance to upgrade our condition. I am a PhD Black woman since 2002, but I am not a faculty yet even though I have applied twice. Why? You need to understand how difficult it is to access good jobs when you have Black skin; however the Black Movement has had successes and the number of black faculty in federal universities is increasing" (R. M., e-mail message to author, July 16, 2009).

With a successful record of research for university centers, large grant-funded projects, and three highly sought-after fellowships (MacArthur fellow;

Ryoichi Sasakawa fellow; Hubert M. Humphrey fellow/Fulbright program), Rosangela has yet to secure a university faculty position at University of Sao Paulo, having tried twice. Faculty positions depend, in part, on ranking high on an admission exam and publications in scientific periodicals, whereas Rosangela has articles published in common books and magazines directed to public teachers and educators. However, the federal higher education institutions have begun opening places for new professors, and with more positions becoming available she continues to pursue that dream:

> I am thinking to start a postdoctorate and after that applying again for a job in a federal university. I do not want to leave my consultancy office. It is a dream too, but I need to keep my feet on the floor and the postdoctorate can give me a score to compete with other candidates. (R. M., e-mail message to author, September 20, 2010)

The prophetic title of Rosangela's dissertation was "Dreams May Come True," and so she continues to move forward, "believing, they really come."

Insights

Rosangela faced the intersection of formidable discriminatory forces in achieving her grandmother's desire—that she have a better profession. These included gender, race, and class. Rosangela was luckier than many, with an intact family, a resourceful father, and a family that was supporting itself, albeit not on a grand scale. The family experience of poverty was relative, but never absolute as it is for many black Brazilians. The current national minimum monthly wage in Brazil is around the equivalent of $285 (Downie and Lloyd 2010). If the quality of schools in high-poverty areas in Brazil matches the pattern in the United States, then the first level of discrimination Rosangela faced may have come from perceptions about the quality of her primary- and secondary-school experience.

Lower-quality basic education in the high-poverty section of the city where her family lives could have kept Rosangela from being among the small percentage of minority students who were admitted to a public university with free tuition. Instead, clearly intelligent and motivated to get a university education and be a journalist, she borrowed money and held a job to pay for her college degree. She may have faced some type of discrimination again when applying for the master's degree. Perhaps Rosangela's undergraduate private college degree did not hold the same level of prestige, or perhaps she was being held to a different standard because of gender and race. Perhaps she encountered years where the typically few graduate student spaces available at flagship institutions were fewer than usual. Her life experiences generally became more positive after she earned a master's degree. Her accomplishment as the first black woman to complete the PhD program in communication and the arts at the University of São Paulo was truly remarkable; she perceives, however, that continuing discrimination against blacks is a primary factor keeping her from securing a faculty position.

As a group, WLE supports and stands for equal educational opportunities for girls and equity in leadership roles for women. As individuals, we have researched and advocated both. We understand that class-based discrimination intersects with gender and racial/ethnic discrimination particularly in less-developed countries. Underlying global poverty are discrimination and violence against women. Kristoff and WuDunn (2009a), who focus attention on women in the economically developing countries of the world, call the oppression of women worldwide "the human rights cause of our time" (29).

Kristoff and WuDunn (2009a) reason that "if the injustices that women in poor countries suffer are of paramount importance, in an economic and geopolitical sense the opportunity they represent is even greater" (28). They observe about countries where girls are uneducated and women marginalized that "it's not an accident that those same countries are disproportionately mired in poverty and driven by fundamentalism and chaos" (28). In fact, they describe women themselves "as the best hope for fighting global poverty" (34), because the money women could make if educated would support their countries as well as their families. Kristoff and WuDunn (2009a, 2009b) describe women who have been successful at turning around lives of poverty. When we increase access to education for girls worldwide, we contribute to making more of these inspiring turnaround stories possible. Voices of educational leaders worldwide must be raised in advocacy to make this happen.

Violence

Every WLE member who submitted a narrative described events that could be classified as critical or pivotal in her commitment toward social justice leadership. For some, critical incidents involved the trauma of leaving home. Others were positively motivated by mentors. Nine narratives described abuse and injustices the writers had either witnessed or experienced. No examples were as "critical" as those that involved encounters with violence. For each woman, observing or enduring these injustices moved her to social justice leadership.

As illustrated by the narratives submitted for this book, violence against women is clearly a global issue. French's (1992) description from two decades ago about the United States still rings true: "Male violence toward women could not be as epidemic as it is without the cooperation of the entire social system—the press, police, courts, legislatures, academia, welfare agencies, the professions, and other institutions. Personal violence against women is a tissue of individual acts given firm backing by entrenched institutions" (182). Additionally, French asserts that these types of situations of equal or greater severity exist throughout the world, that "the climate of violence against women harms all women" (197).

Women are sometime categorized as "collateral damage" when they are hurt from violence of wars. What French (1992) calls personal violence typically happens within the home and is also called domestic violence. We feature a story that illustrates how the violence of childhood sexual abuse affected one woman's entire life and how she has turned that anger into a force for good.

Charol Shakeshaft

The featured example of a leader whose life has been affected by violence against women is Dr. Charol Shakeshaft, whose scholarship about women's leadership is widely read and highly regarded. She published the first comprehensive synthesis of the existing research on women's leadership in education in the United States: *Women in Educational Administration* (1987), which is now in its fifth printing.

Although never a superintendent herself, Charol was honored in 2009 by the American Association of School Administrators (AASA) as one of several winners of the coveted Dr. Effie H. Jones Humanitarian Award, which honors leadership in educational equity and excellence. Criteria for the award include commitment to the advancement and mentorship of women and minorities in positions of leadership and/or commitment to address social justice issues among children, youth, and adults in schools. Charol has done both.

The AASA website describes her accomplishments as follows:

Charol Shakeshaft is Professor and Chair of the Department of Education Leadership at Virginia Commonwealth University. Since 1979, she has worked with graduate students, particularly women, helping to prepare them for leadership in school administration. Dr. Shakeshaft has been studying equity in schools for over 30 years, documenting gendered practice in the classroom and in school administration. She is an internationally recognized researcher in the area of gender patterns in educational delivery and classroom interactions. Her work on equity in schools has taken her into school systems across the United States, Canada and Europe where she has helped educators make schools more welcoming to females and students of color. Shakeshaft gives talks, presents workshops, evaluates programs and curriculum, and conducts gender audits. She serves as an expert witness and consultant in a number of legal proceedings on sexual harassment of students, and works with school districts to develop policies and practices that decrease sexual harassment of all within the educational community. Dr. Shakeshaft was also the principal investigator for the National Science Foundation on a multiyear project to increase the achievement of low-income students of color in science and mathematics and is the principal investigator on a $5.3 million grant for the equitable preparation of assistant principals and principals with a focus on instructional leadership. (http://www.aasa.org/content .aspx?id=3400)

Charol has lived with the reality of violence against women and its repercussions at a personal level since childhood. Now in her early sixties, Charol did not title her narrative, which begins with these lines:

> One event, more than anything else, began a chain of behaviors, reactions, and responses that has influenced nearly every decision I have made, whether consciously or not. I was sexually abused at age three. Although it is always more complex than simple cause and effect, this violation explains my life more than anything else. As far back as I can remember, I was angry.

Born on a farm in rural Iowa, the sexual abuse first started with her grandfather and then a neighboring farmer. When she was four, the family relocated to town. Charol wrote, "Town was still rural Iowa, far from everything, isolated by distance, cornfields, poverty, and ignorance." She continued, "I told my mother what my grandfather had done to me, but she said it wasn't true." Charol said she felt abandoned and "I learned that men could abuse children and no one would stop it." She wrote that her parents "were good, well meaning people who gave me more than they had received from their parents. They did the best they could." Major events and lessons of her life unfold through her narrative, punctuated by the recurring sentence *"And I was angry."*

> I learned that school and teachers were unfair to girls. . . . I learned that a female who stands up for herself is aggressive. . . . I learned that money and privilege didn't protect me from abuse by men. . . . I learned that no one cared if I hurt myself. . . . I learned that writing could be powerful and dangerous. . . . I learned that women who were abused were damaged.

President of the National Honor Society, upon graduation from high school as a National Merit Scholarship Semifinalist, Charol knew she wanted "to have a career that would fight inequality," but she didn't know what that would be. After her first year of college, she wrote, "I gave in to intense pressure and married my boyfriend." On their wedding night she told him about being sexually abused as a child. "He was horrified, not that I was abused, but that he had married someone who was 'used.'" He returned from the honeymoon to stay with his parents, and they were divorced in less than a year.

Charol finished another year of college but was without focus and confused. She decided to go to New York for acting school. That brought another experience with sexual abuse. "Toward the end of the first year, I was gang raped at a casting call. I stopped talking, wouldn't leave my apartment, and eventually returned to my parents' home in Iowa for a summer. I learned that the Midwest wasn't the only place where men were dangerous."

Still wanting to "do work that would change the way that women were treated," Charol returned to college determined to learn to make films. She finished college, married again, and got a job with a filmmaker in New York City. Eventually this scenario unfolded:

> A new boss was hired and on his first day on the job he took me to lunch and told me that I could either have sex with him that night or be demoted to secretary. I quit. I went to the company and told them what had happened. They said grow up. I learned that I wasn't strong enough to be a filmmaker.

It was at this point that Charol, offered a job at a private school for gifted children in Brooklyn Heights, decided to try teaching. "I had always said that I would never be a teacher. I saw it as a stereotypic female career. But I needed a job, so I took it. I came to appreciate the power of teaching and the opportunity to change the status quo." Her experiences in the world of education provided a continuation of "learning" experiences. She tried to unionize the faculty and stop the headmaster and some teachers from sexual activity "with each other and with students. I learned they were stronger than I was and that people willing to speak in private were afraid to stand up in public." Moving to Texas with her professor husband, she began a PhD program and became a graduate assistant. Assigned a secretarial role, she asked instead "to work with a professor just like the male students. No professor would work with me. I learned that speaking out against inequality would result in isolation."

Charol focused much of her class work on women's issues but was not supported in that. One day a male student picked up a table with her materials on it and threw it across the room, saying, "That's what I think of your feminism. . . . I learned that talking about feminism made men violent." When her husband was at a conference, she went to a dinner one evening with a couple who were both university employees. She accepted a ride home with them. The woman drove off, and Charol was pushed into her home by the husband and raped. Bleeding and left with a dislocated jaw, she was "told by university officials not to contact the police. My husband couldn't understand why a smart woman like me had been raped. He couldn't understand why I didn't stop it. I didn't understand either. I learned that institutions protect their own, especially when they are men."

At that point, Charol wrote, "I decided to become a lesbian. It seemed the best decision. No men, no violence, no fear, and no anger. . . . I learned that the only way to be safe from men was to live apart from them." She completed her dissertation on women's leadership styles and took a job at Hofstra University, moving there with her partner, "a gentle, loving friend and partner with whom I lived for fifteen years." The "learning" continued as indicated by the following: "I learned that working in an all male department meant continued hostility and harassment. . . . I learned how universities are able to control young faculty members. . . . I learned that even with a PhD, a job could depend upon sex. . . . I learned that my expertise had nothing to do with my appointment to a prestigious position." Experiences multiplied and the anger continued.

A new refrain begin to emerge after Charol was elected as vice president of Division A (Administration) in the prestigious American Educational Research Association (AERA). She wrote, "I used the position to advance women's issues in a male dominated Division A. . . . I used comedy to talk about gender issues and I talked about my life. . . . Everyone laughed. They thought I made it up." She wrote, "I learned how to channel my anger into humor. *And I was less angry.*" With the safety of tenure and continuing employment she felt she could become a parent. Initially no one supported her, but she began the adoption process and became a mother five months later.

> Everyone thought it was wrong. Some people felt a lesbian shouldn't adopt. Others believed a white person couldn't adequately parent a black child. And still others felt I just wasn't mother material. Time will tell. I learned not to listen to others who get in the way of what I want.

Becoming chairperson of her department at Hofstra, Charol was able to hire people committed to social justice, an equal number of men and women, and an equal number of minority and majority faculty. Building a new department, she wrote, "I learned that there were some men who were decent and caring. *And I was less angry.*" She and the woman who had been her partner separated as Charol "made the decision to come out as a heterosexual." Time and therapy had helped her heal; they continue to be sisters. Moving her research focus to the topic of teachers who sexually abuse students, she testified in trials "when students and parents sue because educator sexual misconduct was not stopped." This has been a significant area of publication and satisfaction for her. She wrote of this development, "I learned that I can use what I know to protect children. *And I was less angry.*"

With this new refrain, the narrative continued. "I met one of those decent and caring men, and I married again. I raised a daughter." Wanting to do something else professionally, she applied to become the dean at Hofstra. Although selected as the top candidate twice by search committees, when the provost

stopped the appointment she left and started a new job at Virginia Commonwealth University in 2007. "I am building a department, working for social
justice, and completing a book." Her narrative ends with this insight:

> My anger served a purpose. It helped me survive an isolated and unsupported
> childhood. It fueled my commitment to change the world for women and girls. It
> pushed me to fight against sexual abuse of children. I learned that I can make a
> difference. I learned that success is measured in small units. I am still angry at in-
> equity and child abuse. I still struggle to get up every morning, to stay and fight,
> and to not hate myself. I don't imagine that will ever change. But I'll keep trying.

Insights

Charol's story personalizes the global issue of violence against women. Information about what happens to vulnerable children and the damage inflicted
by sexual abuse and assault is not new. We know that undoing the stigma can
take a lifetime. The story presents an extraordinary example of an educational
leader and scholar turning great pain into "commitment to change the world
for women and girls." In choosing to write and share this personal narrative
she has courageously raised her voice about a reality many would keep silent.
Raising this subject is significant in the ongoing global struggle to create social
justice for women and girls. If our collective voices can contribute to halting
the diverse forms of violence experienced by women everywhere, we will have
multiplied the outcomes of our individual efforts to shape social justice.

Today, in spite of the Millennium Development Goals to end poverty and
empower women and European Union initiatives to promote gender equality,
the violence continues. In 2008, Human Rights Watch reported soaring rates
of rape and violence against women in the United States in the preceding two
years. Speaking about the world in general, however, Bose and Kim (2009)
write, "Qualified progress has been made in some countries to combat violence
against women" (2). Progress, yes, but in terms of feminist/gender research
concerns that are worldwide, they conclude that "the most universal and critical issue is violence against women" (5).

Education

Every woman who submitted a narrative wrote about an educational experience or opportunity that changed her perspective, opening her eyes to the
reality of social injustice in her own life or the lives of others and moving her
toward a social justice leadership paradigm. Several spoke of understanding
early that education was a way to a better life. Many wrote of being inspired by
particular educational experiences to devote their lives to making a difference.

The WLE group is composed of people who come from diverse backgrounds. Some grew up in poverty, whereas backgrounds of others were more privileged. Investigating why persons from privileged groups support social justice, Goodman (2001) asked people what they thought their motivations were. Findings include that "people's responses tend to fall into three distinct, though interrelated categories" (125). She labels these categories (1) empathy, (2) moral principles and spiritual values, and (3) self-interest. In discussing empathy, she was careful to distinguish it from pity.

> Pity is seeing a homeless person on the street and, while feeling sorry for that person, thinking, "that never could be me." Empathy, however, is more like compassion. . . . Compassion is seeing the homeless person and thinking, "that could be me." . . . Empathy helps us connect with and subsequently care about others who seem different. (127)

Education and knowledge are often the roots of the empathy and compassion that manifest in commitment to social justice leadership.

Saeeda Shah

The featured example of a leader whose education cultivated a commitment to social justice is Dr. Saeeda Shah. Serving since 2003 as senior lecturer in the School of Education at Leicester University in England, Saeeda previously taught for many years in higher education in Pakistan. Her last position there was as professor/dean at the University of Azad Jammu and Kashmir, in Mirpur. A frequent presenter at international conferences, Saeeda has published widely in the areas of educational leadership/management, gender, diversity, faith identity, and Islam and society. Her commitment to social justice is reflected as well in recurring testimony before the United Nations Human Rights Commission, often involving a particular focus on the rights of women and youth in regions of armed conflict.

A respected international voice for gender and human rights, Saeeda describes growing up privileged in Pakistan. She recounts how her prominent conservative traditional Muslim parents and family facilitated her education in a culture that does not encourage public roles for women. Now in her midfifties, Saeeda titled her narrative simply "Selected Chronology." The narrative begins:

> Born in a traditional, religious family who cherish their family tree as descendents of the Prophet Mohammed, I was the second child and the first daughter. Just being a member of the family, irrespective of age, gender, or personal knowl-

edge entitles its members to respect in that society. I was brought up in a house inside a ten-feet-high compound wall, on a hilltop, with a view of a small valley dotted with occasional houses or small clusters of houses, and surrounded by hills with a river flowing by, in a very rural region of Azad Jammu and Kashmir (AJK) in Pakistan. Being perceived as bearers of religious traditions and knowledge, the family enjoyed a religious status and respect from followers who came to seek guidance in religious, social, and even personal matters. Sunday was (and is) the day for the followers to pay visits to seek blessings and guidance, and my earliest memories are of Sundays when hundreds of people—both men and women—would be arriving with their problems, ailments, and worries—women coming inside the compound to Bibi/s (senior ladies in the family) and men going to Pir Sahib (title attributed to male members of the family) in the *Mardana* (male meeting area which was about half-furlong away from the main house in those times). Segregation was a respected tradition.

The Sunday scene imprinted in her memory is of people coming in large numbers to seek advice from her family members, women as well as men, for a variety of problems. Observing her family extend advice and help in this way gave Saeeda an understanding of the meaning and importance of knowledge and compassion.

A second memory is "of the significance of knowledge—the family was respected as perceived bearer of religious knowledge." When asked in a personal communication about the role of her religion in her social justice commitment, Saeeda wrote,

> My religion gives three stages of struggle against injustice—fighting against it, speaking openly against it, and the weakest stage is considering it bad yourself. I am perhaps at the middle stage where I try to highlight these issues in any field when I get an opportunity, whether that has been human rights commission or work in education, and try to raise awareness. Making people think about what is social justice—not just for themselves but for others also—can perhaps lead to better understanding and a better world. Being in education (educational leader?) is an opportunity for me to work towards this shared understanding and conceptualization of social justice. (S. S., e-mail message to author, September 21, 2010)

The family's support for Saeeda's education was extensive. Saeeda's mother was her first teacher, and when it was time for her to go to school her father built a primary school adjacent to the family homes. "It had two rooms within a high compound wall, and a female teacher and a female attendant—initially paid by my father." He extended educational opportunity at a time when there was not a girls' school in the rural region. More than a dozen girls ages five to fifteen started attending with Saeeda. She attended this primary school until she took the year six regional exams offered by a nearby boys' middle school.

Continuing her education from then on required leaving the village and making a variety of accommodations to family and Muslim traditions. Her father rented a house in the district headquarters (Mirpur), and Saeeda "was sent there accompanied by my brother, an aunt, a female cousin, and a servant to attend the school, which I did for the next three years."

To travel escorted from her village home to the city, where the school was, required her at the age of nine to start wearing a burqa. "But my parents permitted me not to wear it while in the city going to and from school. However, I had to be accompanied by a female servant or a male relative when going to school, who would also be waiting for me at the school door every day when the school finished." Her aunt fell ill just before year nine exams, so Saeeda moved back to the family house in the village and was unable to go to school for a whole year. In spite of that gap, she obtained the required permission to take year ten exams and "scored the highest marks among all girls in that region."

From that success followed a succession of firsts: first female in her father's family to matriculate through the formal educational system, as "previously female members of the family were educated only in religious studies and that also within the family compound"; first to go to college; first to be permitted to go to a city in Pakistan to study; first to be allowed to stay in a girls' hostel for her education; and first to complete intermediate education. Finishing a master's in English literature completed the first phase of Saeeda's formal education. Upon returning home after the master's exams, she wrote, "I soon realized that having lived in hostels for education for six years, it was a challenge to spend time 'not doing anything.'"

The family home had shifted to Mirpur, the district headquarters. The conservative family traditions required constraints on mobility and observing *pardah*, plus there were servants to do the household chores. Saeeda decided to enroll for a one-year teacher training program, and then was offered a job.

> The lady principal who was from a city in Pakistan approached my father, requesting him to allow me to teach in the college because they could not find any one in the whole region to teach English. She was clever enough to refer to his commitment to girls' education, and this did the trick. I started my first job as an English lecturer in that college, not as paid lecturer but volunteer. But that was the start. When the job was later advertised I wanted to apply. My mother did a lot of maneuvering to convince my father as she had realized that . . . I would feel useless if I did not have anything to do on a regular basis. Meanwhile my marriage was being arranged with my cousin. I still don't know how, but out of all these negotiations it happened that I could apply for the job. So I applied, had the interview and got the job in another girls' college in a different city in Azad Jammu and Kashmir—becoming the first woman in the family to take up a paid job as well.

In allowing this paid employment, her mother and father both continued to support her quest for a meaningful life.

Saeeda was promoted to assistant professor in three years time and transferred to her hometown of Mirpur. "My daughter was born and that meant that I had to stay in family home where I could get support in looking after her." Involvement in politics created a turbulent time for her family, with various family members (including her father, brother, and husband) facing court cases and in and out of jails for political reasons. After this, her husband stayed mostly in the United Kingdom, and she was demoted by a government order from assistant professor to a lecturer in an action of political victimization, which is common. After years and a court case, the government order was withdrawn, and Saeeda was "reinstated backdated with all arrears paid." In addition to this political victimization, she has experienced pay discrimination. Her first international travel happened in 1984 when she was offered a scholarship to study at University of Manchester in England. The British Council also offered a visa to her mother-in-law so that Saeeda would have help with the children.

Saeeda stayed to complete this second master's degree but then returned to Pakistan, finding life in England with two small children "quite difficult and there was no domestic help available." She resumed her former job and within four years was promoted to associate professor. Three years later she was appointed dean of the University College for Women in Mirpur, a challenging position because of political undercurrents. "The family had a political position and in Pakistan political opposition leads to all sorts of victimization. What supported me was my father's personal reputation and family's socioreligious standing. But that also meant that I have to be very careful in observing family traditions." She negotiated these complexities successfully and was able to fulfill all her professional responsibilities without violating family and faith norms.

"In 1994, a family decision was made that I should move to England with my three children where my husband had been living for some time." She took a study leave from her administrative position and applied for a PhD program at a university close to where her husband was located. Part of the reason for the move was "for the children to get British citizenship through their father."

Saeeda completed a PhD program at Nottingham University in two years and went back to her position in Pakistan in 1998, leaving the children to continue their studies in the United Kingdom with their father and grandmother. She continued as dean and was promoted to professor. She became involved with the United Nations Human Rights Commission and began "traveling to Geneva for the commission's biannual proceedings, which offered further opportunities of stopping over in the UK to spend time with the children."

This arrangement continued for four years until the family situation in England changed in several ways and she decided that the children needed her. Searching the Internet, she found a lecturer position open at Leicester University, interviewed, and was offered the job. She wrote,

> It was a very difficult decision—children on the one side and on the other side a comfortable life with half a dozen servants and a prestigious professional position with the sure opportunity of becoming vice chancellor in a couple of years. An additional challenge was to prepare myself to mentally accept the shift from dean/professor to lecturer. But the decision couldn't be otherwise—I had to be there for my children.

Again she took a five-year leave from her dean/professor position in Pakistan with mixed emotions, planning to return, but that return has not happened.

Since moving to England in 2003 Saeeda has experienced both successes and struggles. Claiming the positive, she wrote, "The more challenges I faced the more determined I became in my work. My concern for people and communities found expression in my writings." When asked to clarify this concern, she highlighted the role of education in forming her commitment to social justice:

> Being positioned as I have been (religious and political context) offered opportunities for seeing and listening to a range of people from a very early life. Having access to education and being an avid reader from very early years helped thinking, and both experiences fed into thinking and raising questions. I am not a "rebel" but I strongly believe that people should have social justice and respect. Why certain people suffer through no fault of theirs but only because of how they are positioned has always worried me. I am a strong believer in education—not just formal education but learning/understanding/knowledge which can give strength and confidence as well as ability to speak and struggle for social justice and equal rights. Lack of knowledge/awareness is one of the major barriers to social justice, and a big factor in submitting to discrimination/oppression/ marginalization. I am not saying that knowledge can eliminate discrimination or oppression (I have seen it being used for discrimination/oppression as well—it is very complex and very political), but it is certainly an enabler in struggle for social justice. (S. S., e-mail message to author, September 21, 2010)

A powerful communicator, Saeeda brings both passion and thought to her work, as shown in these well-chosen words that close her narrative: "To bring people together we need to know and understand people, and distances and exclusions are not contributive to knowing."

Insights

Saeeda grew up in a place with wide disparities of wealth and close to regions of recurring wars. She grew up female in a culture where often traditional Muslim women live outwardly restricted lives, unable to move about in public places without a family member as an escort. Her family, however, supported her education, broadened her world by sending her to the finest schools, and allowed her to become the first woman in the family to take a paid job. She describes Pakistan as "a Muslim society with feudal patriarchal structures and traditions," explaining, "however, women's lives in Pakistan do not form a homogeneous entity" (Shah 2009, 133). Perhaps the stature of the family made possible the freedoms she was given, within the constraints of family traditions, to become an educator with a high-level administrative role at a well-respected university in Pakistan.

Highly educated, Saeeda developed concerns about "selected access to social justice, democracy and equal rights," meaning "not admitting for others what individuals, groups, communities, governments, nations, etc. take for granted for themselves" (S. S., e-mail message to author, September 21, 2010). These concerns ranged beyond gender to include the whole range of diversity. Her experience of place also included a context of political awareness because of the stature of her family and its involvement in politics. All these factors and a sense of responsibility contribute to her ongoing determination to make a meaningful difference in the world by confronting social injustices.

Saeeda's life experiences, reflected upon with her usual thoughtfulness from core values, perhaps continue to develop the empathy and compassion that seem to center her actions. The noun *compassion* is defined as "a feeling of distress and pity for the suffering or misfortune of another" (McLeod 1987, 195). Synonyms for the adjective *compassionate* reveal it to be a word with a stronger and a softer side. On the softer side, synonyms include words such as *pitying*, *lenient*, and *tender-hearted*. The stronger synonyms, however, clarify how it can function as a source of commitment to social justice leadership. These words are *benevolent*, *charitable*, *humane*, and *humanitarian* (McLeod 1987, 97), words and values that lead in the direction of social justice leadership.

In Pakistan, by virtue of her family's position as descendants of the Prophet Mohammed, Saeeda was automatically entitled to and accorded great respect. She left that reality behind when she moved to England in 2003. Living there as a Muslim woman from Pakistan in the post-9/11 world, she is a member of a religious minority group and potentially the subject of suspicion and discrimination. Undeterred, Saeeda not only advocates for education for girls in a multiethnic, multifaith society like Britain; she also teaches about culture, gender, and power issues and is a respected spokesperson internationally for human rights. In other words, her social justice interests and commitments encompass more than gender.

Multiple identities coexist in Saeeda's reality as they do in the life of any woman. Negotiating those often conflicting personal and professional roles and realities can be particularly challenging for Muslim women. Responses to situations are not clear cut. Offering an explanatory framework, Lumby (2009) conceptualizes gender as one of those "multiple identities that comprise the fluid kaleidoscope of an individual existence" (29). She elaborated, "Rather like improvisation in a theater, the performance of gender is constructed in response to others but within the implicit or explicit parameters exerted by the individual, organizational and social context" (29). Saeeda was particularly successful at performing gender in a way acceptable within family and religious constraints, and in a manner that brought her acclaim and success as a university administrator. Her personal skill stretched the given parameters, giving her a world stage upon which to lead for social justice.

COMMITMENT TO SOCIAL JUSTICE: SELECTED SCHOLARSHIP

Current Western scholarship on social justice leadership in education, particularly in the United States, seems more focused on how leadership preparation programs can foster and promote social justice leadership in *future* administrators than on how current leaders for social justice developed that orientation (Brown 2004; Capper, Theoharis, and Sebastian 2006; McKenzie et al. 2008). Only a few examples exist of research focused on origins of an individual's orientation toward social justice leadership. A small qualitative study by Theoharis (2008) focused on seven urban high-school principals in the United States who were reputed models of social justice leadership. He asked the principals directly what motivated their commitments to social justice.

Theoharis (2008) found that they attributed their call to social justice leadership to a variety of personal experiences, clustered into six categories: commitment from family, influence of the social ethos of the sixties and seventies, personal struggle, personal awakening about discrimination and inequity, critical influence of undergraduate studies, and church. Three of the seven principals were women, but he did not report the data about the categories by gender. Two categories Theoharis found in personal experiences of these principals resonate with our WLE narrative analysis findings: specifically, the influence of family and personal awakening about discrimination and inequity.

In earlier scholarship similar to ours, Ah Nee-Benham and Cooper (1998) published an analysis of narratives of diverse women in school leadership in the United States. The book was a deliberate attempt to examine "conceptions of leadership from the margins, conceptions that reflect other cultures and societies than mainstream United States" (ix). From diverse backgrounds and ancestry the women spoke from their experiences as minority women leading in a variety of roles, both formal and informal. Based on extensive interviewing, Ah Nee-Benham and Cooper developed portraits of each woman that revealed new ways of understanding school leadership, as explained in the introduction:

The voices of the women, whose lives unfold within the covers of this book, are fresh and not simply appropriations of white European stories. The message transcends mere reactionary responses to domination. That is not to say that revealing oppression is unimportant but that its existence will present itself in subtle and startling ways throughout each story. (xi)

One of the themes Ah Nee-Benham and Cooper identified in the stories is "the ways in which their difference has instilled in these women a sense of compassion toward all children and a determination to help children to learn, grow, and overcome whatever obstacles are placed in their way. Their sense of equity and justice has been enhanced by their own experiences as minorities" (144). Their stories present a redefinition of power because the leaders profiled did not hold traditional hierarchical posts and also because the power they displayed was as champions of "the moral aspects of equity and fairness in schooling" (vii). Our analysis of the WLE narratives worldwide also reveals that compassion and attention to the moral aspects of equity and fairness were at the center of commitments to social justice leadership.

Campbell-Stephens (2009), director of "Investing in Diversity," a leadership development program for aspiring black and global majority leaders in London schools, "seeks to change both the face and the heart of leadership in London schools" (322). By extension, she challenges us to change the face (and the heart) of educational leadership in other places by including "a Black and global majority voice in its conversation" (321). She explains that "black and global majority people are those who have collectively been referred to in the literature as 'ethnic minorities' within the UK context; [and] minorities, people of colour or racialised groups in America, Canada, and Europe" (323). She argues that the reason for a redefinition in our language, to black and global majority people, is that "peoples of Asian and African descent are the majority on this planet and are increasingly so within the cities of the Western world, joined as they are with a whole range of other 'minorities'" (323). If we listen carefully, we hear them offer a different point of view about the deeper questions of social justice. They define social justice differently.

Spirituality is increasingly associated with leadership by contemporary scholars from both Western and non-Western countries. Shoho, Merchant, and Lugg (2005) place the term *social justice* in a Western context by tracing the historic religious roots of social justice in both Protestant and Catholic theology. In doing so they call attention to what they called "ambiguity" about the meaning of social justice because of differing perspectives, particularly in Western countries, about whether the purpose of society is to serve the needs of individuals above others, or others above individuals. They write, "If individual needs continue to be the focal point of societal concerns, then a definition of social justice must take this into consideration" (49).

Scholars addressing social justice from non-Western or global majority perspectives often acknowledge spirituality as an important aspect of educational leadership and typically put an emphasis on society and education having a broadly defined purpose, serving the needs of others, the group if you will, over needs of individuals. These scholars include the following: Ah Nee-Benham 2003; Ah Nee-Benham and Cooper 1998; Atlas and Capper 2003; Dantley 2005; Fua 2007; Murtadha-Watts 1999; Sanga and Chu 2009; Shah 2009; and Strachan, Akao, Kilavanwa, and Warsal 2010.

The concept of cosmopolitanism is also relevant to the meaning of social justice and points in the direction of taking a broader view. Unterhalter (2008) inserts *cosmopolitanism* into the social justice definition dialogue. The term was initially used by early Greek philosophers to describe "a citizen of the world." The word is "currently emerging as a term associated with global social justice and the problem of thinking of the world as a moral community" (540). Furthermore, she writes, "Debates about cosmopolitanism are concerned with . . . the obligations we owe to those who are not citizens of the same state, but whose lives are affected by our actions, and who in turn affect our lives" (540). According to Unterhalter, "Cosmopolitanism raises a number of demanding questions for comparative education, which has been so strongly framed by the boundary of the nation or locale" (540). It is an ethical orientation, and "thus, the basis for our obligations to all people in the world lies in our common humanity, which is universal in scope" (541).

Cosmopolitanism and compassion clearly are related concepts. Unterhalter (2008) argues that for "thin" cosmopolitans, gender equality is adequate if it "results in a minimal provision of schooling for equal numbers of boys and girls" (543). On the other hand, "gender equality in education is associated in thick cosmopolitan formulations as a substantive idea concerning the global reach of aspirations for equal rights to education, and as a consequence of schooling, a challenge to gendered decision-making structures, opposition to violence against women in all its forms, and a fairer distribution of power" (543).

Unterhalter (2008) concludes by calling consideration of cosmopolitanism to be "a useful way of posing questions about the nature of global social justice and the actions this entails" (551). The stories of Rosangela Malachias, Charol Shakeshaft, and Saeeda Shah bring up for each of us this question: How big are we willing to draw the circle of social justice and compassion? To answer the question requires examining the roots of our responsibilities and our abilities.

CONCLUDING THOUGHTS

We have considered global gender issues for women that are linked to social justice leadership. Rosangela Malachias's story calls attention to discrimination and associated issues of gender, class, and race/ethnicity, conveying poignantly the intersectionality of the forces supporting discrimination. Charol Shakeshaft's story highlights issues of sexual violence, its invisibility, the stigma experienced by girls and women who suffer from sexual abuse or assault, and the strength and determination required to survive and thrive. Saeeda Shah's story illustrates the power of education and knowledge to shape a life. The three narratives collectively demonstrate that gender is a social construction, calling for juggling of multiple identities by women who would lead in cultures and organizations where men, not women, are expected to fill the leadership roles.

In this chapter we also have examined the roots of our responsibilities and our abilities. We have argued that knowledge or experience of localized manifestations of the global issues of discrimination and violence against women, along with transformative education, can move us individually and collectively to leadership commitments that give life the shape of social justice. Problems of discrimination and violence against women are clearly not confined to countries regarded as less developed. The problems are often more difficult to discern, however, in the so-called highly developed countries. Women in positions of leadership at all levels of education worldwide can be the bridge builders, extending equal opportunities to other girls and women as we raise our collective voices.

We framed the chapter in terms of three imperatives for social justice leadership suggested by the collected WLE narratives: discrimination, violence, and education. In conclusion, we turn again to poet David Whyte (2001) to frame how we might think about our own lives in response to the imperatives and stories of the outstanding women leaders featured. He believes that "the pivotal questions to ask ourselves in the mirror every morning, successful or no, are deep, uncompromising ones of personal identity. How much freedom of movement do we find now in our work, whatever the outward trappings? How much of the original person is there?" (155). Advocating a journey of reflection, he suggests that "we must go to the roots of our abilities, a journey into a core sense of ourselves where we can put together an understanding of how we are made, why we have the responsibilities we have, and, just as important, the images that formed us in our growing" (157). Ongoing personal reflection on values and one's leadership journey matters.

4

VALUES CREATE
A LARGER CIRCLE

Until we can understand the assumptions in which we are drenched, we will not know ourselves.

—Adrienne Rich, *When We Dead Awaken: Writing as Re-vision*

Begley (1999) defined values as "those conceptions of the desirable which motivate individuals and collective groups to act in particular ways to achieve particular ends" (237). "The idea that the moral sense is an innate part of human nature is not far-fetched" (Pinker 2008, 5). A common understanding is that values are important to a morality that moves us to act. Psychologists and sociologists have long sought to assess attitudes and values, believing that they could be used to explain, predict, and control behavior. Attitudes proved to be too evanescent, but values have proved useful in understanding behavior patterns in cultures, organizations, and administration. Indeed, the significance of values in the study of leadership has been emphasized and affirmed repeatedly (e.g., Begley 1996; Coleman and Glover, 2010; Evers and Lakomski 1996; Hodgkinson 1991b; Hoy, Tarter, and Hoy 2006; Lazaridou 2007; Leithwood and Jantzi 1990; Leithwood, Louis, Anderson, and Wahlstrom 2004).

We see values as implicit or explicit assertions about what is desirable, important, useful, or worthy. We see them as ranging along a continuum of universality, from purely idiosyncratic preference or taste, through normative or cultural prescriptions, to suprarational moral or ethical principles (Bilsky and Schwartz 1994; Hodgkinson 1991a and 1991b; Kluckhöhn and Strodtbeck 1961). Furthermore, we see values as screening mechanisms that affect awareness and determine the selection of information and definitions of alternatives (Begley 1996).

An aspect of leadership theory that includes values and ethics of leaders revolves around the moral purpose of leadership (Sergiovanni 1992). Leadership scholars and practitioners are refocusing on the question "What is leadership for?" (Blackmore 1999, 2002; Furman 2003). Although leadership for social justice may look different depending on countries' rankings on indicators of development, the underlying values are similar. Clusters of values act as perceptual screens that focus our lives and actions.

VALUES CREATE A LARGER CIRCLE: THE STORIES

Values develop within differing physical, social, and historical contexts; thus they distinguish one human group from another (Hofstede 1980). Values create cultural dispositions, shape behaviors and thoughts, and construct human character. From this perspective, social justice scholarship in educational leadership exhibits some broad, common themes. Featured are moral values like justice, respect, care, and equity. Always in the forefront is a consciousness about the impact of race, class, gender, sexual orientation, and disability constraints on schools and students' learning (Dantley and Tillman 2005). According to Rapp (2002), social justice leadership includes uncovering the value assumptions that underlie "best practices" and sacred cows, the injustices hidden by practices of conventional wisdom.

We found that all the narratives submitted for the book were permeated with indicators of value orientations that affected the participants' lives, their commitments to social justice leadership, and their actions. Values such as honesty, fairness, altruism, equal respect for each individual and his/her abilities, collaboration, efficiency, diversity, integrity, and decency are among those evident in the stories. In general, notwithstanding the diversity in the women's cultural backgrounds, they describe values that originated from influences of family upbringing, economic status, religion, formal education, and career orientation.

In this chapter we discuss how values influence actions by literally and metaphorically leading us to larger circles in which to live and lead. We organize the discussion into three broad thematic clusters: humanitarianism, expanding circles of concern, and developing cosmopolitan consciousness. Each thematic cluster contains values associated with creating a larger circle of life and service. The themes and associated values were evident in many of the WLE women's stories but are illustrated in this chapter by the following featured leaders: (1) Extending Humanitarianism—Elizabeth C. Reilly, United States; (2) Expanding Circles of Concern—Alice Merab Kagoda, Uganda; and (3) Developing Cosmopolitan Consciousness—Marianne Coleman, United Kingdom.

Extending Humanitarianism

The first theme, extending humanitarianism, is associated with kindness, benevolence, and sympathy toward all human beings (Humanitarianism, n.d.). A humanitarian accepts all human beings for what they are and fights prejudice, ignorance, social biases, racism, and injustices. Values include the promotion of human welfare, the improvement of humanity, equality, active compassion, and reform. The latter is the essence of a humanitarian: a passion to change existing social conditions by eradicating or at least alleviating social injustices.

Literature relating school leadership with humanitarianism, though limited, does exist. For example, humanitarianism was an aspect of one study of values that focused on school leaders labeled as humanitarians compared with school leaders labeled program managers. The value chosen most often by the humanitarians from a typology of basic human values was "respect for others" (Leithwood, Begley, and Cousins 1994, 111). This value was reflected in the emphasis these leaders placed on school climate and interpersonal relationships in their leadership practices.

Three assumptions are common to definitions of humanitarianism. The first is the precept that all humans are equal. Aristotle (350 BCE) first articulated this notion in attributing significance to the human soul, while the Stoics extended the notion by arguing that every human being is equal in significance. The second assumption of humanitarianism is an ethic of kindness, benevolence, and sympathy that is applied impartially to all human beings. The third given of humanitarianism is active compassion, a disposition to engage in action to change conditions—particularly social or cultural conditions—that disadvantage human beings. Humanitarianism, then, is concerned fundamentally with reform, and the most potent levers for effecting social reforms are found in education and legislation. Each of these assumptions shines in the first story.

Elizabeth C. Reilly

"Education gives individuals possibilities. From the time I was a young child, this was the message that my mother and father relentlessly repeated." With this statement, Dr. Elizabeth Reilly begins her story titled "Punching Holes in the Darkness: One Woman's Journey toward Leading in a Global Society." Elizabeth's narrative is a collection of vignettes punctuated with poetry and interspersed with quotations meaningful to her. In the narrative she describes the evolution of her career from the early years of teaching in urban schools, to administrative positions in PK–12 education, to her higher education faculty role as professor in the School of Education and former director of the Educational Leadership for Social Justice doctoral program at Loyola Marymount University in Los Angeles, California. The narrative is more than a chronology, as Elizabeth conveys who she is with a writer's literary flair.

Her parents were Elizabeth's first teachers, "the ones who instilled in me the fervent and passionate drive to become educated and to become an educator." Education had helped to raise her mother, a young immigrant, "from the ravages of poverty to a life in which she meaningfully contributed her gifts as a philanthropist." Education had also "led my father from the fields where he harvested crops from the time he could walk, to a prestigious appointment as a jurist." Elizabeth's humanitarianism expressed and extended through her scholarship and teaching seems an extension of family values. Promoting human welfare is her fundamental concern.

Early in her teaching and administrative career Elizabeth realized that "being a teacher meant being above all a learner, and that being a school leader meant being a teacher of teachers." Drawing inspiration from John Dewey, Elizabeth believes that her role is "to see the gifts in others—both children and colleagues," and to help them put those gifts to good use. She elaborates, "I experienced George Eliot's words [from *Middlemarch*, written in 1871] in very real ways. 'What do we live for, if it is not to make life less difficult to each other?' This, then, is the fundamental purpose of education, the goal of teaching, and my work as a teacher, scholar, and educational leader." These humanitarian beliefs suffuse her personal and professional life.

Teaching in the early years was a sometimes frightening and often demoralizing experience for Elizabeth. As a young and inexperienced teacher she was called to join an urban high school where students could not read or write, where riots during lunch times were the norm. It was typical for male students to show their weapons and scars to her and for female students to talk about their pregnancies. Her colleagues also "reflected fear, anger, and a bone-aching weariness with the work at hand." Elizabeth wrote, "My teaching life in those early years resembled in great measure the halls of Hell as I tried valiantly to make meaning of a profession that left me empty." Elizabeth lasted three years in that school and others that were similar, before quitting teaching to take a position as an editor.

Several months into her new position, Elizabeth received a call from a principal of another urban high school who wanted to hire her as a teacher. The school was in the *barrio*, and as they talked she could hear trains speeding by behind the stadium. Persuaded to visit, but with memories from her previous teaching experience still vivid in her mind, Elizabeth walked reluctantly into Sunset High School, unconvinced. "Finding the principal's vision of his school spellbinding, I accepted the position on the spot," she wrote, amazed to find that "the school was indeed a place where both students and staff thrived." It was a true community. She observed emphatically that "from the moment I drove across the railroad tracks those many years ago to this day, I have never again questioned what it is that is my life's work." As indicated in the headings in her narrative, Elizabeth's "winter" ended and the beginning of "spring" heralded the onset of a successful and renowned career.

Elizabeth found in that principal a mentor who "saw in me leadership potential and groomed me to become a school administrator." By the end of her twenties Elizabeth had already held two administrative roles, and by her mid-thirties she enrolled in a doctoral program to pursue an academic career. Although Elizabeth continued to value teaching high-school students, she realized that her work "could benefit far more children if I were to work with their teachers and administrators." Young and inexperienced, she learned soon enough that teaching adult learners had its challenges. She described her work as "daunting" and the needs of urban educators as "vast"; nonetheless, she had found a challenging and stimulating environment that helped her "imagine the art of possibility."

As a young administrator Elizabeth sought advice whenever an opportunity arose. Choosing a mentor became "a habit" for her, using strategies that ranged from subtle request of an individual to teach her to bold assertion that left the other person with no option but to accept. "I would announce, 'You are my mentor. You don't get a vote.'" For Elizabeth it was unthinkable to move forward "without the counsel of others more skillful, wise, creative, and heart-filled." Her mentors frequently were her supervisors while she was in the school system, and later her university professors during her graduate work. Listing notable teachers and guides, Elizabeth wrote, "They each still whisper in my ear more than I can say."

While she was a doctoral student, the world was stunned by the fall of the Union of Soviet Socialist Republics (USSR). Elizabeth decided to conduct her research in Moscow. Having visited the country once before during the Cold War, Elizabeth had developed a sharp understanding at a very young age of "the difference between an ideology and its people." While the whole world was amazed and shocked by televisions images of the marching Soviet army and the lines of civilians waiting for bread, Elizabeth was asking herself, "What of education? Who is telling the story of what it will take to transform a society steeped in Communist ideology into a democracy?"

Taking advantage of an educator exchange program between Russia and the West, Elizabeth traveled to Moscow to present at a conference in Troisk, a scientific community that previously had been closed to Westerners. While there, she was fortunate to stay with a Russian physicist and his family and to obtain their support for her research. "Even in the midst of the most significant change of the twentieth century, the Russians were my selfless and gracious teachers," she recalled. "With precious few basic necessities, they fed me, clothed me, housed me, chauffeured me to interviews and conferences, and treated me as an honored member of their families. I could not help but to be humbled and transformed by the kindness of strangers." Her humanitarian instincts were validated and enriched.

After completing her doctoral program, with the dream of becoming a university professor still alive, Elizabeth looked for opportunities and "taught any graduate course in education I could talk my way into," thus gaining experience and the necessary "curriculum vitae appeal." She reports finding the glass ceiling to be "thick, indeed, and seemingly impenetrable." Elizabeth was gradually changing from being "a consumer of educational practice to an elucidator of theory and practice." The transition was not an easy one, but she was determined and did succeed in finding her way into a full-time appointment in higher education. During her early years in academia, she taught graduate-level courses, advised doctoral students, and got involved in scholarly work. With the help and support of her colleagues, Elizabeth became a full tenured professor only seven years after her initiation into higher education. Her academic obligations were "to mentor, to challenge, to inspire, and to nurture." She embraced them all fully.

The last section ("The Journey Continues") of her narrative begins with a nineteenth-century story attributed to author Robert Louis Stevenson, who grew up with his family in a small town in nineteenth-century Scotland. As a little boy, upon seeing a lamplighter going up a ladder with a torch to light the streetlights, he exclaimed with great excitement to his nanny, "Look at that man! He's punching holes in the darkness!" For Elizabeth the image of the lamplighter captures her conviction that humans have one fundamental task: "I believe it is our task, our moral imperative in our time on earth to punch holes in the darkness—in the darkness of ignorance, of hate, of deprivation, of suffering, and of injustice."

Believing in the lamplighter is the source of Elizabeth's boundless energy, illuminating the places in her heart that whisper, "Here is what you must do in this world, Elizabeth, to make it different, to make it better." Sometime this voice speaks to her as she reflects on her role in the world; at other times it challenges her to seek new paths and choose new directions. "If I approach my work with my heart open to possibilities, then even if many things seem confusing in the moment, over time, clarity emerges and I have a way to step forward with greater boldness." Her recurring visits to Afghanistan, to use one example, illustrate her boldness. Her research there is about documenting the role of women in rebuilding the nation's educational system.

Elizabeth consults and works with leaders from multinationals, government, nongovernment organizations, and education on five continents. Her humanitarian leadership vision is always to serve others. Her words express what she hopes will happen when she works with others to develop leadership, whatever their roles:

If I had to identify what I hope the time we spend together would result in, it would be that when we part, we do so with greater passion for the work that we do: that regardless of our particular positions, we recognize that leadership is what we do, not what we talk about, and that we part more greatly inspired to serve others. It is my hope that we each understand that we have an obligation to serve and to help in raising up future leaders.

Serving others is not the only purpose of Elizabeth's humanitarian leadership vision. Helping people to "possess a larger view of the world" is equally important to her, because such understanding will help individuals "to heal this world." She acknowledges, though, that enlarging worldviews of others is not an easy task. She understands that she is asking others to "possess a larger view of the world—a burden, if you will." The word *burden* underlines for others the significance of this mission and explains further that this larger view of the world entails the "ability to see many aspects of circumstances," the local and the international. Elizabeth describes how she strives to convey this larger view: "Opening our hearts, . . . listening to the inner voices and the outer voices, . . . allowing the muse of inspiration to touch us, . . . feeling the passion to make a difference both locally and globally, . . . and stepping forward with boldness, not alone but with a community of like-minded colleagues . . . this is what the messages of my work are."

Ending her narrative with reflections about where she is today, Elizabeth brings her story full circle to the idea with which it began. "Education gives individuals possibilities." This strong message from her parents has been and continues to be the guiding compass in her life's journey. She wrote, "This is my message as an educator to my students, to my colleagues, and to those with whom I work in our global society. 'You are a gift to the world. I will help you find your gifts so that you may contribute to its healing.'"

Insights

Elizabeth's story conveys the wisdom of an openhearted, generous, and adventurous person who is determined not to waste her time on earth. She is inspired—to list a few icons mentioned in her narrative—by prophets such as Martin Luther King Jr., poets such as Rilke, saints such as Mother Teresa, and mystics such as Rumi. For example, Elizabeth's inspiration to heal the world and to be of service to others comes in part from Mother Teresa—who wrote, "I am a little pencil in the hand of a writing God who is sending a love letter to the world." Elizabeth extends the metaphor, writing, "if my students and I are each that pencil, we are sending not one love letter, but a sheaf of love letters to a world so greatly in need of our care."

Elizabeth's professional journey through various places and spaces has been marked with moments of glory and times of darkness. She embraces both the good and the bad and strives to learn from people and circumstances. She understands that at times there are more questions than answers. Inspired by the truth of Rumi's words, she chooses to "read the book of your life which has been given to you." Her purpose is unfailing: to learn in every opportunity. Echoing Rumi, she writes, "We may not always like nor agree with the questions and the answers, and we may not even see clearly what those questions are at times, but we have the opportunity to learn. We need only cross over and be open. This is a choice, moment by moment."

Elizabeth is an educator whose work displays all three assumptions of humanitarianism—that every human being is equal in significance; that kindness, benevolence, and sympathy should apply to all human beings; and that active compassion creates a disposition to engage in action to change conditions that disadvantage human beings. The phrase that draws the insights shared in her story together is "the art of possibility." She displays rare mastery of that art with words and deeds that draw us into her larger circle.

Expanding Circles of Concern

The second theme, expanding circles of concern, describes a pattern exhibited in the lives of many who submitted narratives for the book. The phrase typifies an individual driven by strong moral principles, one who develops a deep sense of a meaningful life that brings together the personal and the professional through caring into a well-integrated whole. Persons who expand circles of concern find the way to develop beyond the early knowledge and understandings of the local circle into which they were born. Through knowledge gained from experience, their perspectives encompass a wider view as wisdom grows.

In the WLE women's narratives we found numerous examples of women who expand their circles of concern, providing social justice leadership while living with integrity. The process of attaining integrity—achieving a deep sense that life has meaning and that we ought to make a contribution to it (Erikson 1956; Harder 2009)—is inherent in expanding one's circle of concern. Expanding circles of concern, as well as drawing and being drawn to ever-larger circles, contributes to the meaning of one's life and the lives of others.

Such a person is Alice Merab Kagoda from Uganda. She has lived with integrity in an ever-expanding world, guided by strong moral principles, moral uprightness. The word *integrity* derives from the Latin *integer*, meaning intact or whole (Integrity, n.d.). Wanting to be whole is therefore the essence of the value of integrity. A whole person, an upright person, behaves and makes decisions that are in line with strong ethical principles. Values associated with integrity are honesty, faithfulness, consistency, openness, and truthfulness.

Alice Merab Kagoda

 Without Alice's initiative, this book might not have come to fruition because she was the first WLE member to submit her narrative. She titled the 1,300-word account simply "My Story," writing it in English, but "thinking in her mother tongue." Dr. Alice Merab Kagoda is an associate professor and formerly deputy dean of the School of Education at Makarere University in Kampala. She was born and raised in a rural area of Eastern Uganda, in a large family consisting of nine children—seven girls and two brothers. Alice was fifth in the order of birth and describes her family as "very strict Christian."

Her father, an Anglican priest, had high expectations of her but very poor means, as his income from his ministry at the time was very low. Her mother had just basic education and was a trained vernacular teacher. The family was also involved in the cultivation of cotton to support the children's education and raise the money for the tuition fees. Alice's expanded circles of concern today are in stark contrast to the cultural reality for women when she was growing up. As Kagoda and Sperandio (2009) note, "Women were accustomed to a female community-based culture that frowned upon upward social mobility and self-promotion and made it next to impossible to socialize with males in semiformal or informal context" (52).

In a straightforward statement early in her narrative, Alice revealed the conditions and assumptions for education in Uganda, the world into which she was born. She explained that "education in Uganda is a privilege, not a right for most people in rural areas and among the urban poor." For her to get an education was therefore "a miracle" and an "empowering tool." Her elder sisters didn't go on to secondary education because of lack of money for school fees. Alice was grateful for the opportunity to acquire an education, and she seems to have carried that spirit of gratitude throughout her life.

Leaving the small circle of her family and rural area to access schooling, Alice went to primary schools in three rural areas before attending a junior secondary boarding school. Her father supported her financially at that time with the help of a local bursary and the Anglican Church of Canada. She then enrolled at an American senior secondary boarding school in the Tororo district. She was the first daughter to acquire secondary education and benefited from the enlarging circle of people and experience. "I consider my secondary school period a time of awakening," Alice wrote. It was a time when "I set my goals and purpose in life for my future." In developing her goals Alice was assisted by the career counseling she received from the American teachers at her secondary school. During this period she also had opportunities "to study with girls from other tribal groups in Uganda, as well as Indians living in Uganda, which was actually fun, especially during the cultural days."

Alice's future goal at the time was to become a nurse, reflecting a desire to be of service to others. Given the available education at a nurses' training school, she planned to get a diploma in nursing. This was to change, though, because of her father's visit to Makarere University. Here is how Alice described the serendipitous turning point that greatly enlarged the circle of her life and its influence: "He [her father] visited Makerere University in 1969 and on his return he said to me in a letter, 'I saw girls studying for various degree programs. I want you to join this University.' This was my turning point." She wrote that "after reading that letter from my father, my goal changed to that of joining university," making it possible for her to become a teacher.

Alice described both of her parents with great love and admiration. She was especially grateful to her father, whom she described as "a great inspiration because of his love, encouragement, and confidence that I would go to university." Her father's attitude toward education was very unusual, as men in his clan did not believe in girls' education. She may have been the first girl in the clan to acquire secondary education. Alice also expressed gratitude to her mother for giving her "the motherly, loving, moral, and psychological support" that kept her on the path.

Alice was the first woman in her family to graduate from university with a BA, a diploma in education, and later a master's in education, all from Makerere University. After graduating with a BA, she was appointed as a teacher to a girls' secondary school in Jinja district, where she taught for two years. This move again expanded her circles of concern. Her duties, apart from teaching, included being a housemistress and stationery mistress, and those responsibilities introduced her to leadership in schools. After marrying a lecturer at the university, Alice moved back to Kampala and assumed a new post in a secondary school there.

When Alice became a mother she quit teaching for four years and worked for the church for two years as a diocesan mothers/women's worker. Paradoxically this career break enlarged her circles of concern. "This introduced me to the reality of women's world of discrimination, unprivileged positions in society, and my own ignorance of gender issues. I made up my mind from this time to work for women's cause as much as possible," she wrote. Living near the university and enjoying the support of her husband and the sustained encouragement of her father, Alice decided to pursue further education. At the same time the women's movement was also very influential, "encouraging us to go for higher education." Interestingly enough, "higher education at this time was freely available to those who took up this offer; however, very few people took up this privilege offered by the government," Alice wrote.

After graduation, and with "the encouragement of my family and my colleagues," Alice applied successfully to become deputy headmistress of the largest day school in Kampala. Many vacant positions were advertised, but "there were very few women who applied and most of us who applied passed the public service interview and were posted in various schools of Uganda." Once again the circle of her world grew larger. "It was a great and enriching experience working with a very large number of teachers and students who had their unique problems and challenges, which I had to deal with on a daily basis. This gave me the foundation and necessary experience in educational leadership," she recalls.

In 1992 Alice joined Makerere University as a geography lecturer, and two years later she was admitted to the University of Alberta in Edmonton, Canada, to pursue a PhD program. This experience of living a world away expanded her circles of concern beyond her own country and continent. Alice described that time as "an empowering and awakening period" through exposure in her courses to issues related to development, education, gender, peace, environment, and rural sociology. Facts, issues, and challenges of development facing countries like Uganda were discussed at length in each course offered.

One event in particular is indicative of the gender inequalities she experienced during her time as a doctoral student and also her determination to overcome obstacles successfully and to move on. The night before her doctoral candidacy, the transparencies she had prepared for her presentation were taken away from her office by male compatriots who were also students in the program, for they did not want to see her finishing ahead of them.

> The transparencies I was going to use to defend my PhD proposal were hidden by my [Ugandan] male colleagues the evening before the defense. . . . They didn't want to see a woman finishing earlier than them, otherwise people at home would ask them why I was able to finish much earlier. I lost my temper and berated them. I made new transparencies that night and was ready to defend at 10:00 a.m. the following day. It was a great success. (A. K., e-mail message to author, September 23, 2010)

Returning to Uganda with a PhD in international/intercultural education, Alice had a foundation for expanding her circles of concern again. Her civic activities multiplied as her career at Makarere University advanced. Alice became actively involved as a member and in leadership roles with three women's groups: the Uganda Association of University Women (UAUW), Action for Development (ACFODE), and the Uganda Women Network (UWONET). Each provided leadership training experiences that boosted her self-esteem and through which she "acquired the skills of lobbying and advocacy, which have proved to be very helpful in my life." These experiences included attending the Women in Development Leadership Course in Washington, DC, plus a four-day leadership course in Nairobi.

In addition to ongoing activities in these groups, Alice was appointed to leadership positions on governing boards of a national teachers college and two secondary schools. She was also chairperson of the Uganda Association of University Women and belonged to the Mothers Union of Uganda and the Rotary Club of Makerere University. Alice credits her involvement in these activities and positions with helping her develop "the skills of chairing meetings, public speaking, respect for others, appreciation of other cultures and races, and being patient and understanding when dealing with the young and elderly people, which I feel have made me what I am today."

Alice's first university administrative position was in 2002 as acting deputy dean for the School of Education. She was promoted to the rank of senior lecturer in the Department of Social Science and Arts Education in 2004 and subsequently, in 2005, to the position of deputy dean. Recently retired from administration, Alice is an associate professor. She is still a voice for social justice leadership. Her story ended with a list of her promotions and educational and civic leadership positions, followed by this statement: "There are many things I could have written to inform you of the factors behind my success to this level. Because they are many, however, the above are among the most important."

Insights

Alice's story illustrates committed leadership both in education and in the women's movement. According to Tripp (2001), the women's movement in Uganda has grown in strength and autonomy. Tripp explains that in the past, the movement focused on "improving domestic household skills, nutrition and hygiene" (102). However, she continues, "today there is greater emphasis on activities that contribute to women's political participation: civic education, improving leadership skills, and lobbying on particular legislative proposals" (102). Women like Alice Merab Kagoda have contributed to this change in emphasis.

Kagoda and Sperandio (2009) emphasize that "leadership, however defined and practiced, has been a strictly male preserve in traditional Ugandan society, and jealously guarded" (49). In fact, "women are only now establishing civil and property rights in what has traditionally been a male-dominated society" (51). Alice left home first for primary school, took advantage of every chance offered to become more educated, and moved into the larger leadership circles of the Ugandan women's movement and education.

Alice's circles of concern expanded greatly in 2002, when she accepted her first university administrative position as acting deputy dean for the

School of Education. Around that same time, Tripp (2001) wrote, "The fact that there is a larger pool of educated women today than in the past has facilitated the leadership of various organizations. Moreover, cultural openness to women leaders is slowly but surely growing in Uganda and throughout Africa, as many women are increasingly being seen as competent and bold leaders" (104).

Living and leading a life of integrity guided by strong moral principles in ever-expanding circles is the essence of Alice's story. Integrity and gratitude seem to run through her life events. Her family, mainly through the transmission of strong Anglican values, planted the seeds of integrity in Alice. Her journey to independence, the achievement of stimulating experiences, challenging objectives, academic success, and the attainment of social status and prestige—Alice is grateful for it all. Beginning with education, these journeys to ever-expanding circles of people and concerns step by step led her to dedicate herself to others, especially to the promotion of the rights of women and girls in Uganda.

Alice was grateful for every new opportunity, beginning with her parents' encouragement to seek more education than was the norm in Uganda (especially for girls). Their support made possible the "awakening" she experienced at her secondary school and her pursuit of tertiary education to the highest levels in Uganda and abroad. Alice valued achievement and empowerment, evident from the tone of her descriptions of her experiences as deputy headmistress of a large secondary school and as a university lecturer.

Alice's determination to succeed in tertiary education, to enter larger circles of concern, persisted even in the face of obstacles created by conservative countrymen at home and abroad. She valued the opportunity to seek important administrator positions in women's organizations and on various boards and to be a player in those larger circles. Finally, Alice valued caring and justice on a broad scale. This is most obvious in her early plan to become a nurse, in her dedication to women's causes, and later as an active member of a number of women's and other civic organizations.

Living life with integrity means that an individual has a deep sense that life is meaningful—that one can make a contribution to it, especially by dedicating oneself to the service of others. Alice came to that realization while working as a women's worker for the church. Exposure to the realities of women's hardships in Uganda made her see the injustices done to them. She then decided to contribute to bettering their lives and positions in society. Experiencing church-based outreach work was an awakening call for Alice, who sought to take action to lessen or eliminate the injustice that entered her awareness. When one's values are violated, moral outrage drives one to seek social justice (Lambert and Gardner 2009).

Alice knew that to help women's causes she had to climb to the highest point on the educational ladder so that social status and prestige would afford her the levers for influencing people and events. Although she left her rural home behind, her family has always been a source of encouragement, support, and inspiration. Lambert and Gardner (2009) describe how for women leaders "the family environment provides a rich wetland for growth" (46), and Alice's case confirms this. Her strong family values equipped her with strength, direction, and an imperative to live a life of activism and social service. The beneficiaries are her countrywomen, her country, and the world.

Developing Cosmopolitan Consciousness

The values associated with the third theme of developing cosmopolitan consciousness are openness, commitment, productivity, contentment, affiliation, role clarity, industriousness, care, awareness, and justice. Cosmopolitans view themselves as citizens of the world, as in the Ancient Greek meaning of *cosmopolite* (Ribeiro 2005). The term also implies a consciousness of complexity and the interrelatedness of societies, institutions, and peoples. Cosmopolitans feel the need to communicate. Although the focus on a cosmopolitan career may appear to have a selfish bent, "without the notion of selfishness, one becomes 'selfless' and has no 'self' to give away" (Vaillant 2002). Cosmopolitans have a self to contribute to the dialogue needed for peace and community as cultural diversity everywhere is rapidly increasing.

As introduced in chapter 3, the concept of cosmopolitanism is relevant to the dialogue about social justice because it points to taking a broader view. To again quote Unterhalter (2008), the word is "currently emerging as a term associated with global social justice and the problem of thinking of the world as a moral community" (540). Ribeiro (2005) explains the source of ambiguity the term may provoke to be its paradox, "i.e., its unique way of uniting difference and equality" (19). He finds the paradox inherent in the term itself: "The composition of the Greek term, cosmopolis, already indicates this unsolved tension: *cosmos*, a natural universal order, is related to *polis*, society's variable order" (19). The following words of Ribeiro illustrate the relevance of the term to the careers and social justice commitments of WLE members, including Marianne Coleman: "Cosmopolitanism presupposes a positive attitude towards difference, a desire to construct broad allegiances and equal and peaceful global communities of citizens who should be able to communicate across cultural and social boundaries forming a universalist solidarity" (19).

Careers expand an individual's identity and lead the person to assume a social identity within the world of work (Vaillant 2002). Careers exist in a social ethos, and they involve other people. The interactions that take place among people determine the quality of one's career and its contribution to society.

Dantley and Tillman (2005) note that along with moral values, for social justice leaders "always in the forefront is a consciousness about the impact" of their work on schools, students, and learning. Main values and benefits associated with career paths for social justice are affiliation, role clarity, commitment, industriousness, purposefulness, and ultimately the contentment that comes with meaningful work. These values allow the individual to "abandon" the self for the sake of a higher purpose, that of service to others. The WLE women often referred to these values—both implicitly and explicitly—and how they affected their lives and those of other women, too. Marianne Coleman developed a cosmopolitan consciousness over the course of a lifetime that displays "the sophistication that results from familiarity with what is different" (Ribeiro 2005, 20). Beginning in childhood, her developing consciousness of social justice issues and larger worlds qualify her as a *cosmopolitan*. Marianne's career has had a distinctly international focus.

Marianne Coleman

 Marianne's narrative was titled "An Autobiography of Gender." Now formally retired, Dr. Marianne Coleman is an emeritus reader who is still researching. Her position during the last five years of her career was as reader and assistant dean of research at the Institute of Education, University of London. Born at the end of World War II in Leeds, an industrial city in the north of England, Marianne was the only child in an extended family that included her two parents and three grandparents. Her father "came from a line of carpenters and builders, but left school at 14 and mainly due to the depression could not get a job for several years." When Marianne was young, he was working as a bus driver. Her mother had been a civil servant before the war.

Being raised in a household that was occupied almost exclusively by adults, and surrounded by "a lot of illness" had a profound effect on Marianne. It meant that "someone was always having a rest or wasn't very well," so she had to learn early in her life "the importance of playing quietly and amusing [herself]." Marianne had her share of illness, too. At the age of seven she was hospitalized for months with pneumonia. As a result of that, she missed a big part of her schooling that year. Tuition was not then available to hospitalized children, but Marianne "developed a taste for reading," so she managed to overcome this obstacle and had become "an avid reader," something she still carries nowadays.

Growing up in the postwar era in relatively poor economic circumstances made Marianne "conscious of the society" around her. As she said, by the age of five "I had quite a sophisticated understanding of the class system." At that time her family was teetering between middle-class and working-class status. The grandparents contributed to the finances of the family, so after their death Marianne's family had to take in lodgers to be able to make ends meet. Money was very short, and Marianne was aware of it. She also experienced more class issues when she was put in a lower stream (track) at school after recovering from pneumonia. At the time, it was typical for working-class children to be in the bottom stream, while middle-class children attended the top stream. Poverty was another factor Marianne was aware of. "Even in the early 1950s in an industrial urban area like Leeds there were children who came to school dirty and with torn clothes, or who were kept off school because they did not have shoes," she remembers.

When Marianne finished primary school, her family was financially more stable, and she had been able to move up to the top stream, following the persistence of her mother in questioning the school. That move allowed Marianne to take the exams to go to an academic secondary school. This selection process at age eleven dominated the British education system at the time. Her mother's intervention was important to her professional journey because if she had been kept in the lower stream, it is unlikely that she would have had the chance to go to a university. She wrote, "For me and my family [education] was a way to develop and move on, although the restraining influences of social class and gender were limitations."

As a teenager Marianne developed mixed feelings about school. She did well "in English and the humanities subjects, less well in science, badly in math, and abysmally in sport," as she said in her story. Attending an all-girls school, with the entire staff being female, gave Marianne no opportunities to interact with boys or men apart from her father, "against whom I increasingly rebelled." Describing herself as mildly rebellious and somewhat political, she "joined YCND (the youth branch of the Campaign for Nuclear Disarmament) and supported the antiapartheid movement that was growing in South Africa." Marianne's best friend at the time came from a highly political middle-class academic family. This encounter had a profound influence on Marianne, further developing her cosmopolitan consciousness of other worlds. This is how she describes the relationship: "The attitudes and understanding of this family were a huge influence on me. During this period I began to develop critical awareness and a realization that people might be influenced by their circumstances so that society was responsible in part for the problems that beset individuals."

Restless and unhappy, Marianne applied and became an American Field Service (AFS) exchange student in Texas at the age of seventeen. Marianne describes this experience as a "culture shock," and reported, "I think it was this experience and the fact that I was a 'foreigner' myself for a year that has led me to be interested in international work and travel in later years." She built friendships across difference, "established a close bond with my American 'family' and we are still in regular contact nearly fifty years later." She got to know not only Americans "but also people of my own age from a range of countries and continents."

She wrote, "When I returned from the USA, I had to go back to my girls' grammar school, wear the uniform including tie and beret and complete my last year in school taking the A (Advanced) level examinations." Finishing secondary school and doing well in the exams, she then went to the London School of Economics (LSE) to study sociology. She commented that "LSE was a stimulating place to be, particularly as I was there in the early 1960s and my last year, 1967, was the time of the first expression of student unrest that affected universities not only in the UK, but also France and the USA." Courses made the inequalities of society clear, she wrote, and "confirmed and underpinned my political attitudes." She felt that gender inequality was rarely discussed at the time, with class and race being seen as the more important social justice issues. Marianne did not fully enjoy LSE; she felt intimidated and "very much in awe of the academic excellence of others." It was only in her third year that she felt confident academically. Although she could have pursued a master's degree, her lack of confidence deterred her from applying. Thus she left LSE with a "good degree" at "a time when gender issues were just starting to emerge in the academic and political world"–but she felt "rootless, unsure, and lacking in confidence."

In the following postuniversity years she enrolled in a graduate secretarial course and worked as a secretary for a few months, what she described as "a typical woman's dead end route." Being the first person in the family to go to university, she lacked the encouragement and guidance to move her forward. She wrote, "My career aspirations were virtually nonexistent. But my first proper job after the secretarial episode was, unsurprisingly, in education." She thus became a university administrator and supported a distance-learning course, something she continued doing many years later as a distance-learning instructor and designer of distance-learning course materials. As an administrator, she was also involved in personnel selection and recruitment of clerical staff.

Marianne married about three years after leaving the university. Her attempts to move up the career ladder failed, and she realized that her age and marital status were against her. "In every interview, it seemed to me, there was covert or overt concern about my becoming pregnant," she reported. As there was no maternity leave at the time, once she did have a child she was expected to stay home and be a full-time mother. Although her interest in women's issues was alive, her situation as a young mother made her feel somewhat "alienated" from the women's movement since the messages she was getting from the movement at the time indicated that it was impossible to reconcile "being a wife with being a 'real feminist.'"

A turning point for Marianne was a statement her then two-year-old son made. "Men go out to work and 'ladies' stay at home doing the cooking, but that is not work!" Marianne was shocked and frustrated. "I did not want to bring up a son who accepted that as a status quo," so she decided to work part-time as a teacher of economics and politics at a secondary school, finding the position as the result of a chance encounter. With no teacher training, no supervision, and no professional development, Marianne recalled, beginning teaching was "a hard learning curve." However, she continued teaching for thirteen years in the same school. When her second son was born, new legislation had enacted statutory maternity leave with the guarantee of the job upon the woman's return to work. Marianne took advantage of this new legislation and returned to work three months after the birth of her son. "I was the first person at my school to successfully return after maternity leave," she noted.

Managing her teaching job and a family of two sons involved maintaining a "jigsaw of child-minders, nannies, and nurseries," but Marianne made it work. Teaching was a perfect fit for her as it allowed her more time with her two sons, especially during school holidays. She left the school after thirteen years, needing a break and looking for a new opportunity. For eighteen months following her resignation, Marianne worked as an advisory teacher in her county, helping teachers of economics and business studies. She described the people she worked with as "thoughtful and passionate about education," and for the first time she was enjoying her work 100 percent. "The part I enjoyed most was writing reports on the projects and the impact of the professional development that we were delivering. This made me realize that what I would really like to do was research and writing," she commented.

Next another chance encounter led Marianne to work part-time as a research associate for a university professor at Leicester. That post gave her the opportunity to conduct research and coauthor journal articles and a book on school leadership. During that time she also completed an MA course specializing in educational leadership and management. At the end of her contract, Marianne applied for a position and became a lecturer, then a senior lecturer at the same university for the next ten years. Having the full support of her husband, Marianne thrived in that environment. She was actively involved in research and teaching projects in China, Hong Kong, Singapore, South Africa, and Israel—further developing a cosmopolitan consciousness. It was during that time that she also strengthened her interest in women in educational management and leadership, which became the focus of her PhD thesis. Now formally retired, she is enjoying her emeritus reader status while continuing research and publishing several new books.

Enjoying three grandchildren, Marianne wrote, "Every woman who has children and a job or career is faced with difficult decisions." The account of her growing awareness of and commitment to class and gender issues of social justice began with her childhood awareness of class and extended through her educational and professional experiences, including early ambiguity about a career and the challenges faced in combining children and her career. Her life is a story of nascent feminism coming to life as personal experiences, the contemporary social ethos, and international events stimulated her academic interests and focused her commitment to social justice issues of class, gender, and diversity. Reflecting on her life and career, Marianne feels fortunate to have had a satisfying career that she sees as "worthwhile and of some value to others." She also feels fortunate to have had a supportive family who helped her along the way so that she can now "look forward to a future that continues to combine family and work related to gender and other social justice issues."

Insights

Two clear threads run through what Marianne chose to include in her story. One thread is in the elements that reveal how her personal identity developed through increasing consciousness of other worlds and realities; the other is in the passages that describe her journey to a fulfilling career. In regard to "identity," we use the term as Erikson (1956) did: a sense of one's own self; a sense that one's values, politics, passions, and tastes are one's own; a sense of where one's family values end and one's own values begin.

In Marianne's narrative there are numerous comments and experiences that contribute to the identity theme, including references to her awareness of her family's poverty and ambiguous class status, her placement in the lower (vocational) stream in elementary school, the rebellion against her father, and exposure to the values of a friend's academic family, becoming part of an "American family," at the relatively young age of seventeen getting to know people from around the world, and the stimulating intellectual atmosphere at the London School of Economics. Some of these elements in Marianne's story reveal, though, that the development of her identity was not without hiccups—witness her short stint working as a secretary. Ultimately, though, she came to value herself for being someone who could help others and do valuable work. She resisted isolation in domesticity and as a researcher was quick to accept international projects.

The second thread in Marianne's story is in the numerous statements that describe her path toward a fulfilling career. Not surprisingly, these begin at about the halfway mark in her narrative, when she notes that her career aspirations were awakened by the satisfactions of her "first proper job" as administrator of a university distance-learning course and a pronouncement by her toddler son that maintaining a household was not "work." That was when her family's valuing of education as a means for breaking "the restraining influences of social class and gender" was reawakened and she put high priority on further education and achieving success in work that was "worthwhile and of some value to others." Marianne found her true voice through her affiliation with the academic world. She found a clear purpose: to use her knowledge to advance the field of women in leadership positions by bringing to the front issues of inequalities and injustices. This is apparent in her story when she stated: "My education in the social sciences at LSE has had a profound effect on the way that I see the world and stimulated my academic interests." Once Marianne found her true purpose, she worked diligently toward success.

Today Marianne is a well-known scholar on gender issues, diversity, and leadership. Her national and international research has resulted in numerous publications, including her latest book on women in leadership positions (Coleman 2011). Although retired now, Marianne will continue to work on gender and social justice issues. It is important to note that Marianne's narrative also contains somewhat less tangible but important nuances that point to self-transcending values. In the end, Marianne was able to transmit values of her culture and contribute to the betterment of society. She had a broad cosmopolitan worldview, with her more salient values being productivity, care, and justice.

Born before the modern women's movement, Marianne's story is one of expanding consciousness of the world and social justice issues. Even though she came to clarity about her career path later than some, she is an example of how the values of choosing, creating, and exploring a career path with a clear purpose in mind can lead to high achievements and successful performance with the ultimate goal of benefiting women and society at large. In conclusion, it is worth noting also that Marianne made explicit reference to—and appreciated—the role that chance encounters played in her life. Those serendipitous events, reported in other WLE stories as well, showed Marianne the way to go next in order to fulfill her destiny. As she commented, however, these moments have to be recognized and embraced.

VALUES CREATE A LARGER CIRCLE: SELECTED SCHOLARSHIP

Among the best-known conceptualizations of values are Kluckhöhn and Strodtbeck's (1961) typology of value orientations, Hofstede's universal values (Hofstede 1980, 2001; Hofstede and Bond, 1984), Rokeach's system of values (1979), and Schwartz's (1992) universal classification of human values. A less well-known framework is Vaillant's (2002) adaptation of Erik Erikson's (1956) model of fundamental human values. The values referenced in these conceptualizations vary enormously: from conservatism to openness to change; from self-enhancement to self-transcendence; from individualism to collectivism; from dominance and assertiveness to consideration of people; from values that are oriented to the present and past to values oriented to the future; and from universal individual values such as power, security, and achievement to pancultural values such as harmony, mastery, and intellectual and affective autonomy.

Values are the moral compasses that guide us on our personal and professional journeys. Values provide us with a frame of reference for setting priorities and determining right and wrong. Values describe who we are and what we stand for in the world. They give meaning to lives, influence to relationships, and power to actions (Lambert and Gardner 2009). Considering the stories through the lenses of different conceptualizations of values provides readers a way to think about these stories and their own from different perspectives.

First, and one of the best-known values models, is Schwartz's (1992) classification of universal human values, which he derived from surveys of over sixty thousand people. This model suggests another way of looking at the three stories we have examined. Schwartz found ten categories of values, each containing a number of discrete but related values. These categories are power, achievement, hedonism, stimulation, self-direction, universalism, benevolence, tradition, conformity, and security. Schwartz found also that the ten categories, in turn, coalesce into four second-level groups of related categories:

- *Openness to change*: Stimulation, self-direction, and some aspects of hedonism
- *Conservatism*: Security, tradition, and conformity
- *Self-enhancement*: Achievement, power, and other aspects of hedonism
- *Self-transcendence*: Universalism and benevolence

Achievement and power were evident in the three featured stories. Achievement was a potent value in the lives of Elizabeth, Alice, and Marianne, and they pursued power as a means to achieve their goals. They did not, however, use power to dominate others but to attain a degree of social status and prestige through their professions that allowed them to achieve alignments of resources and influence relationships that supported their ultimate goal of a just society. In this way, social justice became their flame. All three sought to help others and were deeply concerned for the general welfare. In that sense, they acted as "earth mothers" (Schwartz 1994) whose purpose is to nurture others.

Schwartz also noted that there are two competing tensions among the four second-level categories of values: self-enhancement versus self-transcendence, and conservatism versus openness to change. The second tension is between valuing independent thoughts, actions, and interests and having a positive attitude toward change versus a submission of oneself, preservation of traditional practices, valuing and protecting the stability in one's life, and attempts to preserve the status quo (Fischer and Smith 2006, 544). It seems that individuals who endorse conservative values are not concerned with justice, whereas openness values lead to a stronger emphasis on justice in general. "Those who endorse conservative values are likely to accept decisions made by their superiors without questioning or scrutinising them in terms of perceived justice" (Fischer and Smith 2006, 544).

Clearly Elizabeth, Alice, and Marianne opposed conservatism and chose instead to tread the road of larger circles to change. They critiqued traditional and conformist structures of society whenever they saw in them injustices that contributed to the suffering of women, and this compelled them to take actions to alter those structures. Thus they chose stimulating careers that would allow them to be independent of the traditional norms, free from the chains of conservatism, and "outside the control of others" (Schwartz 1994). Moreover, they adopted self-transcendent values, which entail not only concern about the well-being of people close to oneself but also concern for all humans and the environment. Self-transcendence values have an egalitarian and tolerant quality, reflecting humanitarianism, expanding circles of concern, and cosmopolitan consciousness.

To explore a second model, we turn to Kluckhöhn and Strodtbeck (1961), who developed another influential theory of human values. The theory posits that there are five fundamental problems that all societies must address and that there are a few fundamental solutions to those problems. The problems are stated as questions in the bulleted list. In each case, embedded following the dash are differing approaches to possible solutions:

- On what aspect of time should we primarily focus—past, present, or future?
- How should humans relate to nature—mastery, submission, or harmony?
- How should individuals relate with others—hierarchically (lineal), as equals (collateral), or according to their individual inclinations (individualistic)?
- What is the prime motivation for behavior—to express one's self (being), to grow (being in becoming), or to achieve?
- What is the nature of human nature—good, bad/evil, or a mixture? (Kluckhöhn and Strodtbeck 1961; Hills 2002)

Applying such questions to the stories of the women featured in this chapter provides more food for thought. For example, in regard to Kluckhöhn and Strodtbeck's (1961) first question about time, Elizabeth, Alice, and Marianne looked to a better future for themselves and society. In the matter of relationships, they valued holism—preferring to see individuals as part of a complex, unified universe whose harmony depends on how all parts interact with one another. When they detected imbalance, they sought to alleviate it, using their unique skills to push for appropriate change. Their motivation was to contribute to society as a whole, again reflecting humanitarianism, larger circles of concern, and cosmopolitan consciousness.

Dantley (2010) adds spirituality to values important in leadership. Specifically, he refers to leadership with critical spirituality, the aspect of character through which we build connectivity and community with others. He contrasts spirituality with religion, which he says is often used to transmit codes of behavior that work in collaboration with civil authorities to "domesticate" a society's citizenry. In comparison, Dantley wrote that spirituality comprises compassion, a sense of equity, understanding, and passion toward others and the life's work to which one has been "called." The strong commitments to social justice leadership displayed in the narratives of Elizabeth, Alice, and Marianne suggest connections between their commitments and spirituality as defined by Dantley. He posits that spirituality is the wellspring of the transformative aspect of a leader's work (214–15). From a different angle, Emmons (1999) defined spirituality as "a search for meaning, for unity, for connectedness, for transcendence, for the highest of human potential" (92), or, one could say, for the larger circle.

Finally, Vaillant (2002) builds on Erikson's work in writing about individuals maturing into "generativity" and "keeping the meaning." It becomes important to the individual to transmit the values of the culture. The prime values here are productivity and care. The most significant relationships are with the workplace, the community, and the family. When the individual attains the "keeper of the meaning" orientation, according to Vaillant, the values of wisdom and justice become important. Justice, unlike care, means not taking sides. The individual strives to produce something that contributes to the betterment not only of the culture but of humanity, the larger circle. Thus there is a "widening of the social radius" (Erikson 1956), such that the individual is concerned about the welfare of the species. Values create a larger circle.

CONCLUDING THOUGHTS

In this chapter we presented the stories of three WLE women to highlight how values create a larger circle within which to live and from which to view the meaning of our lives. Productivity, care, wisdom, and justice were important values to each woman. These and other values associated with social justice affected their personal lives and guided their efforts to attain a more just society. Elizabeth Reilly pursued with passion a goal to unlock the gifts and talents of each individual by opposing injustices, sufferings, deprivation, and hatred. Alice Merab Kagoda pursued social justice through involvement in women's groups—by her advocacy and activism to better women's lives in Uganda. Marianne Coleman pursued social justice through her academic work and her national and international research on gender issues and diversity. Values are the moral compasses and keys to the authenticity and power that enabled them to overcome barriers and use their status, learning skills, resources, and power to influence individuals and lead them toward a more just society.

Families initially formed the values that each woman further developed in her life as she pursued her personal life and career path. For Elizabeth, the privileged environment she grew up in and her parents' unfailing valuing of education ignited the passion to help less privileged individuals to succeed in life. For Alice, working for women's causes came from values developed in overcoming barriers, along with her firsthand experience of helping women in need of support and opportunity. These factors led to her activism to extend equality to other Ugandan girls and women. For Marianne, the value of a more just society, where social class is not an impediment to one's future, was instrumental in her striving for equality.

A dominant impression gained from the stories of Elizabeth, Alice, and Marianne, as well as from others in the book, is that the women engaged in what Sergiovanni (1992) calls leadership grounded in "purposing," leadership that is focused by a sense of what is truly important and what is of paramount value. Fullan (2003) makes the same argument when he argues that social justice leadership requires reassertion of the moral purpose of leadership. Connell, Ashenden, Kessler, and Dowsetts (1982) go a step further, expressing the ideal purpose of education as a call to action that liberates. They write that "in a society disfigured by class exploitation, sexual and racial oppression, and in chronic danger of war and environmental destruction, the only education worth the name is one that forms people capable of taking part in their own liberation" (207–8). If we can lead ourselves and others to a larger view, to an understanding of the interlocking justice issues facing the planet, we will be, become, and build leaders capable of contributing to healing the world.

5

SKILLFUL
AUTHENTIC LEADERSHIP

The authentic self is the soul made visible.

—Sarah Ban Breathnach, *Simple Abundance*

Connecting authentic leadership with social justice, Howell and Avolio (1992) note that authentic leaders are concerned with the common good—and when called on will sacrifice self-interest for the sake of the collective good. Attempts to distill the essence of all positive approaches to leadership (Avolio and Gardner 2005; Luthans and Avolio 2003; May, Hodges, Chan, and Avolio 2003) have coalesced into the concept of authentic leadership, which is thought of as a root concept for positive leadership approaches such as charismatic, transformational, and ethical leadership (Ilies, Morgeson, and Nahrgang 2005). We argue that social justice leadership is defined through actions (Bogotch 2002; Rapp 2002; Strachan 2005) and view authentic leadership as a root concept of social justice leadership also.

At a macro level, Terry (1993) explains that authentic leadership is being "true to ourselves and true to the world, real in ourselves and real in the world" (139). Lyman, Ashby, and Tripses (2005) believe that "integrating doing and being results in authentic leadership. Bringing one's being into leadership is about authenticity, bringing the whole of who you are to your work, not leaving any aspect of yourself at the door" (157). Being an authentic leader means having integrity. Authentic leaders express their "true selves" in daily life. Each lives a "good life" and not only achieves "self-realization" but also has positive effects on followers' *eudaimonic* well-being (Ilies, Morgeson, and Nahrgang 2005). *Eudaimonic* well-being is an ancient concept widely used in discussions of life satisfaction in positive psychology. Peterson, Park, and Seligman (2005) describe the concept as stemming from "the premise that people should develop what is best within themselves and then use these skills and talents in the service of greater goods—including in particular the welfare of other people or humankind writ large" (26).

Focusing on skills is looking at authentic leadership from the micro level. What does *skillful* authentic leadership require? All twenty-three WLE leaders who submitted narratives commented directly on acquiring or using skills of leadership in their social justice work. Skills learned informally from family and role models included taking responsibility, speaking up for beliefs, and acting according to conscience. Skills learned in more formal settings, through higher education and from leadership positions, included: teamwork; developing inclusive communities; political skills such as advocacy and lobbying; and communications skills such as raising consciousness, talking through a problem, building consensus, and facilitating a shared commitment to moving ahead. In this chapter we examine three leaders' narratives through the lens of authentic leadership and associated skills.

SKILLFUL AUTHENTIC LEADERSHIP: THE STORIES

According to Plutarch, Greek philosopher and priest at the sanctuary of Apollo in Delphi, the aphorism "Know thyself" was the first of two phrases that were inscribed in the *pronaos* (forecourt) of the temple by Apollo, the god of light. The proverb was incised into the stonework of many other parts of the temple, too, so that those who visited Delphi to ask Apollo for advice would not miss the message. In fact, ancient Greeks knew and took for granted that both spiritual attainment and catharsis of the soul begin with introspection, self-awareness, and self-knowledge. Through introspection one comes closer to one's true genuine self, and through self-awareness and self-knowledge, in turn, one begins to unveil one's real identity to others. These are the fundamentals, or one could call them the two sides of the coin of authenticity.

Authentic leaders are involved in personal journeys of self-discovery, searching for an ideal but obtainable self or possible sets of selves (Luthans, Youssef, and Avolio 2007). In this journey authentic leaders gain experience, wisdom, and the ability to act with integrity—or what Aristotle (350 BCE) called *phronesis*—in bringing about change that enhances the quality of life of those they serve. Phronesis can be said to mean "practical wisdom." Phronesis is not simply skill in deciding how to achieve a certain end, but also the ability to reflect upon and determine the worthy end itself (Phronesis, n.d.). To the notion of *phronesis*, Aristotle appended the concept of *eudaimonia* or well-being (from *daimon*, meaning "true nature"). Whereas hedonists focused on happiness as the goal of life, Aristotle did not. He stressed that not all desires are worth pursuing; although some desires may yield pleasure, not all produce wellness. Aristotle endorsed finding happiness by leading a virtuous life and doing what is worth doing.

Skillful authentic leadership that typically emerges from a developmental process cannot be oversimplified. We turn to three stories to examine that developmental process and highlight two distinguishing features of skillful authentic leadership. These thematic clusters are evident also in the other WLE narratives. The facets of skillful authentic leadership and the three featured leaders are: (1) Growing into Authenticity—Sister Hellen Bandiho, Tanzania; (2) Developing *Phronesis* (Practical Wisdom)—Pamela Lenz, United States; and (3) Leading for *Eudaimonia* (Well-Being)—Rachel McNae, New Zealand.

Growing into Authenticity

Taking a developmental perspective, a leader's personal history (family, friends, early experiences, educational and work encounters, and role models) as well as trigger events (crises, positive and negative experiences) are catalysts for the development of authentic leadership behaviors and skills. Hoyle, Kernis, Leary, and Baldwin (1999) argue that childhood experiences, family influences, cultural influences, role models, and educational experiences develop the unique lenses that individuals use to interpret life events. Gardner, Avolio, Luthans, May, and Walumbwa (2005) add to the dialogue that the processes of consciously reflecting on such life events and constructively interpreting their meaning are what develop the self and move the leader toward greater authenticity.

However the process unfolds, first and foremost, authentic leaders are true to themselves. They are aware of how they behave and how others perceive them; they know their potentials and their limitations. Ongoing commitment to understand oneself and be consistent are, therefore, at the core of authentic leadership. Second, authenticity has not only cognitive and behavioral dimensions, but relational aspects, too. Thus authentic individuals will likely possess the capacity to develop more valuable and meaningful exchanges with peers and followers. They understand and practice skillful communication.

Two previously featured leaders demonstrate skills and understandings that contribute to authenticity. Katherine Cumings Mansfield (chapter 2) spoke to integrity and social justice in commenting on the skillful use of language. She wrote, "While we may not have originally created the vocabulary we habitually use, like it or not, the language we employ can be healing or injurious. It also has the uncanny ability to reveal the essence of who we are, what we think of ourselves, and what we believe about others." She continued, articulating what can be regarded as a principle of social justice leadership, "We must be attuned to the power of language, and be willing to change how we name people, if we are to be ethical leaders, principled researchers, and decent human beings."

Saeeda Shah (chapter 3) eloquently expressed how leadership is more than skills. She explained, "I believe it [leadership] is a combination of all that a person is—abilities, skills, contacts, positionality—how we position ourselves and how we are positioned by all the stakeholders—that we bring to leadership and not just professional skills that lead to success or failure in leadership positions." The phrase "all that a person is" implies integrity and the capacity for authenticity.

Hellen Bandiho

"Each person has a unique journey." With this phrase, Sister Dr. Hellen Bandiho started her story titled "Personal Journey," which began on the shores of Lake Victoria, in Bukoba, Tanzania, some fifty or so years ago. She wrote her story in the third person, as a formal essay with citations, using the pseudonym Buhinda for herself. Directly addressing readers, she wrote, "It is the hope of this author that her [Buhinda's] experiences, which led her to her current educational position, will shed light and strengthen your own personal journey." Sister Hellen also revealed in the introduction that although there had been male role models in her life, she chose to unfold her story around "female role models" so that young aspiring women leaders might "see themselves using a lens of these outstanding women."

Sister Hellen provides a vivid and colorful description of her early years growing up as the second born of eight children to parents who were "small-scale farmers" in an area "dominated by hills and valleys" and surrounded by banana plantations. She described the village in which she grew up as a "community-oriented" place, where people were bound by strong values—a place where "[raising] children was everyone's responsibility." The first few lines of her story shake us from the realm of what most take for granted and push us to think of how the simplest things for us can be big struggles for others. She expresses that understanding powerfully in a few words:

> Experiences, education, training, and the environment in which people were born and raised contribute immensely to what they are. For some people, basic education is expected and therefore it is acquired naturally; others have to struggle to get an opportunity to learn how to read and write. If you are able to read this, count yourself as privileged.

At that time some girls in Tanzania were denied even primary education. Sister Hellen was certainly not privileged in the usual sense of the word. However, she was fortunate that her basic education was supported and encouraged by her parents. Although they were small-scale farmers and not educated beyond the primary level, they valued education and made sure that their children had access to schooling and the basic conditions to be able to study. They couldn't help their children with school assignments but made sure "that lanterns were filled up with kerosene to enable their children to study at night." The conditions for children attending schools were most difficult. When Sister Hellen began her basic education at age seven, for example, she and her siblings had to walk seven miles every day to arrive at school by 7:30 a.m., and when classes were over at 4:30 p.m. they returned home to help with house chores.

At the local primary school Sister Hellen was taught by *Mwalimu* (meaning "teacher" in Swahili) Suzanna. She inspired Sister Hellen to want to be a teacher herself. Mwalimu Suzanna was among the few female teachers in the area in the 1960s who "were automatically role models to many girls." The impact of those female teachers to girls such as Sister Hellen must have been tremendous as "such women were the only educated women young girls had ever met in their lives." It comes as no surprise, then, that Sister Hellen not only aspired to become a teacher but also years later serves as a role model for younger women.

When she was in primary school (standard 3), nuns from a local community of St. Therese visited her school to talk with the young girls about what they did. This community of nuns sponsored an upper primary school for girls. Her father was determined to get his daughters educated, and so at the age of ten, Sister Hellen left home for this boarding school run by the Sisters of St. Therese. She and her father, and all her belongings, got a motorbike ride from the parish pastor, and all three set off to what would be her new home, located about fifteen miles from her village. This turning-point event was described by Sister Hellen as "a beginning to a new life" through which she would be able to fulfill her career and life goals. "She never looked back either academically or at the route of life she had decided to take." Among other things, boarding school taught Sister Hellen the values of love, caring, responsibility, independence, and "good character," which later helped her pursue her own aspirations and dream to become a teacher. Describing her relationship with the nuns in those early formative years, she recounted how "these women (nuns) were special to me. They were always there for us, day and night, to make sure we excelled academically and were learning good human values" (H. B., e-mail message to author, July 15, 2011).

Sister Hellen had a challenging leadership development experience that very few women in the world get—one year of compulsory military service. Reflecting on this experience, she learned that "certainly, an inspired team is as important to army life as it is to educational leadership." Through tough training and extensive physical and mental demands, she came to recognize "the importance of other people" and teamwork, especially in times of great need and despair. She was particularly grateful to the five young men who felled the forest tree for her when she was unable to complete that required task by herself during the training.

For Sister Hellen, education was "an important leadership tool," one that gave her "status and a voice to express ideas." It was also a tool to be respected. After teaching in grade school for four years, her yearning for further education could not be satisfied in her native land. Tanzania had only two universities (both public), which were reserved for the very privileged few who could attend. However, her religious community took responsibility for the costs of her higher education degrees and sent her abroad. Thus she undertook the long journey to the United States, where she earned a BA and MBA degree from Edgewood College in Madison, Wisconsin, and later a PhD at Duquesne University in Pittsburgh, Pennsylvania. The striking contrast between the green banana fields of Tanzania and that first cold, numbing winter of Wisconsin, a northern state, was a shock for Sister Hellen, a woman who hadn't traveled abroad before.

On her first trip, she landed at an airport not knowing how to proceed. The incident became for her emblematic of how educators today must go the extra mile to help learners deal with ever-changing global complexities. Due to an unexpected delay of her connecting flight, Sister Hellen found herself stranded at a Chicago airport, not knowing how to make a phone call to alert her companion at her destination in Wisconsin. What follows is what she described as "the quarter-dollar leadership experience." First she asked a fellow passenger for help but got only a hurried "take a quarter, drop it in the hole, and follow the operator's instructions" in reply. Undaunted, but not giving up, she wrote,

> Embarrassed to ask more questions, I left the scene wondering what on earth a "quarter" was. I had no choice but to look for more help. I asked a gentleman the same question, hoping and praying that he would not use this "quarter" terminology in his response. Unfortunately, the gentleman responded with the same advice. "Take a quarter and . . ." and so on. But this time I had the courage to ask, "What is a quarter?" At that moment the man . . . must have realized that he was dealing with a person who needed more help than he had originally thought. He went the extra mile, taking me to the store, where he helped me get change. In the process, he taught me not only that a quarter is equivalent to twenty-five cents, but also explained the value of a dime, a nickel, and a penny.

This situation was a learning experience in teaching and leadership, a lesson that upon reflection she credits with illuminating the importance of listening, patience, humility, respect, perseverance, and courage—all valuable skills of authentic leadership.

Upon returning from her studies abroad, Sister Hellen was appointed an assistant lecturer at St. Augustine University of Tanzania (SAUT). It is a secular, nonprofit private institution of higher learning founded by the Catholic bishops of Tanzania in 1998. Sister Hellen gradually worked her way up the professorship ladder, serving for several years as dean of the faculty of business administration. Retiring from that position, she currently is director of postgraduate studies, research and consultancy, and senior lecturer at SAUT.

According to Sister Hellen, teamwork lies at the heart of community life. The experiences of being raised in a small village community and later moving into a religious community are at the core of her life. Her religious community has been a family and source of help for more than thirty years. The women named in the story who assisted her in her life and career journey taught her "to act according to conscience, taking her responsibility seriously, being wise, respectful, and compassionate," all of which she accepts as "good values for successful leadership." The women mentors and role models in Sister Hellen's story are portrayed as women of strength and many virtues, as well as women who are independent thinkers and profoundly spiritual. These women helped Sister Hellen form her own set of values, the most important being integrity, responsibility, commitment, and vision. Sister Hellen is grateful to all these women who were role models for her, who supported her educational and spiritual journey. They shaped her character and fostered her personal growth and development.

Sister Hellen believes "different paths can take you where you want to go as long as you are focused and committed to your cause." She learned early on "that whatever she does, she has to do it with integrity." From her current position as an administrator and educator, Sister Hellen is able to give back to the community some of the gifts she has received during her life journey. Through her education and her leadership position, Sister Hellen has been able to be a role model to younger women who "aspire to become someone in their lives but may be struggling to make it." To help younger women pursue education, she started a scholarship fund for women at her university who lack the resources to continue their education. This is how she explained her motivation for starting the scholarship:

> I knew . . . that when resources are scarce in Africa, a male child will get education and a female child will be left home to help with home chores. I decided to make a difference to a few women by starting a scholarship fund for poor but smart female students who may be lacking the $500 or less towards their tuition and who for that reason may drop out. (H. B., e-mail message to author, July 17, 2009)

Talking with younger women and listening to their stories and problems, Sister Hellen experienced "a wake-up call" about continuing discrimination in education in Tanzania. Although women's lives have improved much since she was a young girl, African women's biggest challenge is still lack of education, particularly postgraduate education. When asked about her interest in gender issues, she wrote that "in Africa and probably in other countries as well, women's education had been neglected for a long time. My mother was not educated, she only knew how to read and write. When I was growing up, I could see how lack of education had a negative impact on her as well as on many other women of her age." She understood that "without education, most women have no income of their own and they depend entirely on their husbands, who can sometimes abuse them because they have economic power."

Sister Hellen was the first woman in her family to earn a university degree, and at the time she submitted her narrative, she was the only female educator at St. Augustine University of Tanzania with a doctorate. In concluding her story she addressed readers directly, beginning with an Asian proverb and ending with a call to action: "There are many paths to the top of the mountain but the view is always the same. . . . Having arrived where we had dreamed of reaching, we are challenged to pave ways for younger women who may be struggling to make it. . . . Let us play our part."

Insights

Sister Hellen's story is confirmation that a critical factor in the development of authentic leadership is exposure to and interaction with supportive and inspirational others. The role of family in supporting and sustaining children's education in the early formative years is of paramount importance to their future success. Also, however, the years at the boarding school were decisive in molding Sister Hellen's character and equipping her with strong moral values. As she described it, "character formation was as important as education itself." Through the caring relationships with the women who surrounded her during her school years, Sister Hellen learned to be responsible, independent, resilient in tough times, courageous in the face of the unknown, and morally strong. These were among the seeds that made Sister Hellen an authentic leader.

Grogan and Shakeshaft (2011) note how "many women of color and many white women are motivated by a strong desire to transform the learning conditions and opportunities for those who have been least well served by current educational policies and practices" (11). Choosing to ease the way for women who would otherwise be denied opportunities for growth and empowerment, authentic leaders are motivated also by the great value they attach to gender equity and equality. For example, the values Sister Hellen internalized ultimately prompted her to help female students attend and continue at the university by establishing a scholarship fund for poor girls. In this, her deeply ingrained moral values were transformed into social action to make a difference. As many scholars have noted, social justice leadership is about having the passion to change hearts as well as minds. Sister Hellen's experiences abroad made her realize how valuable education is for Tanzanian women and how the lack of it has subjected women to a disadvantaged life relative to men.

The story of how Sister Hellen Bandiho came to be a skillful authentic leader has many chapters. Certainly her female teachers and mentors helped her "find her own voice" and develop the authentic leadership capacities that "give meaning to my academic, professional, and religious life." Behaving authentically, according to Kernis (2003), means "acting in accord with one's values, preferences, and needs as opposed to acting merely to please others, or to attain rewards, or avoid punishments through acting falsely" (298). In Sister Hellen's own words, "education, training, experiences, role models, all combine to transform ordinary people into extraordinary leaders." She remembers in her story all the women who have inspired and helped her "to act according to conscience" and who instilled in her the strong moral values needed to become a true authentic leader herself.

Leading with *Phronesis* (Practical Wisdom)

According to Aristotle, effective leadership practices are oriented toward the collective well-being, and *phronesis* is considered a necessary condition for successful social organization and development (Birmingham 2004). WLE leaders have a bias for action—more specifically, for actions of practical wisdom grounded in commitment to social justice. The members of WLE have held a wide variety of leadership positions in the basic and secondary education systems in their countries as well as in institutions of higher education. Reading their stories one can understand things in a new way, interpret a challenging situation from another point of view. Reading their stories carefully, a host of practical skills for authentic leadership are identified. Among others, these include being able to discuss a problem when viewpoints differ, being political through advocacy and lobbying, using a collective leadership approach, having high standards, speaking out against injustice, and fighting for what is right.

Social intelligence is associated with authenticity and practical skills and strategies. Goleman (2006) describes how leaders who have the ability to understand the dynamics of social situations are characterized by empathy, attunement, social cognition, influence, and concern. These traits generate trust and closeness in followers, as the latter feel valued and respected. Lundin, Paul, and Christensen (2000) suggest that authentic leaders find potential in others and act as mentors to help them succeed and reach *eudaimonia* in their lives. Their primary strategies are improving communication through empathetic listening, making work fun, making someone's day in a memorable way, and maintaining a positive mindset and attitude regardless of what is taking place.

Pamela Lenz

Dr. Pamela Lenz was born in Pennsylvania, the first of two girls of an upper-middle-class American family. In her story Pam described herself growing up as a "quirky little kid" whose interests didn't always fit with what others her age liked to do. At school, during recess, she preferred "reading, doing logic problems, or just imagining." Being a curious girl, she loved "knowing how things worked . . . and enjoyed the act of creating"—both physically and mentally—which provided her "a wonderful sense of accomplishment." Her family was not only supportive in what Pam was doing, but also encouraged her to "think outside the box." Family was also fundamental in teaching her the values of integrity and respect. In an early version of her story, Pam referred to the great influence her maternal grandmother, Myrtle, had on her as a child. Myrtle's unique, adventuresome nature and liberated upbringing made her a nonconformist, which is what much later influenced Pam to "march to the beat of a different drummer." Myrtle's influence on Pam is captured best in these words: "Despite her being gone for thirty-three years, things learned from our relationship still guide my daily life."

Much to the chagrin of her father, who believed that the degree did not match her intellectual capabilities, Pam chose a music education major in college and "graduated summa cum laude with a degree in music education, married a music major, and we both immediately completed our music education master's degrees." After graduation, Pam landed a teaching job and taught elementary music for thirteen years. During these years, with her creative and imaginative nature, she managed to enrich the narrowly focused music curriculum of that time with literature, math, science, and other subjects "before it was fashionable to do so." She also proposed trading their traditional marching band uniforms for leather jackets and jeans to complement the show's theme of popular music from the 1950s, something that helped the school band earn first place at championships. Further, when she was an elementary principal, her school implemented co-teaching "before it became the buzzword of special education in twenty-first-century learning."

With further upgrading of her qualifications, Pam became an instructional support teacher, a position she held for eleven years. Then, encouraged by her principal, who saw in her "a good building leader," she got her administrative certificate and was later offered the position of assistant principal. Pam's first year as an administrator taught her "some hard, but good lessons." Pam spent the next two years in that position creating a culture "that was good for students and staff alike." The beginning of her fourth year Pam became principal of another elementary school in the same district. "Thus began some of the most wonderful years of my career." This is how she described this experience:

> I loved the people I worked with. They were caring, creative, and fun loving, yet completely dedicated to the students and community they served. Being eight miles from main campus we thought and worked out of the box. Yet our achievement scores often topped the district charts, and the sense of community shared was beyond compare. It was a building of autonomy, mastery, and purpose.

Pam's teaching and administrative experience span a period of thirty-three years. During most of those years, Pam "remained engaged in [her] passion of working with competitive marching bands—not in the more traditional female role of guard (flag and dance) instructor, but in the decidedly male realm of show design and drill coordination." Her description is illustrative of the tasks she was involved with:

> For those without familiarity, this involves conceptualizing the combination of music and movements on the field. The precise location of every person on the field is individually plotted for every musical phase, with a seven-minute competitive show often requiring seventy discrete pages of drill and choreography.

Although music was a catalytic force in her life, Pam continued to pursue further studies, and in 2006 she enrolled in Duquesne University's Interdisciplinary Program for Educational Leaders, her "best educational decision." The university offered the doctoral degree as a satellite program at Mercyhurst College in Erie, so she attended the classes there except for the weeklong summer residency experiences in Pittsburgh. Helen Sobehart, WLE founding chair, was the director of the doctoral program. From Helen and others in the program, Pam learned "the value of teamwork and trust, as well as how to use all of our resources to lead organizations through the metaphorical woods to a worthy goal." She credits Helen, who also became a close friend, with continuing "to nudge me from my comfortable perch."

Pam's story continued with a thoughtful and reflective account of her current position in a new community as director of curriculum, instruction, and assessment. In this new role she works with the superintendent "to bring autonomy, mastery, and purpose" to their colleagues and families. Pam affirms that it is while in this position that she has come to best know herself as a leader. She explored becoming a superintendent through participating in several districts' interview processes. This experience made her realize that a leader is not necessarily the one at the top of the ladder, and that sometimes leadership is not what is sought out in those positions. She came to realize that deep down she didn't really want or need to be at the top of the ladder in order to feel like a leader because "the noneducational items that occur on a daily basis can crowd your mind, leaving far too little room for thinking, creating, and mastering." For Pam, working with others to implement quality educational practices is the "true essence of school." Proudly she stated that she had "the privilege of leading the best, and making a difference." And "if I had to live my professional life over, I wouldn't trade my colleagues or students for the greatest acclaims the educational world has to offer."

Pam related that "the women leaders who have truly impacted my life have not done so on the basis of position. In fact many have been 'under' me in the traditional hierarchy. Instead, their true influence has come from inner greatness and depth of character." Reflecting on the question "Who in the world am I?" Pam shared what she had learned from women who have been companions on her journey. In her own words, "When I look at my life, I realize how much others have helped me navigate the often rough waters of life. Perhaps the best way to know me is to know some of them." In this connection she named four women who inspired her life: her grandmother Myrtle, her daughter Erin, and her friends Mary Beth Cook and Helen Sobehart. Each of these women impacted Pam at a different stage in her life, teaching invaluable lessons.

Grandmother Myrtle's influence during her early formative years was previously described. Her daughter Erin, "a wise woman and role model," is a living example of resilience and a person who understands "the importance of not allowing one's professional being to overshadow personal relationships and the joy of being alive." This last could not be truer in Erin's case. In a chilling passage, Pam describes how at an eighth-grade dinner-dance, her then thirteen-year-old daughter was standing fifteen feet away from a classmate who took a gun from his pocket and fired two shots that killed one of the school's teachers. As the teacher lay between the students and the entrance to the banquet hall, [Erin] and her friends had to run for cover when the young man then began shooting at random. As one of the prosecution's main witnesses, she was integrally involved in the case for over a year until it was settled. Today Erin is a twenty-seven-year-old forensic molecular biologist who is well recognized in her field, a woman "who cares about others."

Pam's friend Mary Beth taught her "how to listen with one's whole being, how to understand beyond that which is said, how to practice selflessness." Mary Beth was a third-grade teacher at an elementary school where Pam was also teaching and a woman who "emphasized the value of people above all else." In describing their friendship, Pam observed that "we talked, but listened more. Sometimes we just sat together, merely content to be in the other's presence. And it was Mary Beth's arm that I allowed to encircle my shoulders at the unexpected passing of a fellow staff member and close friend." A "stubbornly independent" woman, much like Pam, Mary Beth helped her learn to ask someone else for help. When Pam asked her what path she should take in her life, Mary Beth responded with the following questions: "What is your heart's passion? . . . What fills your life and lungs with breath and joy? What do you believe your purpose in life to be?" These questions have been guiding principles for Pam when choosing new professional endeavors.

Helen Sobehart, who was director of the interdisciplinary program for educational leaders at Duquesne University when Pam pursued her doctoral studies, is described by Pam as "an unconventional woman who had us jumping from heights while secured by a single tether." Pam credits Helen with nudging her repeatedly to venture outside her comfort zone. She described her experiences with Helen as a blessing and empowering. In Helen's case, much as in Mary Beth's, Pam "experienced [Helen's] open arms, uncommon spirit, and kind and caring heart—gifts revealing a depth of character possessed by few." Realizing how fortunate she was to have these women as guides in her life, she wrote, "as I seek to discover myself, I hope that I am the kind of person who leads by listening to others as they have listened to me, one who seeks to make a difference in the world by seizing challenge without sacrificing relationships, and one who accepts unconditionally."

Pam submitted her narrative when she was at a crossroad, struggling with four career choices and how to pick a path that would lead to a greater balance between her career and her personal life—lead to "a place of contentment where I can serve both worlds from the head as well as the heart." Seven months into her new post as the director of curriculum, instruction, and assessment, she shared conclusions about her personal and professional growth, including the understanding that "identifying those who have truly impacted our pathways in life is not always clear." She has learned that "it is just as important to think of those you are leaving, to think of how to do it well, and not to devalue relationships forged over the years." She has been reminded that the essence of true leadership is not position, awards, or name recognition, but the wisdom that comes from the realization that "leadership is a joint venture, often occurring when and where you least expect it, a blending of everyone's future and past into a rich present that serves us all."

An authentic leader who leads with *phronesis*, Pam struggles with questions such as: What type of leader am I? What do I want my legacy to be? What values do I want to embody? Her pursuit of social justice by leading authentically with *phronesis* is a work in progress, "bringing the unconscious to consciousness, so that we intentionally create more equitable opportunities for all" (P. L., e-mail message to author, July 22, 2009). To finish her narrative, Pam shared a quotation from Daniel Pink's *Drive: The Surprising Truth about What Motivates Us*, "The richest experiences in our lives aren't when we're clamoring for validation from others, but when we're listening to our own voice—doing something that matters, doing it well, and doing it in the service of a cause larger than ourselves."

Insights

Pam Lenz's narrative of her personal and professional paths makes us think of leadership not only in terms of theoretical knowledge (*episteme*) or a set of skills (*techne*) but also, as Aristotle described it, a faculty entailing practical wisdom (*phronesis*). Pam's life story clearly illustrates how she acquired *phronesis* through her various engagements with—and leadership of—others toward the achievement of common goals. Her passion for competitive marching bands led her to lead altogether a life that had a clear, driving beat—one typified by thinking out of the box, mastering, inventing and creating, and relationship building. For Pam Lenz, positions, titles, awards, and recognition have not been indicators of strong leadership; rather, relationships are. This explains why her story is largely an acknowledgment of the many teachers and students she worked with over the past thirty years, the people who had an impact on her personal and professional life. Her inner music has the beat of collaboration, openness, willingness, goodness, and togetherness.

In leading, Pam strove to balance what Flyvbjerg (2006) describes as "instrumental rationality" and "value rationality." This balance results in *phronesis* capacity. Her high intellectual capabilities and her yearning for work of the mind have taken Pam to high levels of professional accomplishment and distinction. But it was the additional layer of values, her strong moral inclinations toward meaningful relationships, thoughtful listening, and lifelong learning that proved invaluable, when combined with intellect, in her ability to make a difference in the lives of people with whom she worked. Flyvbjerg argues that striking this balance is crucial to the viability and thriving of any organization. Open-mindedness allowed Pam to be creative and to think outside the box, whereas awareness has helped her see the larger picture—her personal and professional life—in light of her various experiences and interactions with others. In fact, most of her narrative is an account of thoughtful reflection on her life.

Evidence of Pam's leading with *phronesis* is her awareness of her strengths and weaknesses (intrapersonal intelligence), her confidence in her abilities, and her setting of appropriate goals. Zagzebski (1996) states that "it takes phronesis to know how persevering one should be to be persevering, how careful one should be to be careful, how self-sufficient one should be to be autonomous" (221). Perhaps nothing epitomizes Pam's *phronetic* leadership better than her understanding of other people's voices, potentials, and motives. Her leadership is oriented toward the accomplishment of organizational goals and ultimately the common good, by interacting openly and flexibly with others.

Pam's leadership practices comprise what Grogan and Shakeshaft (2011) describe as a form of collective leadership that allows organizations and schools to be viewed as open systems, offering "intriguing possibilities for engaging ideas from the community that address issues of equity and diversity, leading to productive change" (45).

Finally, existentially intelligent persons are characterized by love of freedom, passion, and a strong desire to change situations. Individuals with this capability are able to pose questions about life, death, and ultimate realities (Gardner 1999); they develop a lens through which they are better able to understand human beings; thus, they introduce "authenticity" as the norm of self-identity. When asked about her social justice work, Pam responded by referring to Mother Teresa's words. When asked about her work, Mother Teresa said, "One thing I have done which I believe is important: I have helped people to talk to the poor and not just about the poor." Pam applied these words to herself, saying: "[I hope] that I don't just talk about social justice issues, but that what I do from one day to the next contributes to improving the lives and understandings of others" (P. L., e-mail message to author, September 1, 2011).

Leading for *Eudaimonia*

Shakespeare's famous line "to thine own self be true" captures one aspect of authenticity. Authentic leadership, a relatively new concept in the leadership literature, has raised considerable interest among researchers partly because it relates to the ideals of self-knowledge, excellence of character, and virtuous living. What is not often recognized is that, as noted earlier, authentic leadership differs from other forms of leadership in its focus on *eudaimonia*.

> Eudaimonia or eudaemonia (Ancient Greek: εδαιμονία) . . . is a Greek word commonly translated as happiness; however, "human flourishing" is a more accurate translation. Etymologically, it consists of the word "eu" ("good") and "daimōn" ("spirit"). (Eudaimonia, n.d.)

What the narratives show about *leading for eudaimonia* is that it is important to ensure a balance between one's professional life and one's personal life. There is a need to give equal weight to personal aspirations such as attaining self-acceptance, effective management of one's life and the surrounding environment, having purpose in life, maintaining positive relationships, sustaining personal growth, and assuring autonomy or self-determination. In this connection role models and mentors are once again important. But at least equally important are organizational values, policies, and structures that respect personal rights and moral agency and do not make personal needs subservient to organizational needs.

Rachel McNae

Dr. Rachel McNae is a young woman in her mid-thirties who is a senior lecturer in the Department of Professional Studies in Education at the University of Waikato, in Hamilton, New Zealand. She has worked hard to establish herself professionally in the academic world. She observed that by writing her narrative, she "becomes conscious" of her leadership as it has developed through different stages of her life. Unfolding in different contexts, her leadership journey often took her over rough waters, sometimes has been fulfilling and energizing, and at other times has made her wonder whether academia was the right path for her. Her life story reflects unconventional but satisfying leadership that emanates naturally from the heart and soul of a free-spirited and naturally inclined leader.

Rachel's eloquently written story is a beautiful piece of literature in and of itself and illustrates issues associated with leading for *eudaimonia*. Written as a reflective account of her life as "a woman in education, a woman leading and showing leadership, and a woman empowering other young women to lead," her story depicts the most seemingly "(in)significant moments that have shaped my leadership journey." It has elements of growing into authentic leadership, leading with *phronesis*, and leading for *eudaimonia*. She titled it "My Leadership Stories."

Her narrative is a series of vignettes that describe important events in her life. The first set of vignettes, titled "Wanting ripples but creating waves," is an enchanting description of her experiences with fishing, her favorite hobby, and how such experiences made her aware of how marginalized women are in this male-dominated activity. Rachel begins by expressing her frustration, observing that fishing waders are made exclusively for men's bodies and thus "struggle to embrace the smooth curves of a woman's hips." Then she describes the condescending behavior of a male shopping assistant who "assumes I know nothing about fishing and attempts to sell me everything."

In another vignette she is again frustrated when other male fishermen, upon seeing her preparing her gear to begin fishing, assumed she was awaiting her husband. It was apparent others took for granted that a husband was somewhere around. When they came across her fishing with her husband, others ignored her and instead asked her husband, a novice fisherman, "whether I bait my own hook or does he have to bait and cast my line out for me?" These forms of exclusion and marginalization took much of the joy out of fishing. The following excerpt illustrates how she experiences these feelings of frustration:

> Sometimes I am trying so hard to be validated as a talented fisher, that the experience of fishing becomes lost in my efforts. I no longer hear the trickle of

the stream because I am listening for snide comments belittling my talents, and superfluous snippets of unsolicited advice. I no longer feel the sun on my back, because I am crouching and hiding, leaning into the shadows. My once sure footing on the riverbed is hesitant and I scramble as I attempt to anticipate the change of depth and the fall. And so I question my ability.

Rachel felt envious, marginalized, and angry. However, in her story she acknowledges that her journey has not always been a ride through rough waters as this last example portrays. Nevertheless, she chose deliberately to highlight this aspect in her story because "it has shaped and continues to shape who I am today," and gives a metaphoric insight into aspects of her academic life. In this regard Rachel's story resonates with those of other leaders featured in this book who also endured discrimination and, by means of character, capitalized on circumstances both benign and toxic to grow into authentic leaders.

In another vignette titled "Is it because we are so good at what we do, that we want to have it all?" Rachel described her many conflicting identities: a woman, a new academic, a wife, and a mother. She recognizes that "each of these things pulls me in a different direction, competing for time, energy, commitment, passion, and all the while creating tensions." Rachel wrote that she felt alone at times, even though she knew very well that she was not the first woman to experience these tensions. She felt the need to "recreate" herself, to "re-identify with what makes me who I am," but she was unsure what these things were or how to go about it. These tensions led her to contemplate whether having it all is as good as people think it is.

She described in another vignette the struggles of being a professional woman while at the same time fulfilling the role of the mother. The vignette titled "Wonderwoman? Or wondering why I am doing this?" is a touching testimony of a mother feeling torn between her natural inclination to care for a child and at the same time meet the requirements of a career. Here is how Rachel described the tension of dropping off her son at the nursery school:

> I head back outside to say goodbye. He runs over and clutches at my skirt, begging me not to go. Tears well [mine], tears fall [his]. He hiccups "Mummy stay with Ben." I reply "Mummy has to go to work." A crèche carer comes and picks him up [my heart hurts—that should be me]. I wave goodbye and say "Mummy will be back later." The gate shuts behind me. I can still hear him crying as I cross the road. Ten minutes later, I am standing in front of a class of 160 first year pre-service teachers giving a lecture on building relationships with students and the importance of the ethic of care.

Continuing with her reflection on how she came to be doing the things she loves most, Rachel acknowledges that in the eyes of others she is a lucky woman: she has a job she loves doing (teaching), something she wanted to do since she was twelve years old; she is impassioned with researching in the area of youth and leadership; and she has a family. Yet questions still nag her for an answer: How did this all come about? Why did I make these choices? Have I done the right thing? Such questions hovered over her as from her office window she watched her son playing on the school's playground. "What is it that makes me believe that working . . . is so much more important than caring for my son, teaching my son?" is the most disturbing question she asks herself. It generates feelings of guilt, deceit, and heaviness in her heart.

The path to leadership has been full of emotions for Rachel, but it is second nature for her to be an authentic leader, to lead from the heart and soul. At the age of ten she became the first female Scout in New Zealand, and at the age of fourteen she was a Chief Scout. She describes this experience as "one of the highest honors. . . . I proudly led my troop to their first international jamboree." As a teen Rachel was also made a prefect in her new school only days after her arrival. Her account illustrates how she is able to touch people's hearts:

> I didn't know what a prefect was or what they did. We did not have them at my old country school. I had five minutes to write a speech on why people should vote for me as a student leader. Time passed in an instant. My pen did not work; I borrowed a piece of paper and pencil to scratch some notes down. Before I knew it I was standing in front of the biggest crowd I had ever seen. . . . Words tumbled out of my mouth. . . . My face was hot, I knew I was sweating. Staff nodded in agreement at my statements, students laughed at my jokes. . . . I had no formal knowledge about leadership. No one had taught me to lead. But based on what I had experienced and seen around me, I shared ideas on what I could offer, passionately, honestly.

Rachel was voted in over five other students. To this day she is amazed by how this bent for leadership has helped her throughout her life, and she acknowledges that "serendipitous events" like this have opened doors for her and have allowed her leadership path to emerge.

No one ever taught Rachel about leadership. Rather, "leadership 'came to me' by default through sports teams, class captaincies, and prefect roles." However, she recognized the contribution of others in the formation of her leadership path. "I learned about leadership from the people around me," she wrote, and attributed a great deal of that learning about leadership to her family. Although Rachel did not give a detailed description of her background, she stated that her family valued education, achievement, and independence. She emphasized that her parents "supported me to stand by my own beliefs and make sense of the world in a way that meant something to me." Both Rachel's parents trained to become teachers and taught at high schools. Rachel credited her mother with being "a fantastic role model in both academia and life," furthering her studies with a master's degree in science and completing her doctorate in science education at the age of sixty-three! (R. M., e-mail message to author, September 7, 2011).

Many other role models assisted Rachel at each stage of her life and influenced and helped shape Rachel's leadership path. Because of those women, Rachel came to know what leadership is and how to show it. She came to know that she can choose who she is, what she can be, and what she can do in the world. Those role models demonstrated "an amazing level of kindness, nurturing, caring, knowledge, friendship, morality, gentleness, strength, passion, and desire for fairness and social justice." They also shaped her professional path, influencing her to research passionately about young women and leadership development in high schools. Rachel feels grateful, privileged, blessed to have crossed paths with them. She described the profound effect these women have had on her thinking. "In seeing such wonderful women in action, I have also come to question some aspects of how I now view the world and view leadership, how I want to lead and be led," she reflected.

The modeling of leadership skills that Rachel experienced, however, has not been all positive. She has experienced the bad side of leadership as well. An early negative example happened when, at the age of ten in an attempt to "liven things up" at Brownies, she carved her initials in the top of a wooden toadstool, "doused it with methylated spirits from the Scout cupboard and set it on fire." This caused her to be expelled. She described herself as "the first person in New Zealand to be expelled from such a benign service-learning, and not-for-profit group." At the time, Rachel saw the bad side of leadership in the face of her Brownie leader, who interrogated her after the incident. Rachel remembered vividly how the leader waggled her finger in Rachel's face as she yelled at her. After this, she saw the leader "bully, manipulate, tease, isolate, and torture" others from her leadership position. Rachel knew that what this leader was doing was wrong, she did not like her for that, and she did not want to be like her. This whole experience served as the catalyst for her to join the Scout movement—and although this was a completely male-dominated environment, Rachel found a context where she felt valued as a leader and ironically won an award for fire lighting and group safety!

Rachel finished her story with the insight that her snapshots of her leadership journey present "the complexity of leadership and the challenges one woman has experienced and continues to face." She described the writing of the stories as cathartic for her soul, but she noted that tensions remain and that the experiences she wrote of will continue to shape "interaction, perceptions, and visions" for her leadership journey in the future. She expressed the hope that her collection of vignettes will encourage and challenge other women to examine their own lives and how the stories within *their* stories have influenced their leadership. For Rachel, her narrative is important in her continuing quest to become "conscious *of* and *being within*" her leadership. The last words in her narrative capture important depths in her understanding of leadership's labyrinth:

> I know envy, I know what it feels like to seek and crave. I know guilt, the weight of a heart, a tear in the eye, and a hand in my hand. I know influence, what not to do. I know a shifting identity. I know experience, privileges, pathways, and what opportunity provides or takes away.

Insights

Rachel's narrative provides a good illustration of leadership with *eudaimonia*. In his *Nicomachean Ethics*, Aristotle (350 BCE) defines *eudaimonia* in part as "doing and living well." So eudaimonia equates with the idea of having a good or desirable life. Rachel acknowledges that she has a dream life, a fulfilling and satisfying one. Although she is still in the early stage of her career, she has fulfilled her dream of being a teacher—something she wanted since she was a child—as well as being an academic doing research in the areas of youth and leadership, which fills her with "passion." Furthermore she also has a family life, being blessed with two children and a "wonderful" man. Rachel is very much aware that these are gifts that have given her a good and desirable life.

Aristotle further maintained that to achieve *eudaimonia* one must be actively and fully engaged in intellectually stimulating and fulfilling work and one must achieve well-earned success. In a similar vein, Keyes, Shmotkin, and Ryff (2002) and Ryff and Keyes (1995) suggest that *eudaimonic* well-being can also be conceptualized in terms of realizing one's true potential across one's life span. Rachel seems to have succeeded on both fronts. Her account of her leadership journey is replete with fulfilling actions that earned her success, starting at a very young age with her leadership roles in Scouts, sports, and in school as a prefect and class captain. Building on Aristotle's conceptualization of *eudaimonia*, Ryff and Keyes (1995) posit that *eudaimonia* entails six forms of wellness: self-acceptance, environmental mastery (the capacity to manage effectively one's life and the surrounding environment), purpose in life, positive relationships, personal growth, and autonomy or self-determination. Rachel's narrative illustrates that she attained these forms of wellness. She acknowledges her strengths and weaknesses and understands her emotional reactions to events. She acknowledges the good qualities in herself and the not-so-good aspects of some of her past actions. Although she may at times be unsure of her abilities, her sense of self-determination (autonomy) urges her to delve into new and unchartered territories that contribute valuable lessons for her leadership journey.

While Rachel was on maternity leave following the birth of her second child, Alexis, she closely connected with her academic work and private life as a way to gain a greater sense of her new identity as a homemaker. Humorously, she described herself as working hard on "postdoctoral studies—researching the best Play Dough recipes for [her] daughter and the most effective stain removing detergents" for her son. Notwithstanding, she was also very much involved with social justice work in schools, charitable trusts, and not-for-profit organizations in her community and around the country, assisting young women with becoming conscious of their leadership potentials.

Toward this end Rachel is collaborating with these organizations in designing, evaluating, and contributing to leadership curriculum programs for young women. She now brings a slightly different perspective to women's leadership, knowing that it will be her daughter who will walk down these leadership paths toward destinations that may not even exist yet. She may even tread some of the well-worn leadership trails Rachel herself has walked, a realization that makes Rachel acutely aware of how important her own modeling and living of leadership will be to both of her children. Clearly she is providing authentic leadership, dedicated to attaining phronesis and sustaining eudaimonia for herself and others.

AUTHENTIC LEADERSHIP: THE SCHOLARSHIP

Authentic leadership has been approached from a variety of angles. For example, Gardner and others (2005) proposed a model of authentic leadership development that identified various processes. These include: (1) the leader coming to self-awareness, which includes becoming aware of personal values, emotions, identity, and goals; and (2) the leader developing self-regulation, which includes internalized regulation, balanced processing of information, and adopting openness, self-disclosure, and trust in close relationships. Erickson (1994, 1995) and Avolio and Gardner (2005) agree that leaders develop authenticity over their lifetimes and attain varying levels of authenticity.

Considering approaches to leadership styles, Fris and Lazaridou (2006) articulate the concept of "quantum" leadership. This style operates when control in an organization is highly dispersed, shared equally by all the stakeholders of an organization or group.

> The members of an organization "co-create" their realities . . . control flits among all members of a group insofar as direction is the product of "pushes" provided by individuals . . . hence there is an infinite number of possible paths ("virtual transitions") into the future . . . the "right path" will "emerge" from the interaction of individuals and their contexts. (Fris and Lazaridou 2006)

When the leader is sure of what she/he stands for and is truly committed to furthering the welfare of others, authentic leadership is of the "quantum" type. This form of authentic leadership displays "moral agency." Moral agency is a person's ability and freedom to take action that conforms to his/her sense of what is right. Authentic leadership inheres a core aspect of professionalism: altruism, which is concern for the welfare of others.

Taking a different approach, Cashman (2003) maintains that authentic leadership is characterized by six "seeds": (1) authentic leaders express what is in their hearts; (2) they embrace the good and the bad and are eager to learn from them; (3) they serve the part and the whole through a strong value system; (4) they master the ego and move beyond that; (5) they have the ability to connect with others; and (6) they are able to see potential in others and nurture them. He states that social intelligence is being sincere, honest, open, and truthful to oneself and to others.

In similar fashion, George (2003) affirms that authentic leaders use their understanding and acceptance of emotions positively in their communications rather than allowing themselves to be ruled by emotions. Authentic leaders are not afraid to embrace the good and the bad, learn from these experiences, and use that knowledge to support and advance acts of social justice and fairness. Sister Hellen, Pam, and Rachel were able to embrace the flower as well as the thorn; they expressed their strengths and weaknesses and transformed negative acts into positive work. They emerged stronger and ultimately were able to use their skills and newfound knowledge to better themselves and help others. Authentic leaders are self-aware, willing to admit frailties and share power. That way they engender trust in followers, which is, according to Covey and Merrill (2006), the most effective lever for effecting change in an organization.

Another important aspect of authentic leadership that is noted consistently in the literature is its deep grounding in values. Sosik (2005) notes, for example, that authentic leaders operate from a strong ethical stand. Their thoughts and acts are powered and guided by such self-transcendent values as spirituality, fairness, benevolence toward others, altruism, passion, compassion, and social justice. Such values prompt authentic leaders to shift the focus away from the self toward others, thus showing an understanding of the interconnectedness of themselves and all others around them. Sister Hellen, Pam, and Rachel personify these characteristics. They are leaders who strive to make a difference in each person's life, to allow others to flourish, and to lead a *eudaimonic* life (Shamir and Eilam, 2005).

Aligning behaviors and actions with the true self is at the heart of authentic leadership. Erikson (1950) views authenticity as "one's relationship with oneself," such that an authentic person "acts in accord with the true self, expressing oneself in ways that are consistent with inner thoughts and feelings"

(382). Furthermore, authenticity cannot be forced; authentic individuals express their core feelings, motives, and inclinations freely and naturally (Kernis 2003). Rather than use the words of others, leaders must find their own true voices to gain credibility with followers. They must develop and follow personal moral compasses.

CONCLUDING THOUGHTS

Authenticity is about character and a genuine desire to serve others meaningfully. In this chapter, we presented the narratives of three leaders—Sister Hellen Bandiho, Pamela Lenz, and Rachel McNae—to illustrate how skillful authentic leadership is developed, practiced with practical wisdom (*phronesis*), and enacted with well-being (*eudaimonia*). What does it mean to lead with *phronesis*? Trowbridge (2005) reports that Aristotle emphasized *phronetic* individuals must be well brought up. That is, they require exposure to, and consideration of, examples of well-lived lives: the friendship of good people; temperance, intelligence, experience, understanding, and consideration or decency; and virtue of character. With the current demand for more transparency, accountability, and adherence to ethical and moral standards, authentic leaders are indispensable.

What the successful women's narratives suggest about *developing phronesis* is that the preparation of authentic leaders must pay attention to more than the acquisition of theoretical knowledge (*episteme*) and appropriate skills (*techne*). Preparation must also facilitate the development of *phronesis*, or practical wisdom, that is, tacit knowledge. The narratives also point to a need to encourage leaders in seeing beyond isolated facts, thinking with more than linear logic, and appreciating the whole. For authentic leadership, it seems wholeness may matter more than skills.

Researchers Walumbwa, Avolio, Gardner, Wernsing, and Peterson (2008) have indicated that authentic leadership raises the level of optimism, social intelligence, self-efficacy, and self-esteem, which are all aspects of *eudaimonic* well-being. Sister Hellen, Pam, and Rachel have revealed what is in their hearts, how they live their own words and create authentic choices for themselves and those around them. They manifest their authenticity through their behaviors, exemplifying Aristotle's notion of the *good life* and the *eudaimonic* life. They have revealed that they are also intensely aware of how they feel and how their emotions affect themselves and others.

Authentic leaders are indeed true to themselves and in their interactions with others are guided by their convictions. They go beyond promoting common social causes or missions, bringing about change for the greater good through the kind of leadership that research has associated consistently with effective schools and principals (e.g., Day 2004; Harris 2002; Leithwood, Mascall, and Strauss 2009; MacBeath 2005). At the most fundamental level, authentic leadership is about celebrating the worthiness of human existence, about having integrity, and above all about being real.

6

RESILIENCE

I have learned that leadership for social justice is all about resilience, about pressing on in the face of obstacles, about never feeling powerless, and remaining ever aware of the meaning behind the struggle.

—Joanne Chesley, *Overcoming Injustice: A Tradition of Resilience*

Courage and determined perseverance are inherent in social justice leadership, which by its nature always remains unfinished. Those who wish to shape a more just future by challenging and changing the status quo must speak out and be resilient. Women leaders who trouble the bureaucracy in the name of social justice invite opposition (Blackmore 1999, 2002). Clearly, for women resilience is required for social justice leadership. Many definitions have been advanced, but generally resilience can be defined as the ability to overcome challenges, turn them into opportunity, and be transformed by the experience.

Resilience calls on intellectual, psychological, and spiritual qualities. Researchers suggest that resilience can be learned (Richardson 2002). According to Coutu (2002), "More than education, more than experience, more than training, a person's level of resilience will determine who succeeds and who fails" (3). She describes resilience as the capacity for making meaning, a "way resilient people build bridges from present-day hardships to a fuller, better constructed future" (4). The meaning of the quest is why leaders for social justice remain resilient in the face of the distance between the present and the future they envision.

In the words of Bateson (1989), "Because we are engaged in a day-by-day process of self invention—not discovery, for what we search for does not exist until we find it—both the past and the future are raw material, shaped and reshaped by each individual" (28). As illustrated by the narratives of women featured in this chapter, resilience is something we can find, and resilient is something we can become as we live into the personal and professional transformations of our lives. Kleinerman (2010) believes that "to truly know your identity, you must first know your voice" (18). To transform opportunities for others to lead and learn through social justice leadership may mean we first transform ourselves, find our own voices.

In this chapter we focus on three qualities of resilience that recurred in the WLE narratives of intertwined personal and professional journeys. These qualities associated with resilience are courage, perseverance, and speaking out. Although these and other qualities, beliefs, and behaviors that resilience comprises have been identified from a variety of perspectives, no formula for resilience exists.

RESILIENCE: THE STORIES

Becoming energized instead of overcome by the immense challenges of social justice leadership demonstrates resilience. For many leaders, the qualities undergirding their resilience developed with the support of family and mentors over time in response to recurring adversities. A few seem to have been born with perseverance and the courage to speak out. Although each life story in this chapter illustrates multiple aspects of resilience, one story will be featured for each of the qualities. The qualities and three featured leaders are: (1) Courage–Diane Reed, United States; (2) Perseverance–Panpim Cheaupalakit, Thailand; and (3) Speaking Out–Joyce Wilson-Tagoe, Ghana.

Courage

Early etymology of the English word *courage* reveals French, Italian, Spanish, and Latin words that all essentially mean "heart, which remains a common metaphor for inner strength" (Online Etymology Dictionary). In Middle English, courage was "used broadly for 'what is in one's mind or thoughts.'" Once associated primarily with mind, disposition, and spirit, today courage is most often associated with bravery and actions. Writers of seven narratives used the word *courage*. Actions of courage sometimes come from those discussions we have with our inner selves. Courage is manifested in the world but comes from the heart.

Courage is required when adversity and disruptions, both planned and unplanned, require resilience to survive. "Disruptions mean that an individual's intact world paradigm is changed and may result in perceived negative or positive outcomes" (Richardson 2002, 311). Examples of disruptions expected to result in positive outcomes—such as a new job, getting married, or going to school—sometimes have unintended consequences in our lives. Disruptions less positive include losing a job, family difficulties, divorce, or illness to name only a few possibilities.

In retrospect, such disruptions are often labeled turning points. Whatever their cause or label, courage is called for when facing the adversity of an experience that dissolves a comfortable paradigm. Resiliency is "the ability to accept adversity as part of life, and to step through it and beyond it with courage and determination and trust" (Baldwin, Maldonado, Lacey, and Efinger 2004, 19). Major life turning points requiring courage to step through and beyond were described in sixteen of the WLE narratives. Many of these were times of self-searching, looking for the way forward. Ten of the stories included descriptions of the process of reintegrating after confronting challenging personal situations, such as divorce.

Diane Reed

Dr. Diane Reed titled her narrative "A Story for my Daughter Ashley," prefacing it with a reflective quotation about life's journey from a book of meditations that included this line: "It is in the end—in the bittersweet of looking back—that you can see the true beauty of the journey" (*Moments of Peace* 2005, 242). In her thitynine years of experience as an educator, Diane served as an elementary teacher, secondary English teacher, elementary-school principal, assistant superintendent, and superintendent.

From 2003 to 2010 Diane was a member of the governing board of the American Association of School Administrators (AASA). As a member of that board, she traveled extensively internationally. She worked in schools and met with various ministers of education during these travels that took her to eight countries: Peru, Italy, Ireland, Argentina, China, Thailand, Australia, and New Zealand. She emphasized, "I am deeply committed to supporting education for children throughout the world, because education follows birth as the greatest gift anyone can receive." Finally fulfilling a lifetime dream of teaching at the college level, since 2005 Diane has been an associate professor and co-director of the Graduate Education Leadership Department at St. John Fisher College, located in Rochester, New York.

Diane's narrative begins with the circumstances surrounding the marriage of her parents and her birth. Her father's family was from Muncie, Indiana. Her mother was the youngest daughter of first-generation immigrants from Germany who came to New York City to start a new life. Her grandfather was a waiter at the Waldorf Astoria Hotel in New York City. Her parents met there, and her mother was eighteen when she married. Her father was serving in the US Navy during World War II, so her mother moved to Indiana to live with her father's parents and go to college. Diane wrote, "When my mother found out she was pregnant she was most upset because all she wanted was to finish college and graduate with a BA degree. She left and moved back to New York with her parents." Diane was born in New York City on December 6, 1946.

Challenges surrounded Diane from the time of her birth through her childhood. Her father found out he had a daughter through a communication from the Red Cross when Diane was nine months old. Her parents divorced, and a difficult custody battle lasted for many years. Basically, Diane lived with her mother and her parents for the school year and with her father and his parents for the summer months. She explained, however, "I always had much family support and was loved." Her father remarried and had three sons. Her mother did not remarry until after her father died. Diane shared that "he committed suicide. I was very close to him and was devastated." She was eleven years old when she lived through this major untimely loss.

Although each began well, Diane's three marriages to educators added to her experiences of adversity. In each case differences in values took Diane and her marriage partners on different paths. When she was in college Diane married her high-school boyfriend. After they put themselves through college, Diane began teaching middle-school English when she was twenty years old. During her eleven years of teaching she earned a master's degree in reading and then went back to school to earn the administrative certification required to be a district reading coordinator. Her husband, on the other hand, started teaching but did not like it. Instead of teaching, she recounted that "he then became a buyer of men's clothing for a department store and started traveling. We grew apart and did not share the same values, so we divorced when we were in our twenties."

Diane remarried at twenty-nine and became an elementary principal when she was thirty-two, serving in that position for nine years. She wrote about the new marriage, "My second husband had a large, very close family and I loved being part of them." During this time she and her husband tried to have children, eventually adopting "a newborn healthy boy." As a busy elementary principal, she described herself as "a driven person and a workaholic" who struggled with balancing her career and family. "I loved being a mother, yet wanted to continue my education and earn a doctorate in curriculum as I always knew I wanted to eventually teach full-time at the college level. While I was a successful administrator I never really wanted to be one. My real passion has always been teaching."

Adding doctoral study to raising a child and being a principal increased her stress. Balancing a career and family became increasingly difficult after Diane finished her doctorate and became an assistant superintendent in a new district in upstate New York. When she was forty-two, she and her husband adopted a second child—"a beautiful newborn baby girl." At this point, she described her husband as being "about image and making lots of money." Describing their life, she elaborated that "once again our values were different and we grew apart. My core values are family, spirituality, and education. People and relationships are a top priority. Money has never mattered to me and with all the areas I was juggling I was just trying to survive and keep it all together and be successful." Meanwhile, "my husband wanted little to do with family responsibilities as he was struggling to make his fame and fortune."

Diane developed what she called a "super woman" routine, "doing night baby feedings while developing curriculum management systems and proving myself in a man's world." She was offered the superintendent's position after five years in the district. Initially reluctant, she was persuaded to apply when asked by a few of the board members, and found herself in the top six of over one hundred applicants. Living outside the district, in the final interview she was asked about residency. "I told them it had not been a requirement when I applied for the assistant superintendent job and the answer I gave them was I was not going to move. I only lived thirty minutes from the district," she explained. Diane got the call with the job offer at midnight and the invitation to start contract negotiations the next day. She noted, "My husband was less than happy. It really was the final straw in our relationship."

Assuming the new position, Diane quickly understood that "I did not know anything about being a superintendent." One neighboring female superintendent called the first morning and gave her advice on negotiating her contract. "She saved my life on a number of occasions. She was a pro at negotiating in a man's world," Diane summarized. In the beginning she also relied on her exceptional administrative assistant to help her handle tasks of both her old and new positions. The process of hiring a new assistant superintendent took six months. In Diane's first year as superintendent, the budget was defeated and all her contracts were up for negotiations. She wrote that "it took two and one-half years to settle the teacher contract. We only survived because of the relationships I had built as assistant superintendent with the union and staff." With a focus on student achievement and teaching and learning, she built a successful administrative team through emphasizing team building and resiliency.

Diane's second marriage ended in divorce as her successful superintendent career unfolded. She faced it courageously, ending up declaring financial bankruptcy, while "he went on to build a highly lucrative business." Her first marriage lasted seven years, and the second lasted twenty years. The third time, she married a successful superintendent for whom she had worked. He took a new superintendent position in downstate New York. "He lost that job and went through a period of depression" before finding another position, she observed. Then for seven years they had a commuter marriage until he retired as a superintendent, took an administrative position with a local college, left Diane, and filed for divorce.

Speaking for herself and other women who have faced divorce, Diane wrote, "Divorces are costly financially, costly emotionally, and costly for the children. Many have paid a high price for professional successes." Summing up her experiences with marriage, Diane underscored an irony, writing, "I have chosen to marry traditional men who want strong women, until they marry them."

Mentoring and networking were at the heart of Diane's success in the superintendency as she joined local, state, and national leadership organizations, achieving leadership roles at all levels. For six years she was on the executive committee of the New York State Council of School Superintendents (NYS-COSS), where she held the offices of treasurer and vice president and was president-elect when she retired from the superintendency in January 2006. For four years she was cochair of the New York State Association of Women in Administration (NYSAWA). During this time she became most aware that "women and minorities need a champion."

It was because of her experience in this statewide organization that Diane began to focus on social justice. "Social justice became a passion of mine and led me to an ongoing annual national conference on women in educational leadership at the University of Nebraska, Lincoln, which led me to WLE and Helen Sobehart." In 2011 Diane was one of two women honored by AASA with the Dr. Effie H. Jones Humanitarian Award for leadership based on her advocacy, mentorship, and advancement of women and minorities as well as her commitment to address social justice issues. Diane has made over one hundred presentations to local, state, national, and international groups on social justice issues regarding women's/racial equity.

Diane has also conducted workshops and presentations for thousands of educators and other leaders on leadership development, personal and organizational resilience, and strategic planning to get high student achievement results. A professional contact through AASA with Dr. Jerry Patterson led Diane to the study of resiliency. A retired superintendent and professor at the University of Alabama at Birmingham, for over ten years Dr. Patterson worked with Diane's district to facilitate the yearly administrative summer training programs on his research specialty—resiliency.

Given her multiple experiences of adversity, Patterson's programs about resiliency had a profound influence on Diane and changed her life both personally and professionally. "He coached me through many difficult situations that I encountered with the Board of Education throughout my fourteen years as superintendent." When she was offered a full-time college teaching position, he helped her to "let go of the superintendency as I struggled to reinvent myself professionally." She credited Dr. Patterson with mentoring her through the transition to being an academic, teaching her how to write and publish, and coauthoring publications centered on resiliency and leadership (e.g., Patterson, Goens, and Reed 2008; Patterson, Goens, and Reed 2009; Reed and Patterson, 2007).

Looking back on her life, Diane feels "blessed in so very many ways." She has "two wonderful and successful children," her health, and a meaningful professional career. She wrote, "I am at the stage in my life where mentoring future educational leaders, particularly women, is a high priority." Diane proudly described her daughter as she ended her narrative with hopes for the future success of all women leaders.

> Ashley is definitely a feminist who will find her passion and I am confident will champion women's leadership in a global twenty-first-century world. She is a fearless woman and hopefully will continue the work of her mother and WLE and women throughout the world to promote education for all and support female leaders as they continue the progress made by our generation. There are many miles to go before we get there and we need both males and females to advance this most critical cause of educating and supporting all women in every country of the world.

Insights

Diane wrote about the adversities she experienced in a matter-of-fact tone conveying realistic optimism, a characteristic of resilience (Patterson, Goens, and Reed 2009). The endings of each of her marriages could have crushed her spirit. Instead, she took "partial responsibility" for the marriage failures and sought counseling. She did not dissolve but persisted in a process of reintegration, maintaining her priorities. Each time a marriage ended, she demonstrated the resilient reintegration that "results in growth, knowledge, self-understanding, and increased strength of resilient qualities" (Richardson 2002, 310). Realistic optimism and strong values led her in the tasks of courageous decision making. She moved forward personally and professionally. She lived courageously and remained guided by her core heart values—"family, spirituality, and education."

Diane believes "role models and networking continue to be the key" to inspiring both individual growth and transformation of society. She confronted a variety of challenges and crises in her fourteen years as a superintendent. The reality of transformation through resilience that she studied and wrote about was something she lived as a superintendent. She demonstrated personally that "resilient superintendents possess the ability to recover, learn and grow stronger when confronted by chronic or crisis adversity" (Patterson, Goens, and Reed 2008, 28). A quality that supported her during both the personal and professional experiences with adversity was her faith. She shared that "to this day I am a deeply spiritual person and have a deep faith in God. This has and continues to guide me through my successes and struggles."

Leadership in AASA transformed Diane's view of the world, broadening her horizon to include a vision of what education should be for children all around the world. She calls "fanning the flame for social justice" the number one priority in her life professionally at this point. Her story offers insights into how resilience is developed and can lead to advocacy for social justice causes. In the end, actions born of resiliency are what matter. A book she coauthored offers this insight: "But if the leader does not *act* on the courage of convictions, especially during difficult times, then everything else is just talk" (Patterson, Goens, and Reed, 2009, 10–11). Diane continues to act on and live the courage of her convictions.

Perseverance

Perseverance is considered an action skill of resilient leadership by scholars and former practitioners Patterson, Goens, and Reed (2009). Challenging the status quo requires strength in the form of perseverance, which they define as people's ability to "pursue a course of action, consistent with their core values about what matters most, and without regard for discouragement, barriers, or previous failure—unless it is absolutely clear all realistic strategies have been exhausted" (106). In a study of resilient women administrators, Christman and McClellan (2008) asked the seven participants to identify components of their own resiliency and engaged them in a process of rank ordering all responses from the group. The quality of perseverance was ranked second overall. Perseverance functions as an internal resilience sustainer, whether it is something innate or a quality instilled by family and arising from life circumstances (Baldwin et al. 2004).

Perseverance is particularly important for women leaders in cultures and fields where men are clearly dominant and in positions of authority, as is true in educational leadership in both developed and developing countries. The WLE narratives collectively support the idea that perseverance can be instilled by family. Writers of twenty-one narratives described support from families, and eighteen identified one or more mentors who inspired their strength. Supporting family and mentors were important in developed countries as well as in cultures that do not generally support education for girls. For example, Marianne Coleman (chapter 4) described both family support and professional mentors in these words:

I have also been incredibly fortunate in the people that I have met who have given me chances to change and to develop, my parents who supported me in going to the USA and to university, my husband who supported me in my work, particularly when I changed careers into higher education and research, the mentors in the early stages of my academic career, and the chance meetings which resulted in my career taking fresh directions.

Panpim Cheaupalakit

 Dr. Panpim Cheaupalakit was born in Tah-Sao, a town of three thousand to five thousand in Uttaradit province in the northern part of Thailand. Hers is a story of perseverance, illuminating how resilience arises from the interaction of internal qualities and external supporting factors. Now in her early fifties, she lives in Bangkok, where she is a senior lecturer in the International College for Sustainability Studies and the Department of Educational Administration at Srinakharinwirot University. Previously she had served in university administrative positions, including being dean of the International College for Sustainability Studies, director of the Office of International Relations, and chief of finance. She titled her narrative "The Journey of Life."

"I grew up in an ordinary Thai-Chinese family where the children took care of each other during the day as both our parents worked," she began. Her Thai mother married her widowed Chinese father when her mother was twenty and her father was forty. "My dad was handsome and relatively wealthy and had been chosen by my mother's parents in an arranged marriage. She was actually involved in a relationship with another man, but at that time a young woman was not able to choose her own husband." When her parents married, Panpim's father already had six children, the eldest a girl who was only a year younger than Panpim's mother. Then seven more girls and one boy were born to this Thai-Chinese family, making a total of fourteen children, ten girls and four boys. Panpim considers her mother to be her first role model, describing her as "full of passion, strong, and thoughtful." Continuing, she wrote, "Undeniably, my early years had considerable influence on my beliefs and aspirations and helped to make me who I am today."

In many families, girls were not encouraged to study because in the Thai-Chinese culture a girl would no longer belong to the family once she married and moved out to live with her husband's family. "Unlike other Thai-Chinese families, we were fortunate that our mother wanted all of her kids to study as much as they could. She also encouraged and supported one of her stepsons who performed well in school to study further." Panpim observed how "at that time my mother's passion for education was rare and even weird in some people's eyes. Although she was mocked, mom continued to believe that education could help her kids to be productive members of society."

When Panpim was between three and four years old, the family house accidentally burned down. Her father had not bought insurance. The family suffered a lot from this, even though her father was able to rebuild the house with the help of grandparents. To help the family financially, her mother moved back to her family in Pah-Kluay to generate income through her parents' farming business. Except for a brother, who went to Bangkok to pursue his studies, all of the children stayed in town with their father. She wrote, "Dad took us to see mom approximately once a month. She worked very hard to make sure that she earned enough to fully support my brother's study." The distance to where her mother lived was only about five kilometers, but it was on the opposite side of the Narn River, and the walk took an hour or more (P. C., e-mail message to author, June 28, 2011). Her parents lived separately until Panpim was twelve to thirteen years old, when some of her stepsisters married and moved out.

Panpim's education began when she was four at a home school near her house, a place where about fifteen four- to six-year-olds were taught in one large room in three groups separated according to age. Panpim wrote, "I was a sociable child and I quickly became accustomed to the school environment. I even helped the teacher take care of some new students who were upset and crying for their mothers. I was more mature than other children, perhaps because of the way I was raised at home."

When she was seven, Panpim entered compulsory basic education at a grades 1–7 school within walking distance of her home. She took on a leadership role as the head of the class almost every year except when she was in first grade. At school she did better than her male classmates. She was an excellent math student but performed poorly in English. By sixth grade, she started helping friends who were not good at mathematics and geometry. They would do homework together, and her friends would buy her a meal after school. It was at this time that she began thinking she wanted to become a teacher when she grew up. How she moved from this childhood dream to her present university teaching position is a story of perseverance.

"In our family, the parents never spent leisure time with their young kids," she wrote. Panpim began taking care of her two-year-old sister when she was eleven. Looking back, she sees this as one of her first leadership roles.

> The free time that I had previously enjoyed after school became a thing of the past when my babysitting role began, but I didn't really feel bad about it. It was something we were prepared for by our culture. At that time, my older sister took care of me. While I was babysitting our youngest sister, my older sister helped me with my homework and taught me how to take care of the baby. All of my mom's seven girls had some chores to do besides their studies.

In fact, it was only her brother who had no domestic duties. He needed to study hard to perform well at school.

After finishing basic education, Panpim entered a high school in town for girls from grades 8–12. Panpim demonstrated her strength and ability to speak out against injustice in grade 11 when she led a group of students in a protest against an election for student president.

> We were unsatisfied with campaigns which were unfairly supported by the deputy principal for student affairs and we fought for a new election. Although we lost the battle, we had set the standard for the next elections to come. School administrators and teachers are supposed to dispense justice rather than take sides.

She wrote, "Dad didn't like it when I got myself into trouble but mom never complained as long as I could give her good reasons."

When Panpim finished high school, her "academic performance was believed to be too good to become a school teacher," so the Thai system did not allow her to enter a school of education to become a teacher. Instead she moved to Bangkok, where she entered a business administration program majoring in accounting. Once again she had free meals in return for tutoring her friends, which "convinced me that I really could become a good teacher in the future." When she graduated from college she decided to work as an accountant for Srinakharinwirot University, a public university, although she could have made more money with a company. Perseverance was a factor in her choosing a job at a university. She had not given up the dream of becoming a teacher.

Panpim took the university accounting position so that she could continue her studies there and be qualified to become a university professor. A year later she enrolled in the master of educational administration program. It was difficult because she didn't have enough work experience and she was also the youngest student. She wrote that "it was the first time I felt completely inferior." However, she persevered. She tutored classmates on statistics and research methods, and in return "my senior friends welcomed me to their groups." She learned much through determined hard work and from her classmates. Continuing to work at the university, she was promoted to head of the Office of Finance.

In 1994 the university campuses within Bangkok were consolidated. Panpim was moved to the main campus and transferred to the Office of International Relations, where she worked with a vice president from whom she learned how to think "out of the box." Eventually she was promoted to director of the Office of International Studies. Because of continuing challenges with English, "I wasn't comfortable with the new assignment and wanted to quit," she admitted. The first female university president personally asked Panpim to persevere, becoming her second role model after her mother. The president encouraged her self-confidence and hired an English expert to facilitate running the office. Together they arranged several international conferences. Panpim explained that "working closely with her I learned so much about trust and empowerment. She opened my eyes to a lot of things."

With her English gradually improving, Panpim was awarded a graduate assistantship to pursue a PhD at Illinois State University in the spring of 1999. She met with the president prior to taking a study leave of absence, and the woman's words still echo and have kept her at Srinakharinwirot, although she has had better financial offers. The president said, "I wish you well in your studies, as if you were my blood sister. Promise that you will come back and never leave the university. Listen, someday you will become somebody important and you will make us proud."

Doctoral study was not difficult for her in terms of subject matter, but Panpim found the English challenging. Characteristically, she persevered. She worked hard, taking two to three times longer to do the reading and writing than her native English-speaking friends. Through this hard work her English improved, and once again she made use of her strength in mathematics to succeed and help others be successful. "My numeracy skills enabled me to assist my professor to prepare for her research methods classes. I was also popular among my close friends as I helped them with statistics and research methods. In return they edited my pieces of writing."

During doctoral study she was assigned to read Mary Wollstonecraft's *A Vindication of the Rights of Women*, first published in 1792. That assignment raised Panpim's awareness of gender equality. "I was shocked at first, but eventually came to realize that I had actually experienced 'gender inequality' throughout my life without knowing—at home and at university. The Thai-Chinese culture inculcated me to comply with the norms of Thai society." She continued:

> I thought of my mom and wondered if she were me now, would she stand up and fight for her rights. I ended up choosing gender and leadership for my dissertation. Through my research, I learned so much about gender issues, oppression, and barriers . . . I felt like I had awakened from a good dream and faced an unknown, unjust world. I didn't know yet what to do about this.

A classmate told her, "Panpim, when you go back home, your folks will notice that you aren't the same person they knew." Panpim agreed, "This class changed us a lot." Having earned a PhD, Panpim returned home in 2002 to her post as director of international relations. She also became part of the team establishing a new international college for sustainability studies, where she later became interim dean. She reported, "I did not forget to add gender issues into the course curricula in the new program."

In 2008 Panpim decided it was time to follow her childhood dream of becoming a teacher, so she entered the teaching ranks at her university after twenty-five years in higher education administration. Now she has time to conduct research and do the social justice work that she has always wanted to do, including research on women leaders in education in Thailand. She has researched, spoken, and written about other social justice topics, such as sustainability studies and ecotourism in the Western Forest Complex in Thailand. She is also working with her colleagues on a research grant on domestic violence, including violence affecting female prisoners. She wrote, "I fully hope that our research will have an impact on waking up women as well as bridging the gender gap." In closing her narrative, Panpim looked back reflectively.

> I don't know which experiences have most influenced my ideology. What I know is that experiences I gained throughout my life have still reverberated back and forth in my heart, at different times, and during different experiences. For one, my mother's experience of married life encouraged me to stay single. Definitely, I am the sum total of all my past experiences."

Insights

Panpim's leadership story is a journey of perseverance and hard work. Her narrative illustrated internal qualities and external factors that contribute to resilience, suggesting that resilience in her case was perhaps both innate and learned. Perseverance was definitely instilled by her family. Panpim's leadership qualities and maturity already were showing by age four, when she first went to school. Her home responsibilities developed internal qualities such as self-efficacy, determination, and dreams. Her strong mother valued and supported her educational journey. Panpim has survived and grown through disruptions, such as the approximately nine years in which her mother was away, the time she was blocked from studying to be a teacher, and the years English continued to challenge her as she continued her education all the way to a doctorate. She reports being changed by the knowledge of how she had experienced gender inequality throughout her life, unknowingly, as she complied with the norms of Thai society.

Panpim's perseverance and administrative career in academia are unusual for a woman in Thai culture, where male domination of top leadership roles is the norm at universities and elsewhere. In her dissertation examining the glass ceiling in Thai culture, she used a Thai saying to illustrate how the gender dynamic works: "Men as those who lead are like the forelegs of an elephant, while women, as those who follow, are the hind legs." She continued, explaining that "most Thai people live in a Thai-Chinese culture in which men are head of the household and women are placed in a lower status. Men focus on career success, knowledge seeking, and freedom, whereas women emphasize love, family, and are dependent on their husbands" (Cheaupalakit 2002, 72).

Although still widely believed to be inferior to men, Thai women are seeking equal status, so this is changing. Panpim (2002) reported in her dissertation as a sign of progress that "today women administrators no longer consider themselves abnormal" (75). Nevertheless, career advancement for women has been and continues to be blocked by cultural barriers.

Today some women are choosing to reject administrative roles because of difficulty in creating a balance of career and family responsibilities and priorities. Having chosen to remain single, Panpim's motivation is different. In shifting her position from administration to teaching, Panpim is actualizing a childhood dream of becoming a teacher. In some cultures, moving from administration to teaching would be considered strange. Panpim (Cheaupalakit 2009) explained, however, that "Thai culture inculcates women to believe that they can be successful without having to be in administration" (30–31). In making the choice to teach she is transforming her life to be in greater harmony with her values and desire to contribute to social justice outcomes for women in her country.

Speaking Out

In connection with women's development, Belenky, Clinchy, Goldberger, and Tarule (1986) wrote that "women repeatedly use the metaphor of voice to depict their intellectual and ethical development; and that the development of a sense of voice, mind and self were intricately intertwined" (18). Kleinerman (2010) understood that "without question, women in every age have fought for the right to be heard, to participate in the leadership of their societies, to have voice both metaphorically and literally" (2).

Speaking of the institutions of higher education, Chan (2010) asserted that "voice is constructed in terms of self-expression, talking back, speaking out, and breaking silence. . . . Voice highlights the issue of speaking for oneself and the ability to declare that there are injustices and problems within the institution" (2). She continued, "The concept of coming to voice can be used to acknowledge that many women and minority groups have been silenced by the power of institutional discourses" (2). Ultimately leadership for social justice requires us to consider larger social issues and the power of institutions in our countries as we work to reduce inequity of opportunity for girls to be educated and women to lead.

Across many cultures, speaking out by women has historically been associated with bringing shame to one's families. Jamieson (1995) identified silence/shame as one of the double binds faced by women who wanted a life in the public sphere. A double bind with its two alternatives sets up a limited reality, with "one or both penalizing the person being offered them. In the history of humans, such choices have been constructed to deny women access to power and, where individuals manage to slip past their constraints, to undermine their exercise of whatever power they achieve" (13–14). Jamieson gave examples from history of how women who have risked speaking in public have been characterized or labeled as whores, as heresiarchs, as witches, and as hysterics. In the United States, she observed, "even after women were granted access to higher education, their right to present their own ideas in public was denied" (83).

The importance of speaking out is embedded in all twenty-three narratives in descriptions of the growth of feminist perspectives and awareness of gender inequalities. For many, these new perspectives typically reflected both educational and intellectual passages. Narratives of nine women referred specifically to voice or speaking out. One positive example referring to voice was Sister Hellen Bandiho (chapter 5), who said that through her doctoral study she "was able to find her own voice on issues." Risks of speaking out still include types of retaliation by those in power. As a graduate student Charol Shakeshaft (chapter 3) requested to work with a professor, as the male students were, instead of in the secretarial role to which she was assigned. Discovering that no professor would work with her, she wrote, "I learned that speaking out against inequality would result in isolation." Women educational leaders around the world take risks through speaking out to challenge the status quo and to protect their rights. Speaking out is an action central to descriptions of social justice leadership included in the narratives.

Joyce Wilson-Tagoe

A woman who understood speaking out at an early age is Joyce Wilson-Tagoe from Atorkor, Ghana. Her story illustrates multiple risks by an outspoken woman who has tenaciously pursued the right to be who she is and achieve her goals. Her story illustrates courage and perseverance as well as speaking out. Joyce is actively involved with teacher education and with student and community activities. A full-time lecturer at the University of Education, Winneba, she is a member of the University Teachers Association of Ghana.

Joyce has facilitated collaboration workshops on school leadership and teaching English in secondary schools with the Ghana National Association of Teachers and other teacher organizations since 1994. "Her interest in gender issues was aroused when she started tertiary education and realized the unfair differences that existed between males and females within the job sector and the huge conflicting economic and domestic roles that women twirl in. She has always tried to look at the role gender plays in all the activities" (WLE conference program 2009, 32).

Joyce titled her story "Decades of My Life" because every ten years she found herself going through a change. Both of her parents were teachers, and she grew up with three sisters and one foster brother. When she was born as the third child and second daughter of her parents, she was christened "Joyce" because her mother "read a story and liked what the character Joyce was—a strong character." The name seems to have been prophetic. She comes from Atorkor, a small coastal town in the southern part of Ghana in the Volta region. Joyce is from a royal family, the granddaughter of Torgbui Amegashie Aweku I, a chief of Keta, the administrative headquarters of the Trans Volta Togoland, and the great-granddaughter of the first prominent ruler, Torgbui Ackumey Geli Adjorlolo I, of Atorkor, which was a former trading post during the transatlantic slave trade.

"My childhood was full of adventure," she wrote, "and I remember they were years when I freely spoke my mind without inhibition. There were arguments with my dad about stories I read and what I thought about the characters." She began reading at the age of three, starting school at the age of six. Her teacher parents were frequently transferred to other towns or regions of the country. By age ten she had moved several times to six of the nine regions then existing in Ghana. She enjoyed the traveling and meeting new people so much that she once wanted to be a journalist. She learned to speak several languages and dialects. During a period of being homeschooled along with her siblings, her parents allowed Joyce to read a lot of fiction and gave her the opportunity to try her hand at anything, including "cooking very sumptuous dishes, singing solos and acting in school dramas." She speculated that "those early years of my life maybe introduced me to what I would now call some qualities of leadership."

Along with this freedom to explore her interests, however, she lived with a father who was a very strict headmaster of the school he administered and who carried that strictness into his home. Joyce explained, "My mother had to always agree with whatever decision he took, but he found himself saddled with a daughter who had a mind of her own. At an early age I found myself not conforming to rules and was fond of asking why I should be compelled to do as others say when I needed answers to why I should do such things anyway."

Joyce's mother, who preferred not to rock the boat, called her headstrong. She was always more like her paternal grandmother, who was very outspoken and resilient in the face of troubles. Writing about her grandmother, Joyce said, "I understand that she hated injustice and would fight tooth and nail to see justice accorded where it was due, and she would beat her chest to show the men that they have no business toying with her or she will teach them a lesson or two." Everyone in the family recognized that Joyce took after this grandmother who had died when Joyce was just two.

The decade of her adolescence began with a major military coup, led by a native of her town, to remove Dr. Kwame Nkrumah as the president of Ghana. She wrote that "the 24th of February, 1966, was just like any other ordinary day. We went to school very early and as usual my class joined the middle school for morning assembly. Then the news about the coup flashed! The first coup in Ghana! It was led by a native of our town! What was going to happen to us?" People were killed, and the whole community "was jubilating over the overthrow of a so-called dictator of Ghana."

Against a backdrop of communal celebration, eleven-year-old Joyce loudly asked an impertinent "why" question about the violence. She reports that her mother nearly died of a heart attack hearing her speak out openly, and the family decided it was "time to make me learn from my experiences." Her father said to her mother, "she must go with me on my transfer." And so the family was separated for several years, with her mother and two younger sisters staying in her home town while she went many miles away with her father to Saltpond, where he joined the Ministry of Education's Curricula and Courses Division.

During this time with her strict father, Joyce learned patience and how to talk through a problem and find solutions to it. She learned about life's injustices when she was not well accepted at a girls-only Catholic middle school. She spent much time with books brought by the mobile library service of the Ghana Library Board. Entering secondary school at thirteen, she honed her leadership qualities, did well in final examinations, and could have continued to college. She got married instead after finding out that she was pregnant and "had a beautiful baby girl" when she was twenty. Her father was unhappy about her decision to be a housewife, believing that she would make a fine lawyer since she excelled at speaking out.

When her husband went to the United States to attend college, Joyce moved back with her parents. Her mother retired from teaching prematurely to look after the baby so that Joyce could go back to school to study to become a teacher. However, her husband was not happy about the idea of a working wife. She explained,

We never seemed to agree on anything and he kept deriding my "clowning" in front of children in the name of teaching. I found out too late that he [my husband] had no respect for women who want to stand for their rights as sensible, thinking beings. I was so disappointed at his disrespect and abusive ways that it took me five long years to realize that I am a strong woman who can achieve anything I want if only I persevere and work hard at it.

In the teacher training college she served as "head girl," and the male teachers who ridiculed the girl students provided Joyce with an incentive to work harder. In the end, she "was the only girl alongside nine boys who had outright passes" in the courses.

Joyce's first teaching job was at an army base school with wonderful facilities. The classes were small and the parents were willing to help. She put in long hours and was happy even though exhausted. Then a new station officer arrived who required everybody to take instructions about how to teach whether they believed in his methods or not. She could not stand the interference and speaking out clearly voiced her disagreement one day in front of the commanding officer.

The result of speaking out was an interdepartmental transfer to a poorly equipped army school, so Joyce decided to seek further education to be able to teach in a secondary school. A hundred and twenty people took the entrance exam, and only twenty-five people were admitted. "By God's grace," she wrote, "I did very well and was one of three women who got admitted." At this time she decided to get a divorce. It was time to speak out against her husband's disrespect. She called the divorce "messy and traumatic," but she resiliently carried on and studied hard to achieve her goals.

After graduation Joyce was appointed to Adisadel College, one of the best boys' secondary schools in Ghana, to teach English language and literature. In addition to teaching, she served in a variety of leadership roles, including being assistant housemistress. She coordinated educational trips for the boys and organized voluntary work in the community for them. The headmaster of the school was wonderful, and she was mentored by her department chair. She fell in love and married one of her coworkers. He has been a source of encouragement and joy for her, often telling her she can do anything. With his encouragement she decided to get a degree in teaching, entering the university at the age of thirty-four.

Back in school again she faced challenges. She juggled the study, a sick parent, looking after her home, and teaching part-time in an Anglican seminary. Working with the wives of the student priests, she helped set up fund-raising activities to help the poor in the north of the country. After this experience she wrote, "I realized that women need to be emancipated from some of the traditional roles that have been foisted on us by the men folk."

When she graduated, Joyce returned to Adisadel College to teach and began a period of activism. For example, she started a study group for teachers on the staff and introduced them to the labor laws operating in the country. She joined the Ghana National Teachers Association and became a member of a group of eleven other teachers who went around the country to teach school leadership courses to secondary teachers. She continued to do community service, talking at seminars for the youth on HIV/AIDS and doing voluntary work on sanitation in the school and the village in which the school was located. Her ability to speak out served her well in these social justice leadership pursuits.

In 1999, after ten years of marriage, Joyce's husband retired as assistant headmaster of the school, and she planned to go back to school to take a second degree in educational administration so that she could join the Ministry of Education. Discovering that her husband had an incurable eye disease that would lead to blindness, she was going to put her quest for more education on hold. He insisted instead that she give it a try, and he studied Braille.

The next decade of her life was about "charting a new course," Joyce wrote. Beginning study for her masters at University of Cape Coast, she had to take in her mother, after losing her beloved dad, "who had been my mainstay through thick and thin." Her continuing work with students in the seminary taught her about fortitude and perseverance. Gathering data for her thesis, she was employed by the university to teach communication skills to first-year undergraduates. She was hoping to finish her thesis in record time so that she could teach at the university, but then in 2003 her internal assessor for the thesis created obstacles. She has never learned why. He rejected parts of her thesis, which she quickly rewrote and submitted. Then the thesis got lost for two years and could not be found anywhere.

She spent some time away in England with a cousin to decide what to do next. Then she returned home in April 2004 and took a job as a research assistant at University of Education, Winneba. "The thesis vanished for two years and then resurfaced after I threatened to take the university to court." Her decision to speak out forcefully made a difference. Having the thesis again in hand, she continued speaking out. She related her ordeal to the vice-chancellor of University of Education, Winneba, who had been one of her lecturers when she was an undergraduate. He took up the case and got the dean of faculty to appoint a new internal assessor to look at her thesis. Her work was finally submitted to the graduate exam board, but the submission did not meet the deadline, so she had to wait an additional year, receiving the degree finally in 2007. In 2008 she was invited to interview for the position of research fellow at the University of Education, Winneba. She was confirmed as a full-time lecturer in March 2010.

Today Joyce's research is concerned with the underrepresentation of women in academia. She is still facilitating leadership development with teachers, especially females in the secondary system. She began a PhD in leadership and management in September 2011. Her PhD thesis will be on mentoring female faculty to enhance and improve scholarship in the public universities. Joyce came to the WLE conference in 2009 in Germany after discovering the WLE organization online. Inquiring about attending, she was invited to participate and present her research. Her paper was titled "Women in Leadership and Management in Higher Education in Ghana: Meandering the Curves."

Joyce ended her narrative with these words, "Our journeys take us through so many paths but our resilience, determination, hope and fortitude see us traverse these paths without thinking of shirking our responsibilities. We hold out in the darkness and God lights up the path and we see our way through the tunnel."

Insights

Joyce is a woman who has meandered many curves—asking questions and speaking out when dealt or dealing with injustices. Her ability to speak out was nurtured by her family. As a young girl, an impetuous Joyce spent time with her father learning how to handle conflict and speak out effectively. She spoke out and chose not to remain with an abusive husband and his disrespect. She spoke out when a supervisor insisted that everyone teach his way. In workshops across the country she introduced teachers to labor laws and concepts of school leadership, teaching them how to speak out. She spoke out against the injustice of a male internal assessor's loss of her master's thesis by threatening a lawsuit and enlisting the help of a mentor to complete the degree. Joyce's innate comfort with speaking out protected her in a variety of situations. Her strong voice was important in her resilient transformation and reintegration from the first marriage and other adversities. Speaking out, she has persevered courageously to actualize her dreams.

Women in Ghana have a long cultural history of speaking up and participating in decision making and leadership. Whereas speaking out seems at first a heritage from Joyce's family through her royalty and outspoken paternal grandmother, speaking out by women seems to have a larger cultural context as a result of the important traditional roles of *queenmothers* in Ghana. The traditional institutions featured "parallel structures of male and female representatives existing in each family, and headed by the royal family with the chief and the queenmother" (Müller 2003, 333). Providing more details, Müller elaborated that "in the history of Ghana, women's organizations played an important political role during the struggle against British colonialization at the beginning of the 19th century and up to 1957, the year of Ghana's independence. Collective military actions were organized by female heads of towns or villages called queenmothers" (333).

At this time these traditional structures of power for women are regaining local political relevance. Today the queenmothers (female heads of towns or villages) and subqueenmothers (female heads of families) have organized to participate in economic development initiatives and decision making. "Subqueenmothers are, in comparison to subchiefs, a new phenomenon, as the first woman was elected in 1985. . . . Subqueenmothers are now trying to extend their spaces beyond the family context" (334), according to Müller's research.

The existence of the queenmothers provides additional insight into Joyce's strong voice for social justice. In response to a question about whether she had been influenced by the queenmother phenomenon, Joyce acknowledged having queenmothers to be a very important part of the history of Ghana. She explained,

> They play a significant role in the enstoolment of the chiefs and kings. Without them no chief or king will be enstooled. . . . They lost their voice for some time when Western education or schooling was introduced but with the new crop of educated Queenmothers fighting for inclusion in the house of chiefs their voices are now going beyond the palaces and into the public domain. I believe if I had stayed long in my hometown I might possibly be a Queenmother because the members of my extended family keep asking me to come home. (J. W. T., e-mail message to author, June 4, 2011)

RESILIENCE: SELECTED SCHOLARSHIP

Two scholarly frameworks, Patterson, Goens, and Reed (2009) from the field of education and Richardson (2002) from psychology, provide additional insights into resilience as described in the chapter stories. Two main concepts from the work of Patterson, Goens, and Reed (2009) particularly apply—phases of resilience and resiliency skills. They explained five phases of a resilience cycle. The first phase begins when adversity strikes and interrupts normal conditions. Typically a deteriorating phase comes second, and for some people unable to claim resiliency the path leads ultimately to dysfunction. However, another choice is the cycle of survival that leads to stability. Growth begins with a third or adapting phase, moves to a fourth or recovering phase, and finally culminates in a fifth growing phase (5). These phases serve as a backdrop against which strengths found in resilient leaders unfolded, viewed in three broad categories of skills and qualities: resilience thinking skills, resilience capacity skills, and resilience action skills.

Each category of skills is displayed in the stories shared in this chapter. Resilience thinking skills include two dimensions (Patterson, Goens, and Reed 2009). The first is taking a clear-eyed look at a present reality or adversity to understand it accurately; the second is to interpret future possibilities optimistically in spite of what may be a negative situation. "Resilient leaders demonstrate an optimistic view about what's possible" (9). For example, Panpim displayed resilience thinking skills in continuing her education in spite of challenges with English. She stayed positive, had a clear-eyed view of the reality of her talents, and was able to use her mathematical skills to compensate for her issues with English. She envisioned a future as a teacher that she eventually actualized.

Patterson, Goens, and Reed (2009) characterized what they called resilience capacity-building skills as a skill set able to become stronger over time. They identified four basic resilience capacity-building or fuel sources: "personal values, personal efficacy, personal well-being, and personal support base" (9). Diane demonstrated the resilience capacity-building skills of a value-driven leader. She emphasized the importance of her core values clearly throughout her narrative. She made decisions and lived by her educational and ethical values. Her personal efficacy was maintained in part by her spiritual well-being. Her strong confidence was also supported by the lived experiences gained in "leadership competence in serving others" (10).

Resilience action skills were defined as perseverance, adaptability, courage, and taking personal responsibility (Patterson, Goens, and Reed 2009). Joyce's narrative painted a clear portrait in words of resilience action skills. She was adaptable to new situations and persevered toward her goals, taking personal responsibility for making her desired future happen. Over and over again her story illustrated acting on "the courage of convictions" (11) through speaking out. In terms of social justice leadership, speaking out is an action, an essential skill that can motivate others to action. Joyce possesses a clear voice and is not afraid to use it. These skill sets of resiliency have broad applicability within and outside of the field of education.

A second important scholarly framework was developed by Richardson (2002). His metatheory of resiliency provides a "big picture" historical frame from which to understand what has been written about resiliency and its significance in human lives. He conceived of it not as a problem-oriented theory, but rather as "something that provides a needed paradigm to incorporate postmodern thinking" (307). He elaborated, "Resilience metatheory embraces semantic variance and validates the unique academic paradigms, whether that force is called chi, collective unconscious, energy, oscillations, motivational force, neuropeptides, spirit, human essence, or resilience" (317).

Richardson (2002) described three waves of resiliency inquiry existing in the literature. The first wave of research identified resilient "qualities, assets, and protective factors that help people grow through adversity" (308). Lists of multiple personal resilience qualities were the chief outcome of this wave of inquiry. Examples are the qualities of courage, perseverance, and speaking out that framed this chapter. Whether qualities of resilience are innate or learned is a debate that continues.

Many of the earlier studies of resilience focused on high-risk children and youth, including their lives over time, in efforts to understand how they were able to overcome adversity experienced in childhood and youth. The question was (Richardson 2002, 308), "What characteristics mark people who will thrive in the face of risk factors or adversity as opposed to those who succumb to destructive behaviors?" These studies have been important to educators and resulted in a movement toward professional development programs focused on developing resilience in teachers, as well as curriculum created to support resilience in young people (Henderson and Milstein 2002; Milstein and Henry 2008).

Richardson (2002) explained that the second wave of inquiry focused on discovering how people developed these resilient qualities through the process of coping with adversities. The question was (310), "How are resilient qualities acquired?" Richardson presented an illustrative model of the process that begins with a negative disruption to *biopsychospiritual homeostasis*, followed by choices "between resilient reintegration, reintegration back to the comfort zone, or reintegration with loss" (308). His resiliency process model is similar to the phase model described by Patterson, Goens, and Reed (2009). Each model encourages viewing resilience as a path that can be chosen and suggests strategies.

The third wave explored innate resilience to help persons "discover and apply the force that drives a person toward self-actualization and to resiliently reintegrate from disruptions" (308). The question explored by the third wave included (313), "What and where is the energy source or motivation to reintegrate resiliently?" With the third wave of research, the source of this energy to grow began to be viewed as "a spiritual source or innate resilience" (309). According to Richardson, "there is a force within everyone that drives them to seek self-actualization, altruism, wisdom, and harmony with a spiritual source of strength" (309).

Richardson (2002) advanced two postulates in support of this "force within everyone" concept. The first was that "a source for actuating resilience comes from one's ecosystem" (314). For example, he argued; "The more that physicists seem to learn, the more they allude to a driving force that controls the universe. . . . From physics, we learn that it is *quanta* that is the energy required for resilient reintegration" (314). He compared that with the view from Eastern medicine or Taoism that "all things connect with a flow of energy termed *chi*" (314). This energy circulates within and around individuals and can create patterns of flow that provide strength.

Many subjects of resiliency inquiry reported belief in God or a creative force as their source of strength. Richardson summarized his ideas regarding ecological sources: "The energy or force that drives a person from survival to self-actualization may be called quanta, chi, spirit, God, or resilience" (315). The second postulate is that "resilience is a capacity in every soul" (315). Richardson defined his use of the word *soul* as follows: "In resilience theory, soul refers to the whole integrated being of an individual with one's transpersonal nature or human spirit as the primary guiding force of the system" (315). Supporting his second postulate are citations of scholars of quantum mechanics, the new physics, and psychoneuroimmunology.

We have presented Richardson's metatheory in some detail because it underscores that our stories have many layers of meaning, whatever our cultures, experiences, and languages. We are born with or can develop the personal qualities of resilience that support our growth in the face of adversity. Becoming resilient is a process with predictable stages that can be studied. Resilience supporting the growth of life can take many forms and is a capacity each person can develop. Resilience is as mysterious as the essence of human personality, arising from the depths of ultimate reality, whatever name that is given.

CONCLUDING THOUGHTS

Coutu (2002) addressed how resilience works, stating with some irony that "resilience is something you realize you have *after* the fact" (3). She reported that "an increasing body of empirical evidence shows that resilience . . . can be learned" (3) and confessed that all the theories she has reviewed in her own research just make common sense. Continuing, she asserted,

> But I also observed that almost all the theories overlap in three ways. Resilient people, they posit, possess three characteristics: a staunch acceptance of reality; a deep belief, often buttressed by strongly held values, that life is meaningful; and an uncanny ability to improvise. You can bounce back from hardship with just one or two of these qualities, but you will only be truly resilient with all three. (3)

By including the ability to improvise, Coutu (2002) echoes the metaphor that Bateson (1989) developed about women's lives as improvisations. Bateson wrote that "the compositions we create in these times of change are filled with interlocking messages of our commitments and decisions. Each one is a message of possibility" (241). We believe the life experiences of each of the women in this book offer a message of possibility. The three women featured in this chapter—Dr. Diane Reed, Dr. Panpim Cheaupalakit, and Joyce Wilson-Tagoe—represent quintessential survivors whose lives and leadership for social justice display all three of Coutu's characteristics of resilience.

Gilligan (1982) argued that women speak in a different voice, a voice grounded in a preference for decisions based on values associated with social justice. A thought we take away from this chapter is that "resilience is not an all-or-nothing, fixed characteristic. Resilience is a relative concept" (Patterson, Goens, and Reed 2009, 4). It will manifest itself differently in women's lives as well as in different cultures. It will manifest with different strengths in different people. We believe that resilience is a necessary ingredient of social justice leadership. Courage and perseverance work together for good when we speak out as advocates for social justice.

7

MULTIPLE PATHS TOWARD ADVANCING SOCIAL JUSTICE OUTCOMES

As a way of making meaning in their work of leadership, women discuss their desire to "make things better," to right social wrongs, and to increase support for underserved groups. . . . Whatever the explanation for women's social justice emphasis, the reality remains that working for social justice means working for change.

—Margaret Grogan and Charol Shakeshaft,
Women and Educational Leadership

Each leader who submitted a narrative has found a path that is uniquely hers, that feels right in its combination of activism, mentoring, and scholarship. Their narratives described periods of introspection that led to turning points, transformation, and renewed commitment to advancing social justice. For some, these were intellectual or spiritual passages; others happened through physical passages to new locations. Many leaders left home literally, willing to leave the familiar to expand their worldviews and opportunities. Their geographic moves have led to both personal and career development. Other women have metaphorically "left home" in their public sphere work to increase gender equity for women in educational leadership and access to educational opportunities for girls.

Members of WLE walk multiple paths to advance social justice outcomes and bring about change. They have wrestled at some level with cultural expectations and limitations related to gender. On the other hand, they have understood the advantages of the "outsider status" they can bring to change processes as women. They have not limited their social justice work to issues of gender nor even to issues of education. Career paths differed, but in thinking about how these leaders have advanced social justice outcomes, a preliminary pathway seemed to lead inward, followed in the life story narratives by some combination of three pathways of social justice work in the world: activism, mentoring, and scholarship.

ADVANCING SOCIAL JUSTICE OUTCOMES: THE STORIES

All twenty-three women earned higher-education qualifications to develop their careers and advance their social justice work. Each woman heard a "call to action," sometimes a loud banging on the door and sometimes a persistent whisper in the ear. In this chapter three pathways of social justice work will be illustrated and discussed. The three women whose stories are featured in this chapter come from different backgrounds and countries but are equally committed to advancing social justice outcomes.

As is true for each leader profiled in the book, multiple pathways to advancing social justice outcomes are embedded in their life experiences. Each narrative is presented, however, to highlight a particular pathway. The pathways and featured women are: (1) Activism—Vanita Richard, South Africa; (2) Mentoring—Jill Sperandio, United Kingdom, now a resident of the United States; and (3) Scholarship—Margaret Grogan, who has dual citizenship in the United States and Australia.

Social justice work is a journey rather than a destination (Strachan 2005). In the narratives, fifteen women referred to a "journey" to describe both their personal and their professional lives. For example, both Margaret and Jill left their countries of birth to move to faraway destinations where they experienced new cultures very different from the ones in which they were raised. Vanita's path led her away from internalized oppression in apartheid South Africa toward freedom of spirit, self-confidence, and activism in postapartheid South Africa.

Activism

Social justice work is an action, informed by strong values, beliefs, feelings, and emotions. The women's narratives are rich with illustrations of feeling passionate about their social justice work and angry about injustices that are then important motivators for social justice leadership (Rapp 2002). Feelings have consequences. As Zembylas asserts (2010), "Emotions in leadership, therefore, are not only a psychological matter for individuals but also a political space in which school leaders, teachers, students, and parents interact with implications for larger political and cultural struggles for change" (613). The stories from many WLE women mention being motivated by their anger at personal injustices. Being raised in apartheid South Africa, Vanita had many unpleasant memories that exposed her internalized oppression and motivated her activism.

In fact, Zembylas (2010) suggests that the preparation of leaders for social justice must engage with the emotional aspects. This engagement helps to provide the leaders with "the emotional tools to navigate effectively through both the personal and structural/political challenges of leadership" (613).

Vanita Richard

 Dr. Vanita Richard is an educator whose career has had many facets, just like the diamonds mined in South Africa. Today she is senior project manager for leadership programs at the Matthew Goniwe School of Leadership and Governance in Johannesburg, South Africa. In that capacity she facilitates an elective on gender for school principals and also manages a support program for the Principals in Leadership program. As will be shown, the programs help to heal the scars of apartheid. Vanita has also been an elementary teacher and became part of the largest teachers union in South Africa during the "free Mandela" years, chairing the gender committee in 1988.

Vanita titled her narrative "Memories," illuminating her choice of the title with the words that follow from Lewis B. Smedes: "Forgiving does not erase the bitter past. A healed memory is not a deleted memory. Instead, forgiving what we cannot forget creates a new way to remember. We change the memory of our past into a hope for our future." Recalling her early years, Vanita began the narrative by stating that growing up in South Africa significantly influenced her thinking.

The oldest of four children and the only girl in an Indian family, Vanita was born in 1952 in Sophiatown, which at that time was a multiracial environment. She was from a working-class background. Her father worked in a factory, and her mother became a primary school teacher once her youngest child started school. "She quickly built a reputation for being a hard-working teacher dedicated to learners and to learning." Vanita attended school in a colored township until grade 2, when the Group Areas Act was introduced, meaning that members of every race had to attend their own racially exclusive schools. Vanita's family was told to move to an Indian school some distance away.

When Vanita was eight, the Group Areas Act was more strictly enforced, and they were "forcefully removed to Lenasia, an all-Indian township," where they lived temporarily in an army barracks with two families sharing living quarters. At that time both her mother and aunt were in an advanced stage of pregnancy. She reflected,

> Thinking back I wonder how they managed to pack and move and share a barracks in their state and still take care of us. We were five children, all under the

age of nine living together. As children, however, we had great fun in the army barracks. We played many games, some initiated on the spur of the moment. We had no television or TV games so we really enjoyed the outdoors.

The location meant "all the children in the camp walked five miles to a pre-fabricated school containing asbestos. We had to cross railway lines to get to the school." Later the family moved to a house in the township, where Vanita lived until she married in 1973.

The apartheid regime socialized nonwhites to believe that they were inferior. She characterizes the apartheid government as wanting black people to be "hewers of wood and drawers of water" (King James Bible). Vanita believes this made her a tentative child lacking confidence:

> In the apartheid years we were socialized to believe that we were inferior. We had separate entrances to all public places such as banks, post offices, separate toilets, separate transport, separate schools, etc. We could only go to the parks on certain days of the week and faced many other barriers. Subconsciously, I grew to accept my subordinate position, whether I admitted it consciously or not.

She elaborated with this memory: "I remember when I was very young walking behind my dad (a tall, stately, proud man) going into a café to buy ice cream and my dad telling my mum he does not know whether we will be served or chased out of the shop."

However, there were powerful positive influences in her life that countered the oppression and led to her questioning the way things were and her place in apartheid and postapartheid South Africa. The first influence was her parents' belief in the importance of a good education. She understood that "education was the only thing that could not be taken away. It reflected pride and accomplishment that could not be eroded." She struggled at school with self-confidence and "only began to become assertive and somewhat rebellious in grade 11," she wrote. Finally performing better at school, she became a teacher, continued to study part-time, and gained her PhD at the age of fifty. Achieving this goal reaffirmed her belief in herself and led to her life work. "Affirming the potential of people has become a passion and is the work that I engage in at Matthew Goniwe in a leadership programme," she explained.

The second powerful influence in her life came from the antiapartheid movements within the country—such as the United Democratic Front (UDF) and the Transvaal Indian Congress, as well as the Free Mandela worldwide campaign that provided a worthy cause to fight for and stimulated the struggle within the country. She elaborated, "We felt hopeful that things were going to change. We rebelled against the school inspectors, against their autocratic and prescriptive attitudes. We worked with the school representative councils comprising senior learners to bring about democratic changes in the school system."

Happening at the same time as the Free Mandela campaigns was a third powerful influence, an educational experience. During her honors study at the University of Witwatersrand, Vanita became engaged with many ideas, including Marxism. She described the course as "extremely unorthodox" as the articles and discussions focused on "the evils of apartheid . . . [and] I really began to understand the social engineering of apartheid." Vanita's understanding of her internalized oppression grew. Reflecting this understanding, she quoted Steve Biko: "The most potent weapon in the hands of the oppressor is the mind of the oppressed" (speech in Cape Town, 1971). Her university professors were courageous. Should they have been discovered teaching antiapartheid material, they risked losing their careers and being arrested. Married with two daughters, Vanita experienced this period as both exciting and dangerous. She wrote, "I felt a real sense of freedom at this time even though we had to be extremely careful with what we said and who we spoke to because of the risk involved."

The fourth powerful influence was postapartheid, the time after Nelson Mandela was released. There was a new feeling of freedom, and opportunities for activism and social justice work were abundant. The work was huge. In 1997, Vanita was appointed as a life skills facilitator to the Department of Education. This was also the first time she was able to freely have contact with other races. She visited African, colored, and white schools and was shocked at the poor state of the African schools. Robert McNamara, who was the ex-president of the World Bank, visited South Africa in 1982. He described educational conditions in the country at that time in these words:

> I have seen very few countries in the world that have such inadequate educational conditions. I was shocked at what I saw in some of the rural areas and homelands. Education is of fundamental importance. There is no social, political, or economic problem you can solve without adequate education.

These four major influences fueled Vanita's activism and were turning points in her life. Violence in schools was prevalent as a legacy of the violence and brutality that children had been exposed to during apartheid. Vanita was involved in establishing support groups where healing was discussed. Her social justice work at this time also involved attending human rights and antibias workshops with education officials. The intention was for those attending the workshops to transfer the information to those working in the schools.

According to Vanita, the hurt and damage perpetrated by apartheid is still evident, and there is still a great deal of social justice work to be done. Steve Biko was a courageous activist much admired by Vanita. He still has a powerful influence on her work: "I do love Biko. I have just reread *I Write What I*

Like' (V. R., e-mail message to author, August 4, 2011). His words that follow guide her:

> It becomes more necessary to see the truth as it is if you realize that the only vehicle for change is these people who have lost their personality. The first step therefore is to make the black man come to himself; to pump back life into his empty shell; to infuse him with pride and dignity, to remind him of his complicity in the crime of allowing himself to be misused and therefore letting evil reign supreme in the country of his birth. (Biko 1978)

Vanita currently teaches leadership and works with women managers through a gender course, helping to erase the hurt and build their confidence to manage holistically, and quoting Biko, "to infuse him [the black man] with pride and dignity." Another aim of her work with the women managers is to empower them "not to have the prejudices that we were confronted with while growing up," so that they don't perpetuate the injustices in their schools to which they were exposed. Vanita sees her own life story reflected in the lives of the women in her gender courses.

Jansen's (2006) study of white South African principals whose social justice leadership was aimed at transforming their schools into "racially diverse communities" (37) observed that "leading for social justice meant coming to terms with the leaders' own past" (46). Similarly, Phendla (2004) found in her research on black women principals that "particular life experiences (profoundly affected by race, class, gender and language) affect individuals in their professional lives and in their political commitment to social justice" (abstract).

Although recalling and discussing memories can be painful, Vanita believes examining such memories is absolutely necessary to enable the women she is working with to understand their oppression so that they can move on and find themselves. She explained how the emotional aspect of social justice leadership is often hidden and ignored: "Recalling unpleasant memories and experiences can sometimes be difficult to deal with." She feels close to the women and is proud to be associated with them as they have battled against enormous odds to become leaders, showing immense courage in the process.

Looking back, Vanita observed, "My history makes me very passionate about gender issues. I realize now how internally oppressed I was and how the early messages influenced my thinking and attitudes. I understand how black women were doubly oppressed: first as blacks and secondly as women." The powerful positive influences in her life countered the oppression that surrounded her growing up. In her story's conclusion Vanita expressed a broad vision of social justice:

> We have to ensure through telling our stories that the young boys and girls we interact with in our schools, in our homes and colleges, know that oppressive

cultures and negative attitudes regarding gender, race, ability, and sexual orientation undermine the transformation of a society. Creating this type of group consciousness will contribute immensely to liberation and empowerment, particularly among women.

Insights

In their research exploring black women's activism, Brooks and Hodgson (2007) highlight how the political climate and "key political events" (7) can provide the trigger and motivation for people to involve themselves in social justice work. This was certainly true also for Vanita as an Indian woman. The oppression and discrimination she witnessed under the apartheid South African government was a significant motivating factor in her call to social justice work. Experiencing injustice, oppression, and discrimination firsthand can also "motivate women to resist actively racial-gender discrimination" (Brooks and Hodgson 2007, 8). Vanita's experiences were both oppressive and transformative and fueled her passion for advancing social justice outcomes.

Vanita's story illustrates that for some of the women in the WLE group, advancing social justice outcomes was dangerous and emotional work requiring courage and determination in highly volatile contexts. Her pathway involved painful reflection that helped her to understand her internalized oppression and use that understanding to empower others. She explained,

> We have to work through this layer of oppression to really free ourselves and this work I am passionate about. The reality perspective is get over it—apartheid no longer exists. Internalized oppression is not dealt with and continues to influence generations. We see this evidence in the world. (V. R., e-mail message to author, August 4, 2011)

Realizing and overcoming oppression is an important precursor to moving on, using past experience for good rather than for perpetuating oppression on others, as noted by Biko (1978). Applebaum (2008) explains that social justice must "emphasize not only how experience constitutes who we understand ourselves to be, but also how we interpret whatever happens to us" (410).

Risk is part and parcel of social justice leadership. According to Donnell, Yang, Winfield, Canestrari, Marlowe, and Kamii (2008), "Taking a stand, actively opposing injustice, teaching for social justice is a highly politicized, controversial, and dangerous pursuit" (38). The social justice work undertaken by Donnell and her colleagues was in the United Kingdom, and it is unlikely that their perceived danger was on a scale that Vanita experienced in apartheid and postapartheid South Africa. The level of risk and danger is relative, dependent upon the cultural and political context and the enormity of the task to reform education unique to postapartheid South Africa. Culture and context matter (Crossley and Jarvis 2001).

However, it is unlikely that imported Western solutions to complex national problems will be appropriate (Gewal 2008). The curriculum reforms in South Africa were intended to eliminate inequities in education (Jansen 1998), important social justice work. However, outcomes-based education has been imported from the West and, according to Jansen (1998), is inappropriate for the context. So the "how" of advancing social justice in education has been at the center of considerable debate in South Africa, including whether to transform or reform. In 1998 Enslin and Pendlebury wrote:

> Under apartheid, education was a site of contestation. Now it is supposed to be a site of transformation, not only for its own sake but also because it is crucial to transforming other spheres. A primary goal of the ANC's policy framework is to transform the institutions of society in the interests of all and so enable social, cultural, economic and political empowerment of all citizens. Many South Africans see educational transformation as the key to transforming society at large. (Enslin and Pendlebury 1998, para. 2)

Unterhalter (1998) is doubtful that the intended social justice outcomes embedded in the South African National Qualification Framework (NQF) will deliver gender equity. More work will be needed for the goals of the framework to be realized. She reasons,

> For the social justice advocates the NQF the needs of women (sic), subject to discrimination and exploitation under apartheid, are a matter of concern . . . the nature of particular gendered needs have not been explored in any depth in the policy documents of the NQF. (para. 3)

Christie (2010) claims that educational inequities persist along racial lines in South Africa and that although all children have the right to basic education, it has not delivered equality. What these scholars suggest is that the legacy of apartheid continues; the environment in which Vanita works is unstable and paved with disagreement as to how progress should be made.

Yet despite these differences of opinion as to how education should be transformed to better deliver social justice outcomes in South Africa, Vanita is doing the transformative social justice work that is important to her. So often the narratives of the WLE women revealed how their personal life experiences drove their commitment to advancing social justice outcomes. Nowhere is this more obvious than in the women's stories from economically developing countries like South Africa, where issues of culture, poverty, and violence compound and deepen social injustices (Strachan et al. 2010).

Mentoring

The literature on women and educational leadership speaks to the powerful impact mentoring has on advancing women's careers (Gardiner, Enomoto, and Grogan 2000). Women leaders who have a commitment to advancing social justice outcomes will mentor other women to help them advance their careers. Either being mentored or mentoring others, or both, were strong themes to emerge from the women's stories: nineteen of the WLE women specifically refer to mentoring in their stories.

Mentors are invaluable in helping women, especially minority women, to gain access to leadership positions in male-dominated organizations (Enomoto, Gardiner, and Grogan 2000). For the WLE women, sometimes the mentor was male, sometimes female. Some of their mentors were professional colleagues, sometimes a family member or a friend. Sometimes women come to understand the power and importance of mentoring through international experiences that introduce them to discrimination and injustice, thus fueling their commitment to social justice (Larson and Moja 2010). Seventeen of the WLE women had such international experiences that heightened their awareness of and sensitivity to discrimination, contributing to their commitment to advancing social justice outcomes for women.

Jill Sperandio

Dr. Jill Sperandio is featured as an example of how extensive international experiences can shape women's commitments to social justice and how mentoring can be one strategy for advancing social justice outcomes. She titled her narrative "Lifestory—through a Gendered Lens." Following a career of teaching and administration in international schools, and after a brief period of time as an administrator, program evaluator, and teacher educator for the International Baccalaureate Organization, Jill obtained an academic position at Lehigh University in Pennsylvania.

Jill is now a tenured associate professor teaching in the educational leadership program, including Lehigh University's program for international school administrators. Her academic profile states:

Dr. Sperandio's primary research interest is focused on gender issues in educational leadership in both developed and developing countries. She is currently exploring aspects of women's motivation and journey to become educational leaders, together with their access to leadership training and the role that mentoring plays in this training, in Uganda, Bangladesh and urban school districts in Philadelphia. Secondary research interests include the development of international and global citizenship programs, international school leadership, and the historical development of education for girls in developed and developing countries. (Lehigh University 2011)

Jill was born and raised in England. Her parents met in Cairo during World War II, and Jill believes that their stories and photographs instilled in her a desire to travel. Throughout her life Jill has traveled extensively, living and working in many different countries. These experiences raised her awareness of gender inequity. She commented:

> [In Kuwait] I learned not only what it meant to be a second-class citizen, but as a woman to sit in separate areas of the bus, go to separate sections of the banks and government buildings, and watch women swim fully covered in black robes off the beaches under the scrutiny of male relatives. Other positions abroad followed—to Malta with our young son, back to Africa, to Venezuela, Azerbaijan, and the Netherlands. Sensitized now to discrimination, each stop along the way showed me more of how it works, sometimes blatant, at others subtle, and often unconscious.

As a baby boomer, Jill considers that she and her family benefited from the socialist reforms of the post–World War II government:

> [The] new schools and progressive teaching, free university places, health care and union protection for workers. My father and mother, both forced by family circumstances to leave school at fourteen, thanked the war for providing opportunities to move out of their working-class environment and into solidly middle-class lifestyle in a newly built garden suburb in the town where my father grew up.

Jill was successful at school, and her gift for writing helped her to gain entry to university. However, her parents, who had both come from working-class backgrounds, assumed that Jill would not be attending a university, that maybe she would be a primary school teacher or a secretary, as was the lot of "clever" girls of that generation. But when her father overheard his workmates discussing their children's applications for the university, fate took a hand. He realized Jill had not applied. With his encouragement she did, explaining that "belatedly I obtained a coveted place [at university], one of the 4 percent of my national peer group to do so, and one of considerably less than 4 percent of women to qualify."

Jill describes her university years as "golden." She studied geography and American studies and traveled overseas every summer. She volunteered in the United States, had a study scholarship in Israel, and experienced hitchhiking in Yugoslavia. At the end of her degree she trained as a high-school teacher, even though "I had no desire to teach, but was hooked by the university lifestyle, and was becoming increasingly aware of the limited opportunities for women in the job market." To her surprise, she enjoyed teaching. She also realized that teaching provided her with opportunities to travel, something she still craved.

During the 1960s and 1970s many British colonies were gaining their independence, and many British teachers went to these colonies to help support their education systems as there was an extreme shortage of trained teachers. Jill was offered jobs in a number of countries but finally opted for a position as geography teacher in Uganda. She taught at a coeducational boarding school "on the edge of the Great Rift Valley—a geographer's paradise."

While she was still in the United Kingdom Jill had a somewhat sheltered understanding of feminism and discrimination. She accepted this as "the natural order of things." Her experiences in Uganda changed that view. As an expatriate she lived a privileged lifestyle.

> We lived in a world of our own, the war in Vietnam a million miles away, tie-dye tee shirts and miniskirts, parties, travel, houses on school compounds, housekeepers and gardeners part and parcel of our everyday existence. I was on a lower pay scale to that of my male colleagues but it didn't matter—even the basic allowance of a volunteer allowed a lifestyle unthinkable in the USA or the UK.

However, life for Ugandan women and girls was very different. Jill saw how hard they worked and how they were subject to cultural customs abhorrent to her "such as genital mutilation, early marriage into polygamous relationships, domestic violence." Men had all the power and control over women's lives. Few girls accessed education; boys' education was privileged. Girls' aspirations were limited to being teachers and secretaries, for example, much like Jill's parents had foreseen for her. However, the boys aspired to and got plum government jobs. The boys also did not like being taught by an expatriate woman, even if she was well qualified.

Jill married a Peace Corps volunteer from the United States, and when Idi Amin came to power they left Uganda for Kuwait, beginning a career teaching in international schools in many different parts of the world. While her husband's career accelerated quickly into administration, Jill's did not. "I waited for my hard work and dedication to be recognized as younger, less qualified, and less experienced men were tapped and promoted above me, and eventually I learned I had to ask, to demand, if I was to progress professionally." Otherwise, it was as if she were invisible.

After many years teaching and leading international schools around the world, fate brought Jill to the United States, where, to her surprise, she was accepted at the University of Chicago and encouraged to pursue her PhD, successfully completed in 1998. Uganda was returning to peace, and her doctoral research gave her the opportunity to return there. As Jill said,

> I wanted to see whether the education system had survived, how those women I had taught in the sixties had fared, and learn about the expectations and aspirations of a new generation of female secondary school students. I was given the means to spend three months in Uganda doing fieldwork in the company of a young Ugandan woman, my research assistant. Together we traveled the country, visiting schools, observing lessons, talking to women teachers, students, and school administrators, listening to amazing stories of hardship, determination, perseverance, and dreams of future success.

It was international experiences of discrimination in developing countries that fueled Jill's commitment to mentoring women. She now relishes the opportunity in her academic work to continue to research and publish with women in developing nations, particularly in Uganda. Her latest work has been the development of a grounded model to contribute to understanding and "awareness of how cultural contexts can mediate the factors affecting women's access and journey to educational leadership" (Sperandio 2010, 722). The model considers the interaction of international-, national-, and personal-level variables. It is an example of scholarship with a mentoring value.

Wherever Jill was in the world, she initiated mentoring activities. As principal in Azerbaijan, she introduced a community service program linking the international school community to local Azeri schools and institutions—formalizing a mentoring role for her international school. In the Netherlands, she served as deputy headmistress and involved parents from the different national groups represented at the school in an innovative "out of class" weeklong interdisciplinary program experience for children who were eleven to sixteen years old. Essentially, this experience was a week of mentoring for the young people and their parents.

Although Jill recognizes that she was discriminated against in her career, she considers that to some extent her privilege as a white, educated woman has protected her when compared with the women in the developing nations where she has worked. She wrote, "Only now, forty years on, do I really understand the need for activism . . . to make discrimination visible." Even though she has had no female mentors, mentoring is an important aspect of her activism:

> One of the joys of my current position is the opportunities it has offered to me to help other women realize their dreams—women attempting a higher degree that they have put off while they took care of families; young women in the international schools who would like to lead to bring about change, but don't believe

they have the skills; women considering taking on leadership roles in challenging urban schools in the States.

The girls Jill taught many years ago still remember her and are in touch with her today, commenting on the profound influence Jill had on their lives, something Jill did not realize at the time. One young woman Jill taught in Kuwait over thirty years ago recently wrote, telling her,

> You were a great teacher. . . . I loved those geography lessons! . . . I am one of five or six women in our class who never got married. I think we are all stuck between the east and the west. I love that you focus on girls. Anyone that empowers women has my respect.

Such is the power of mentoring.

Insights

The WLE stories are a testament to the complexity and power of mentoring. Each of the women who acknowledged the importance of mentoring had unique mentoring experiences. Women who are in the early years of their career spoke of being mentored, rather than of mentoring others, and the affirming and empowering effect of that experience. Often the mentoring relationship was informal, not arranged. Rather an older, more experienced person, sometimes male and sometimes female, saw potential and took on the mantle of a mentor.

There were also descriptions of formal mentoring, often in the supervisor-student relationship when undertaking postgraduate study. None of the women described being part of a formal women's mentoring program. Such programs have been used and seen by many as an important strategy in advancing women's careers. However, there has also been criticism of women-only leadership development, particularly in developing countries, where it is seen as important to get men on women's side. Women-only leadership programs may be seen as threatening by men and viewed with suspicion. Mentoring is very often utilized in women-only programs as an important support strategy (Strachan, Saunders, Jimmy, and Lapi 2007).

Instead of relying on women-only programs, gender mainstreaming has been suggested as a strategy to help improve women's status, including women's representation in leadership positions. The United Nations Development Programme (UNDP) defines gender mainstreaming as

> a strategy for making women's as well as men's concerns and experiences an integral dimension of . . . the policies and programmes in all political, economic

and societal spheres so that women and men benefit equally and inequality is not perpetuated. (United Nations Development Programme 2011)

According to the UNDP, gender mainstreaming is also falling short of expectations in achieving gender equality because of poor accountability mechanisms, poor resources, and lack of commitment. In reality, often a dual approach is used, both women-only and gender mainstreaming. International statistical data on women's underrepresentation in educational leadership positions (Sobehart 2009) attest to the need to continue with activist strategies, including mentoring. Yet, despite the very slow improvement in women's representation in senior leadership positions in education, the WLE women continue their work to dismantle the systems and attitudes that are barriers to women's advancement.

Scholarship

A third pathway to advancing social justice outcomes for the WLE members was through scholarship. This occurred in two ways, either through study at university and/or by researching and publishing. For many of the WLE women, studying provided an awakening of not only their lived realities as women striving to find and make their places in the world, but also of the lived realities of others far less privileged. Through scholarship the women had become what Freire ([1970] 2002) called conscientized, that is, they had learned to "perceive social, political, and economic contradictions—developing a critical awareness" (Anon, n.d.).

There was an awakening in the women's understanding of feminism and what it meant to be oppressed. Some of the WLE women came to know feminism later in their lives; that is, they were aware of it but had not really engaged yet with its ideas. Embracing feminism later in life is visible in the literature. Even the well-known feminist activist Charlotte Bunch didn't initially see her activism as feminist (Brooks and Hodgson 2007).

Often the women were busy with marriage (sometimes divorce), raising children, study, and work. They were in survival mode. When they took the opportunity or made the opportunity to do further study, their embryonic understanding of feminism and oppression blossomed through their engagement with the academic world or their personal experiences with discrimination (Neville and Hamer 2006). Producing scholarship was another pathway to advancing social justice outcomes. WLE group members are actively and extensively involved in researching and publishing and are highly regarded scholars in the field of social justice and educational leadership.

Margaret Grogan

The featured example of a leader who has used scholarship to advance social justice outcomes is Dr. Margaret Grogan. Margaret chose to write a letter to her adult daughter Klara to tell her story. The longest of the twenty-three narratives was titled "The Short Version of how I got from Queensland to California: A letter to our daughter Klara." Margaret is professor and dean of the School of Educational Studies at Claremont Graduate University in California. During her academic career Margaret has been recognized for her excellence in teaching and scholarly research. She served on the executive committee and as president of the University Council for Educational Administration (UCEA). An excerpt from her university web page chronicles other impressive achievements:

> She [Margaret] has also been an associate editor and/or editorial board member of two of the top journals of educational leadership. She has chaired more than 25 doctoral dissertations. She has received high-flyer awards for her teaching at the University of Missouri. In 1997 she received the Willower Award of Excellence to honor scholarship in the field of leadership and ethics in education. (http://www.cgu.edu/pages/5658.asp)

Margaret has specifically been recognized for her contribution to research on women and educational leadership. In 2005 she and Cryss Brunner were recognized by the American Association of School Administrators (AASA) for ten years of research in the field. Margaret has published five books, twenty-five book chapters, and seventeen refereed articles. "Her current research focuses on women in leadership, the superintendency, the moral and ethical dimensions of leadership, and leadership for social justice. She also edited a series on Women in Leadership for SUNY Press for over 10 years" (http://www.cgu.edu/pages/5658.asp).

Born in Bundaberg, Queensland, Australia, Margaret came from a lower-middle-class family that valued education. Her father, Pat, came from a background on the land and, having gone to college to get his BA, became a senior lecturer at the Queensland Agricultural College. Her mother Mollie, who had been a bank teller in Bundaberg during the war, ran a part-time bank agency for students of the college from their house. A steady job and a good education were important in their family.

Margaret was educated in the Catholic school system and the prevailing career at that time for clever girls was to be a teacher or a nurse. She didn't want to be either; she wanted to be a lawyer. When she told her father, he laughed: "Honey, he said, we don't know the kind of people who could help you get a job. You better be a teacher and marry a rich man." During her high-school years she left home to attend a Catholic girls' boarding school in Brisbane, calling it an enjoyable but sheltered experience.

Winning a scholarship to study at Queensland University, Margaret completed a BA in English, ancient history, and Japanese. Her choice to study Japanese was to say the least very unusual in 1970s Australia. Still fresh were memories of World War II, including a rumored possible invasion of Australia by the Japanese, the bombing of the city of Darwin in the north, and Japanese concentration camps. As a result, she met some opposition; however, studying Japanese proved to be an inspired choice for Margaret. The options for a career that used her ancient history and Japanese majors were very limited, so Margaret trained as a secondary school teacher. Her first teaching position was in Townsville in the far north of Australia. Despite her earlier reservations about being a teacher, she loved it:

> I had a great time. I lived near the water, rode a bicycle to school and fell in and out of love at least three times during the eighteen months I was there. I went bushwalking most weekends—often barefoot—to show I was as tough as the rest of them (pretty weird when you think about it).

Encouraged by her principal, in 1975 Margaret headed for Tokyo to teach English as a second language. She stayed for seventeen years. Her time in Japan included meeting and marrying her husband, who was from Germany, in 1977. She was teaching part-time at the Mitsui Company, working in radio and television, narrating films and doing voice-overs, and doing commercials and radio English lessons. She was hired as a teacher at the International School of the Sacred Heart (ISSH) in Hiroo. "Sister Ruth Sheehy from Dublin was head of the school and I found her to be a breath of fresh air. She was very smart, very well read, and very dedicated to providing the best education possible for the girls at ISSH—from about fifty or sixty different countries."

Margaret and her husband decided to stay in Japan. They lived a Japanese lifestyle. "We didn't live like wealthy *gaijin* who worked for the embassy or a big corporation. It was a much more Japanese lifestyle—*tatami* mats and *shoji* sliding doors upstairs in the room that became yours [Klara's] with a sunken *kotatsu* to warm ourselves." Promotion followed, and Margaret became the head of the English department and co-coordinator of the International Baccalaureate. It was at this time that she also completed her master's degree in curriculum and instruction from Michigan State University, a program offered at one of the American bases on the edge of Tokyo. Margaret taught at ISSH for fourteen years. Recently she has reconnected in California with some of the girls she taught in the 1980s. She finds she remembers them well, even their sisters and their friends, stating, "It was undoubtedly the best time of my life."

As for other WLE women, a turning point for Margaret in her understanding of feminism and gender equity occurred serendipitously rather than through planning. She became involved in the Seeking Educational Equity and Diversity (S.E.E.D.) project with faculty at ISSH. She explained, "I had never really thought much about feminism or racism or homophobia or any of the marginalizing structures in society. Coming from a privileged background, I pretty much took for granted that I was doing well based on my own merits." The S.E.E.D. project sparked some spirited debates on race, class, gender, sexuality, and religious differences, and Margaret considered that she learned from her students, "who embodied many of these differences."

Being involved in the S.E.E.D. project over a number of years was the beginning of Margaret's extensive scholarship on gender equity and social justice in education. Even though working at ISSH provided Margaret with "a huge sense of fulfillment," she had been thinking about pursuing a PhD. Her interest in educational leadership was sparked not only by her many responsibilities but also by some of the Sacred Heart sisters with whom she taught. "Ruth taught me that to lead others is a great privilege to be undertaken with humility and care."

Although it was hard for her to leave ISSH, in 1992 Margaret and her daughter Klara left Japan for the United States, where Margaret would study for her PhD at Washington State University (WSU). Having taken WSU classes for several years, she had completed all the WSU leadership courses through off-site intensive seminars held in places like Singapore and Hong Kong. She had also spent a couple of summers taking courses at WSU in Pullman in the United States. Margaret decided to study women aspiring to the superintendency because at that time so few women were superintendents:

> I had always thought the US was a shining example of equal opportunity for men and women when I lived outside the country. How amazed I was to find out that in 1993, the year I did my study, only 5 percent of US school districts were run by women.

Even though Margaret was not yet actually considering an academic career, some of her professors warned her that she was unlikely to be appointed as an assistant professor if she researched "just women." She paid no heed to their advice, as "I'd read the research and the critical feminist theories. I understood that if I let them discourage me, I would be maintaining the status quo." Before Margaret graduated in 1994 she discovered that she loved research and writing:

> I fell in love with doing research. It was another epiphany—the first had been finding out that I had a passion for school leadership when I was at ISSH, and

now this one was finding out that I wanted to spend the rest of my life engaged in research! And writing! . . . the analysis of data and sense making was a blast. I can still feel goose bumps when I think of the excitement of doing that dissertation.

On completion of her doctorate and even though Margaret had never envisaged living in the United States, she applied to over fifty universities, most of which did not reply, she noted, as well as for principal positions in the area. Ultimately, she was offered and accepted an assistant professorship at the University of Virginia (UVA). The family bought a house and settled in Charlottesville, where they stayed for eight years. She observed that "those eight years at UVA provided me with an excellent start to my academic career. I worked alongside some of the best professors in the field of education."

Margaret knew that if she wanted to gain tenure she had to publish. Despite a heavy teaching load she published her dissertation as a book. Working seven days a week, she also coresearched with colleagues, and from that research wrote more books and articles. She avoided taking leadership roles at UVA because that would have made it difficult for her to carry on with her research and publishing and would have jeopardized her ability to get tenure. However, soon after she was granted tenure she took on the role of program coordinator at UVA, a role she enjoyed and that served as her introduction to higher-education administration. Margaret's leadership abilities were being recognized, and in 2002 she was encouraged to apply for and was successful in winning a department chair position at the University of Missouri-Columbia. Appointed as a full professor, Margaret's academic career was continuing to accelerate. She wrote, "I soon learned that leadership in higher education was a delicate balance of building consensus and facilitating a shared commitment to move ahead."

The position at the University of Missouri was challenging, but Margaret continued to publish. She participated in a number of the department's Educational Leadership and Policy Analysis (ELPA) projects, including the partnership statewide cooperative EdD program, which allowed her to travel all over the state of Missouri. She was also involved in dissertation supervision and codesigning the principal preparation program. Margaret's publications, mainly but not solely, focused on women and educational leadership, gender equity, and diversity. After six years at the University of Missouri she was appointed professor and dean of the School of Education Studies at Claremont Graduate University, a position she currently holds. The long letter to her daughter ends with these words: "I think we are done with moving. Well at least with finding new jobs. I like this one and hope to be doing it in ten years from now."

Insights

Being raised in an open, supportive environment meant that as an intelligent, young Catholic woman growing up in Australia in the 1950s and 1960s, Margaret dared to dream of stepping outside the normal life path of young women of that time—early marriage and babies. Although studying at a university was becoming more common during those decades, it certainly was not the norm and without a scholarship would not have been possible for Margaret. Unbeknownst at the time, it was that early foundation plus her time in Japan that paved a pathway to a possible academic career.

Margaret's story echoes that of other WLE women who have used scholarship and research to advance social justice outcomes by making visible discrimination and injustices. Like other WLE women, her conscientization came from her international experiences and by engaging in research and graduate study. The process of conscientization was not rapid, but once undertaken there was no turning back; you can't unknow what you know.

In order to gain tenure, Margaret knew that she had to publish and in doing so worked seven days a week. Scholarship suggests that the strong emphasis on research as a promotion criterion disadvantages women, who also usually carry the bulk of domestic responsibilities at home (Guth and Wright 2009). In so doing, they either limit the time they have available to focus on research, or they work exceptionally long hours. Guth and Wright (2009) conclude from their research on UK women in higher education that universities usually have fair policies, policies that in theory promote equal opportunities for female academics, but they raise this issue:

> This discrepancy between policy and lived experience raises questions about the effectiveness of law and policy alone in ensuring gender equality. This is partly because the university is unable to make any changes to its employees' private lives and how they are organized. (142)

We are not suggesting here that Margaret carried most of the domestic responsibilities in her family. In fact, Margaret commented, "my wonderful husband does and has done for years the cooking and grocery shopping"; rather, we are suggesting that for many women academics the personal cost can be very high. However, once Margaret gained tenure, her leadership qualities were quickly recognized and she was rapidly promoted.

International research reveals that for some women experiences of teaching in higher education, also called "the academy," are not as positive as Margaret's. For example, some research on US women academics found that for many women the tenure process was very difficult and the academic environment toxic (Cooper and Strachan 2006). Other WLE women experienced discrimination and violence while working in academia. Those women needed to be particularly strong and courageous to survive in such hostile workplaces. Stress levels can be very high, especially if women are trying to balance family and career responsibilities.

Women are underrepresented in faculty positions and particularly under-represented in senior positions (Fitzgerald and Wilkinson 2010). Demograph-ics of the WLE group displayed in table 1.2 (See chapter 1) reveal that seven-teen of the twenty-three women, including Margaret, are over the age of fifty. Because many will retire within ten years, we need to be vigilant in finding ways to make the teaching in higher education more welcoming to women. We need to encourage and support young feminist academics to advance their careers so that they can carry on with social justice scholarship to advance so-cial justice outcomes. The production of social justice scholarship is important feminist work.

The women's stories bear witness to the profound reflection and question-ing that takes place as they study and/or teach. Two important aspects of advancing social justice outcomes are (1) making visible both injustice and oppression, and (2) questioning how feminism and activism are theorized (Gewal 2008). To ensure that the WLE group does not perpetuate the hege-mony of (older) white middle-class feminism that so concerns Gewal (2008), a conscious decision has been made to include in WLE younger women (and some men) from diverse cultures around the world, from both developed and developing countries.

The scholarship of all twenty-three of the WLE women featured in this book has at some time been focused on an aspect of gender equity and social justice in education. WLE as a group has also been involved in social justice research. For example, with the assistance of funding from the Commonwealth Council for Educational Administration and Management (CCEAM), a group of WLE researchers is charting the representation of women in educational leadership in the Commonwealth, thereby filling a gap. The WLE group is using scholar-ship to advance social justice outcomes in this project and others.

ADVANCING SOCIAL JUSTICE OUTCOMES: SELECTED SCHOLARSHIP

Scheurich and McKenzie (2006) offer four imperatives that they consider es-sential to advancing social justice outcomes. They state first that social justice work is ongoing as "oppression, injustice, and inequity continue in old forms and new" (10). The second imperative is that we must deepen our understand-ing of social justice. They pose the question of whether we really understand the complexities of discrimination, racism, homophobia, and other lived reali-ties. The third imperative is that we must engage in self-critique and examine our own prejudices. Finally, the fourth imperative is that we must be activists. The social justice battles highlighted by Scheurich and McKenzie in 2006 are very similar to those Anna Julia Cooper was waging one hundred-plus years ago (Johnson 2009).

Johnson (2009) reports on how Cooper, an African American feminist educator born around 1859, challenged the status quo. "She was engaging in a social justice strategy that attempted to empower her students' and teachers' dreams, desires, voices, and rights to have access to an equitable educational experience" (78). She was an activist, a mentor of girls and women, and a scholar. At the age of sixty-six she gained her PhD from the Sorbonne. She was a woman who was ahead of her time. Despite great opposition she continued to fight for social justice in education until her death at age 105.

The discrimination and social injustices in education that Cooper was so concerned about all those years ago are still prevalent today in what is proving to be "a difficult and lengthy struggle" (Scheurich and McKenzie 2006, 12). Also, the strategies that Cooper utilized then, the scholarship suggests, are still relevant today: "Cooper utilized pedagogical practices and thoughts that were focused on transforming the educational experiences that circumscribed the lives of marginalized groups. Her pedagogy was political in that it was rooted in an anti-racist, anti-sexist, and anti-classist battle" (Johnson 2009, 78–79).

Transformation and transformative leadership are often mentioned in the literature on advancing social justice outcomes. Scholarship suggests that transformative leadership is essential to advancing social justice outcomes (Shields 2009b). A critical question is how do transformative leaders become transformative? Educational leadership preparation programs that utilize critical reflection can play an important role. Shields (2009b) provides us with an explanation of transformative leadership:

> [It] begins with questions of justice and democracy; it critiques inequitable practices and offers the promise not only of greater individual achievement but of a better life lived in common with others. It inextricably links education and educational leadership with the wider diverse social context within which it is embedded. (55)

The importance of educational leaders developing a critical consciousness is echoed by McKenzie and colleagues (2008): "[T]he role of a critical consciousness in a leadership preparation program for social justice is to motivate students to become social justice leaders in their schools and communities" (124).

McKenzie and colleagues (2008) posit that a social justice–oriented preparation program for educational leaders needs to select students who already have a social justice orientation as this means they can move more quickly to "become advocates and leaders of change" (118). In addition, they argue that for the students in the program to develop a critical consciousness they need to study in-depth injustices and inequities and how education practices can compound those, much in the same way that Vanita worked with the women leaders in South Africa. Most importantly, developing critical consciousness is an essential forerunner to becoming an activist leader of change (Cambron-McCabe and McCarthy 2005).

Preparing transformative leaders requires academic faculty who engage in critical pedagogical practices (Johnson 2009), model "the kinds of organizations they expect their graduates to create" (Cambron-McCabe and McCarthy 2005, 216), and are politically active and advocate for changes in educational policies and practices (Cambron-McCabe and McCarthy 2005). That means, in summary, they must practice what they teach.

Social justice outcomes are hard to achieve. Shields (2009a) suggests that educational leaders will need to "develop four dispositions and skill sets: an awakening of global curiosity; the ability to establish strong dialogic relationships; a transformative approach to leadership; and a willingness to take a stance as a public intellectual" (138–39). It is not enough just to develop critical consciousness in educational leaders and point them toward the path of advancing social justice outcomes: they need to be equipped with skills to support them in their work.

CONCLUDING THOUGHTS

This chapter has explored how Vanita Richard, Jill Sperandio, and Margaret Grogan advanced social justice outcomes. Vanita's story speaks to the powerful influence that discriminatory political practices had on motivating her to engage in action. Courage is featured in the literature as an important quality for those engaged in social justice work (Lee and McKerrow 2005). Detention by the authorities for engaging in antiapartheid activities often resulted in torture and death, as happened to Stephen Bantu Biko.

Vanita's activism was motivated not only by the oppressive government policies but also by her personal experience of discrimination. Vanita's story also explains how engagement with radical ideas through graduate study helped her to understand her internalized oppression, a powerful weapon in the hands of the oppressor. She found inspiration in the actions of courageous people such as Stephen Bantu Biko. The context is an important consideration when planning social justice actions. It influences the "what" and the "how" of advancing social justice outcomes. What is possible in one context may not be possible or appropriate in another context.

Prior to her work in many different countries, Jill had also internalized oppression of women as, in her words, "the natural order of things." While Jill admits to having experienced discrimination she also acknowledges that, in comparison to most of the world, as a white educated woman she is very privileged. The impact of context on Jill's experience of discrimination is evident. Jill's story illustrates also how international experiences exposed her to practices that significantly discriminated against women and girls, to an extent beyond anything she had personally experienced. Her conscientization and embrace of feminism, as for Margaret and other WLE women, was a gradual process. However, even if Jill did not overtly embrace feminism, she did do feminist social justice work as her mentoring of girls and women in many countries attests.

Margaret's story is illustrative of what Hart (2005) refers to as "professionalized activism . . . [that] focuses on tactics that mirror the professional work in academe in order to advance [a social justice] agenda" (7). An important aspect of professionalized activism is engaging in high-quality research and scholarship that exposes and makes visible discrimination and injustice. Findings of such research can then influence policies that are aimed at eliminating discriminatory practices. Feminist academics like Margaret who take on leadership responsibilities and who are committed to advancing social justice outcomes influence the shaping of equitable organizational practices. Their power and influence gives feminist leaders "opportunities to open up access to knowledge and resources to those with less power" (Lee and McKerrow 2005, para. 5). How they do that is, according to Hart (2005), dependent upon their professional socialization.

The stories of Vanita Richard, Jill Sperandio, and Margaret Grogan show that the shaping of strategies and the multiple pathways used to advance social justice outcomes are also influenced by powerful personal experiences and by context. A quotation about the meaningful connection between women leaders' work for social justice outcomes and women's leadership for change opened the chapter. We conclude with these words of urgency, also from Grogan and Shakeshaft (2011), that call leaders on multiple pathways to come together to work for change:

> Individuals having leadership responsibility must understand what diverse collective leadership is, and must create opportunities for it to occur. Moreover, only by deliberately drawing on diverse perspectives can organizations gain the best effect of collectively derived directions for change. We hope that the old texts that situate leadership in the individual are abandoned. We need the strength and power of numbers and a variety of lived experience. . . . There is not a moment to lose. (106)

There is not a moment to lose in the United States or any other country. Through our leadership practices, pathways, and passion to advance social justice outcomes we make the meaning of the future.

8

ACTIONS DEFINE SOCIAL JUSTICE LEADERSHIP

Perhaps the greatest challenge for educators committed to social justice, then, is to remember that our actions can inform our theories as much as theories inform our actions.

—Dana Rapp, "Social Justice and the Importance of Rebellious, Oppositional Imaginations"

Stories from personal narratives grounding this book tell how social justice leadership opens opportunity, expands rights, reduces poverty, diminishes violence against women, extends dignity, creates communities of difference, and becomes a force for good in the larger society. Seventeen of the participants have clearly been activists in pursuing social justice in education and the larger society. What social justice leadership means to them is defined by their actions in both their personal and professional lives. They are living their values, whatever their country or pathway. Our actions are always the real story and the realization of our motivation and values.

Making a difference is a commitment strongly evident in the leadership of the WLE women. Action, sometimes courageous, is required if a difference is to be made (Shields 2009b). Grogan and Shakeshaft's (2011) review of scholarship on social justice leadership suggests that "women, more often than men, talk about having entered teaching to change the lives of children, to make the world a fairer place, and to change institutions so that all children have a chance" (11). WLE women have been about such actions in their professional and personal lives. Whereas the previous chapter examined social justice actions in terms of the pathways of activism, mentoring, and scholarship, in this chapter we focus on particular themes, angles of activism, that were conveyed in the narratives. The themes that illustrate the actions of women committed to achieving their goals of making a difference are "doing" feminism, engaging in political activism, and using power to make a difference.

TAKING ACTION TO MAKE A DIFFERENCE: THE STORIES

The WLE stories are full of examples of commitment to inclusive social justice action that goes beyond a concern for advancing women in educational leadership. Although each life story in this chapter illustrates aspects of all the themes, one story will be featured for each. The themes and featured leaders are: (1) Doing Feminism—Jane Strachan, New Zealand; (2) Engaging in Political Activism—Anastasia Athanasoula-Reppa, Greece; and (3) Using Power to Make a Difference—Helen Sobehart, United States.

Doing Feminism

Some women leaders use the social justice values of feminism as a leadership platform. "Feminist leaders are motivated by fairness, justice, and equity and strive to keep issues of gender, race, social class, sexual orientation, and ability at the forefront of what they do each day" (Barton 2006, para. 32). While all the WLE women featured in this book were activists, not all used "feminist" to describe their activism. Six women do identify as feminist, and all are older (sixty-plus years), white, and middle class. This perhaps reflects the discomfort that some women have with owning the word *feminism* as many view feminism negatively and do not wish to be labeled feminist. Violent reactions of others can cause many women to shy away from the label.

Some women prefer to describe themselves as passionate about "social justice issues" or "gender" or "equality and equity" rather than as feminist. Resistance to being labeled feminist and resistance to social justice work are themes evident in the literature and are explored later in this chapter. Jane Strachan, like some other WLE women, came to know and embrace feminism later in life. Her journey to "doing feminism" came from personal and professional experiences that fueled her passion to lead in socially just ways. Her feminism informs her leadership and her life actions.

Jane Strachan

Dr. Jane Strachan retired at the end of 2011 from her position as associate professor in the Faculty of Education, University of Waikato, in Hamilton, New Zealand. Her career in education spans over forty-five years. She taught in high schools, served as a guidance counselor, and finally became a university professor. She has an undergraduate qualification in physical education and teaching, a graduate qualification in guidance and counseling, and both master's and PhD degrees in educational leadership. Jane's university web page stated: "My teaching and research interests are focused on educational leadership, social justice, gender, women, policy development and Pacific education" (http://edlinked.soe.waikato.ac.nz/staff/index.php?user=jane&page_id=2545). Jane's story was written in two parts. She describes the first part as her "journey to feminism" and the second part as her "doing feminism."

Jane was born in England into a middle-class family and has one older brother. She remembers her childhood in northern England as happy. In 1957 at the age of eleven, Jane moved to New Zealand with her family. Now, after fifty-five-plus years in New Zealand, Jane thinks of herself as very much a "kiwi," the commonly used, affectionate term for a New Zealander. Initially, adjustment to the New Zealand culture was not easy; she "spoke funny" and found it difficult to make friends. In an effort to be befriended by another girl at her school, Jane went along with a suggestion that they commit acts of vandalism in a local park. Jane ended up in court, and her parents were fined.

This was a huge disgrace and embarrassment for her family, and Jane was very ashamed. "I ended up trying to be the model teenager as I wanted to make up for what I had done and avoid hurting my parents again. My parents were proud of me. They were good, kind and loving people." With the wisdom of hindsight, Jane thinks this brush with the law helped her to identify with the "underdog." Throughout her life she has involved herself in supporting and taking action on behalf of the less privileged and the marginalized. She calls this "doing feminism," even though in the earlier years of her life she did not know what feminism was.

In 1968 Jane started her first teaching position in a working-class, coeducational high school. Her teaching career in high schools spanned twenty-two years in both coeducational and single-sex schools in mainly poor communities in New Zealand. It was during those years that she first came into contact with feminism and feminists. However, like other WLE women, her embracing of feminism was slow. She explained,

> I had been well socialized to behave and look like a lady by my traditional, English, middle-class family background and the private single-sex, girls' schools I attended for fourteen years. I fully expected to teach until I married and had children, at which time I would leave teaching and stay at home to raise my children. I did not view teaching as a career in terms of promotion to a senior position. I loved to teach and that was enough for me.

In the early 1970s Jane followed the "expected" path of marriage and children. Although she continued to teach physical education until she was seven months pregnant with her first child, she then resigned her teaching position, cashed in her superannuation (something she now regrets in retirement), and bought an automatic washing machine ("for nappy [diaper] washing") with the money. She settled down to enjoy being a wife and a mother. However, the reality was somewhat different; "within three months of the birth of my first son, I separated from my husband and was living with my parents. I was now a single parent with very little money."

Jane looked for a part-time teaching position. Fortunately, during the early 1970s finding a teaching position was not difficult; finding quality child care was. The "women's liberation" ideas debated by her friends, by those early "women's libbers," and by the media, began to make personal sense for Jane. She was catapulted into an awareness of how women were oppressed and experienced other people's prejudices about single parents. She personally felt a mixture of relief about having a break from her baby (her mother and a friend cared for him) and guilt about being a working mother.

The years between the early 1970s and 1990, when Jane left high-school teaching, were a time that included another child and a marriage that also ended in divorce, full-time teaching with two young children to support, and further study at graduate level. By now her understanding of oppression was more sophisticated and much broader. Her years as a secondary-school guidance counselor had brought her face to face with the disadvantage experienced by minority groups, and Māori in particular. She wrote, "I worked hard to try and change attitudes and systems within the schools where I taught in order to make the opportunities for all people fairer and more just."

During the 1980s Jane held middle management positions in the schools in which she taught. She still did not see herself as moving into senior management positions. She was in survival mode teaching, studying, and raising two children. However, a number of things happened that increased her awareness about attitudes of some people to women in leadership positions, and the unfairness of the promotion system in schools that were very male dominated. First, she applied for and was accepted to attend a teacher in-service course on middle management in education. A male colleague commented that he thought by wanting to go to the course she was "blatantly ambitious"; he also asked, "What makes you think that you are good enough?" Jane was angry.

Second, the school where Jane was teaching was appointing two new staff members to the senior management team. The process that was used for the appointment meant that for the final interview, only men had been short-listed, and therefore the senior team would have been entirely made up of men. This was in contradiction to the school's equal opportunities policy. She was angered by this and rallied the staff to protest, which they did. There was significant resistance by the board of trustees to the staff's request to start the appointment process again. However, the board of trustees did rethink its decision and readvertised, and a woman was appointed to the assistant principal position. Jane wrote, "This incident sharpened my understanding of how women were disadvantaged by promotion systems, how collective action could make a difference, and what it felt like to experience resistance from those in power."

In 1989, Jane took a year's leave without pay to embark on her master's degree. "I was burnt out from my work as a guidance counselor and needed a break. Much of my counseling work had been supporting and advocating for girls who had been abused. I was exhausted." At Waikato University, Jane chose to study educational leadership and was amazed at how invisible women's writing was in her courses; "it was as if women did not write about educational leadership and that women were not leaders in schools," she observed. Jane persuaded her lecturer in educational leadership to include women's scholarship. Later she wrote about this experience and published a journal article titled "The Man in the Literature" (1993). During this period of study she also began "to understand the different feminist theoretical positions and how each explained the experiences of women educational leaders."

Having completed her master's degree, in 1991 Jane was appointed to a tenured position as a senior lecturer in the Department of Professional Studies in Education at the University of Waikato. Throughout this period, Jane's feminism was strengthening, as was her activism. This involved working with groups of women in high schools, being active on the university's Equal Opportunity and Freedom from Harassment Committee, and, with the support of another feminist colleague, introducing new courses at the graduate and undergraduate levels that had gender and equity in educational leadership as their foci. In these courses, literature written by women scholars formed the core of the required reading.

For her PhD topic Jane decided to investigate the feminist educational leadership of three women high-school principals. The topic fascinated her. Describing the principals, she wrote that "the women participants all self-identified as feminist, acknowledged that their feminism informed their leadership practice, and all practiced their feminist educational leadership in very different ways. They were courageous, outspoken, immensely hard working, and inspirational. They were doing feminism."

The second part of Jane's story she titled "the doing of my feminism." On the completion of her PhD, she became the chairperson of the Department of Professional Studies in Education. It was a large department that focused on professional teacher education and was an ideal opportunity to practice her feminist educational leadership and also add valuable experience that would assist in her promotion. "I loved the job, which I found surprising as many others saw it as something to be avoided. I tried to practice my feminist educational leadership in ways that empowered and supported others, was efficient, was socially just, built relationships and offered others opportunities."

Two years later she applied for and was appointed to the position of assistant dean of graduate studies. This position helped her to understand the wider university context and brought her into contact with many international students who had come to New Zealand on scholarship to study at the graduate and postgraduate levels. She supervised many of them throughout her career. Jane saw this supervision as part of her social justice work, explaining, "For most of these students English was not their first language; sometimes it was their fifth or sixth language (I was in awe). However, to write a thesis in English was very difficult for them and required extra support from their supervisors."

For ten years Jane enjoyed her work as an academic. She was comfortable, and she enjoyed good working conditions, great friends and colleagues, stimulating work, a new apartment, and two grown sons who were about to explore the world. So she was surprised when she wanted to respond to Volunteer Service Abroad's call for a women's advisor to the Department of Women's Affairs in Vanuatu. "I couldn't resist. This was a chance to 'walk the talk.' To do feminism." Fortunately, the University of Waikato agreed to give her two years leave without pay. Jane was supported by her feminist dean and PhD supervisor, Noeline Alcorn. "I had a safety net, a job to go back to. The decision to spend two years as a volunteer advisor to the director of the Department of Women's Affairs in the Vanuatu government turned out to be one of the best decisions I have ever made," she commented.

Jane had to establish her credibility, and this took time. She was working out of her comfort zone, culturally, linguistically, and climatically. She explained, "My taken-for-granted ways of operating were challenged." During her time in Vanuatu Jane and the women she worked with experienced significant resistance to their work to improve the status of women. For example, the policy they developed to increase women's representation in government was stalled on a regular basis by male politicians, as "women were not meant to be leaders." Their work challenged the cultural norms of the role of women.

On her return to New Zealand Jane took up her academic position again, teaching, research, and to a lesser extent administration. However, her supervision of thesis students increased hugely as international students approached her to be their supervisor, particularly students from the Pacific, who perceived she now had some understanding of their lived realities. Within two years of her return to New Zealand another opportunity presented itself. The Faculty of Education at the University of Waikato won a multimillion-dollar New Zealand Aid Programme contract to capacity build teacher education in the Solomon Islands. Jane managed the project for four and a half years. The Solomon Islands is a very poor country and has experienced huge ethnic conflict that has seriously damaged the morale of the people and the government infrastructure, including teacher education. Jane wrote, "My work was social justice work. It was the doing of my feminism, and I feel so privileged to have been involved in this work in the closing years of my career."

Jane is now retired. In preparation, she decided to work three days a week. "I thought it time to put something back into my local community so am now a volunteer support worker for refugees who come to New Zealand. Their stories are truly heart wrenching." She sees supporting and mentoring other women academics as important work, too. "We need younger women to carry on the feminist work, helping them gain entry to women's networks and to publishing. Mentoring them and supporting them has been a key part of my work, in New Zealand and in the Pacific." She is also a grandmother and emphasized that "another key part of my life is being a grandmother and helping to raise grandchildren who like my two sons have strong social consciences."

Insights

Jane's story offers a number of insights that help explain how and why women leaders use a social justice platform for their leadership actions. Social justice leadership is not just put into action by women from underprivileged and marginalized backgrounds; women of privilege can also be passionate about and active in social justice leadership work. The literature points to a strong link between moral purpose, ethical leadership, values, and a commitment to work in socially just ways and for socially just outcomes. Jane speaks of a loving family who supported her when as a young girl she let them down by breaking the law and ending up in court. Her parents, although very disappointed, showed compassion. Bandura's (1997) social learning theory explains how children and adolescents learn behavior and values by observation and modeling. In this context, privilege can be reframed from one of high socioeconomic status, that is, economic capital (Jane's parents were economically comfortable but not wealthy) to one of family capital (good parenting).

Jane's feminism was a powerful motivating force in her social justice leadership. Her "doing feminism" was action based. Feminist leadership is built on a foundation of social justice and wanting to make a difference, to help improve the lives of the oppressed and the marginalized at both individual and institutional levels (Grogan and Shakeshaft 2011). It involves speaking out, and it requires courage. Although Jane publicly owned her feminism, others in this book did not; yet their leadership is based on the social justice principles of feminism. Whether women identify as feminist or not is not the issue; their actions are of importance and define them as leaders for social justice.

Jane's story also highlights that women who are activists will face resistance and need to prepare themselves for that. When cultural norms are challenged, people can feel threatened and may react against proposed changes; sometimes that reaction may involve a personal attack. Fear of being personally attacked can discourage women from taking action and can also take an emotional toll. As they strove to advance their social justice agendas, resistance was also experienced by Anastasia and Helen, as illustrated in their stories to follow. Resistance from others is a consequence of social justice activism.

Political Activism

In a passionate plea, Rapp (2002) exhorts educational leaders concerned with social justice to "more forcefully fight injustices from platforms of constitutional authority and civic responsibility in locations around and outside of schools" (227). Stories of WLE women who were politically active included membership in political organizations and participation in a variety of protest movements. Other WLE women protested against the Vietnam war (called the American war by the Vietnamese!) and Iraq wars and advocated for abused women and women in prisons. Their social justice leadership was not confined to the educational setting. Some of these wider political activities were dependent on what was happening on a local or world stage at the time. Anastasia Athanasoula-Reppa's story is peppered with descriptions of the political activities she has engaged in throughout her life. As with other WLE women, her first foray into political activism was dependent upon what was happening in Greece at the time she moved to Athens to attend university in the 1970s. These experiences as a student fueled in her a passion for social justice action.

Anastasia Athanasoula-Reppa

Dr. Anastasia Athanasoula-Reppa is a retired professor and former president of the Department of Pedagogical Studies at the School of Pedagogical and Technological Education (ASPETE) in Athens, Greece. Although now retired, Anastasia continues to work as a visiting professor and volunteer tutor at several universities and institutions around the world.

Anastasia was born in Arta, a small town in western Greece, in 1954. Greece had just emerged from World War II and the Greek Civil War. This was a time when Anastasia described conditions as "very bad for our nation . . . poverty and underdevelopment were everywhere . . . many people were forced into internal migration and external immigration." In 2011, things are once again economically very bad for Greece, and Anastasia has been forced into early retirement from her faculty/administrative position. She is a victim of Greece's serious economic woes and public service cutbacks.

Titled "My Monologue," Anastasia's story tells of a loving, extended family that was seriously affected by the difficult economic and social conditions in Greece post–World War II. Many of her family emigrated. "A characteristic example of the size of the emigration that took place is my father's family; they came from a very small village. The family had nine children and all of them left the village. Three of them today live in Canada and the rest of them live in the capital of prefecture Arta. Things were easier for my mother's family as they had fields for growing food." The social dislocation was huge as Greeks spread out across the globe in search of a more prosperous life.

The Greek cultural context (region of Epirus) into which Anastasia was born was very traditional. Yet despite this cultural conservatism the women of Epirus were very well known for their heroism during the war years of 1940–1948 (World War II and the Civil War), when they carried ammunition and clothing for the soldiers, sometimes in appalling and cold conditions. Anastasia explains the role of Greek women:

> The position of women was very difficult. Males were considered to be the boss in the family. A woman should attend to the house and participate in the agricultural and veterinary household duties without having the right to express her opinion. Families were extensive and a woman lived with the parents-in-law and the siblings of her husband who weren't married. All marriages, except for very few exceptions, came from matchmaking and not out of love between two people. Seldom were women sent to school.

Anastasia was the oldest child in her family, born to parents who were struggling to make a living in farming.

> It was really hard for my parents to nourish three children. So, they decided to send me at the age of four to live with my father's parents in the mountainous village of Makrykampo. My father was an exceptionally intelligent and skillful person (he later became a priest). He made a tank in order to irrigate the property and my mother, who was a dynamic and worthy woman, worked the property with a cow. Life there was very hard but at the same time beautiful.

Her younger brother died tragically in an accident. Later, another brother and sister were born. However, her parent's property was not producing enough for them to live, so they rented a coffee shop with money from a brother of her father's from Canada. Years later, the state granted to her parents some land near Mytikas village of prefecture Preveza. Her parents and grandmother (who died in 2010 at the age of 112 years) continued to live on the family properties.

The time she lived with her grandmother was a very special and influential time in Anastasia's life. "My grandparents were exceptionally dear and hard-working people. I learned from them to love and to respect each person, to have deep faith in God, and to be optimistic. Grandmother, Anastasia, was my first educator." During her first three years in primary school she had a remarkable young schoolteacher who, in addition to classical teaching, also taught them how to behave and survive. She wrote, "I remember the mornings that characteristically he used to, no matter how cold the weather, send us to the forest in order to bring timbers to turn on the heating. Afterwards we would begin the studies. The school was one teacher only for all classes and children were like one family."

At age ten her family's economic situation had improved, so Anastasia returned to live with her parents and attended a new school, which she did not enjoy. The culture was very different from what she had experienced at the small school in her grandmother's village. "The atmosphere of my new school was completely different. There the children were competitive, people were not polite, and I felt like a stranger," she explained. Despite this, Anastasia did well at school and, unlike many girls of her generation, went on to high-school education.

Her years at high school were exceptionally difficult for Anastasia because she had to live away from home, because of the military dictatorship, and because of poverty. She puts her survival down to practicing the virtues and values taught to her by her grandmother. Her time in high school coincided with the dictatorship of Georgios Papadopoulou (1967–1973). She experienced military law, being deprived of freedom of expression, and a strict education system. Boys and girls went to separate schools. It was at this time that Anastasia came into contact with a series of influential teachers and professors who encouraged their students to be politically active. "In the school among our professors were three liberal teachers who taught us to claim our rights."

Anastasia's political activities started in earnest in 1973 when she entered Panteion University of Political and Social Sciences. This was the year that the student movement arose against the dictatorship. She reported, "From the time I became a student I got active in the student movement against the dictatorship. With other students we created the Student Independence Movement (S.I.M.)." These students, who like Anastasia were involved in the fight against the military dictatorship, went on to be "exceptional scientists, journalists, politicians, ambassadors of state, and public servants."

During this time Anastasia shared an apartment close to Panteion University with her brother and one sister. Their apartment was a meeting place for other students and professors involved in resisting the dictatorship. In 1974 there was a change in the regime; democracy, human freedoms, and parliament were a reality again. With the return of democracy, some educational changes took place that included universities' return to academic freedom.

Anastasia was immersed in a political movement that was exciting and brought her into contact with influential people she greatly admired. Key professors supported and fueled her political activism. "My professors (to whom I am immensely grateful) gave me the best intellectual tools (cognitively and sociopolitically)," she wrote. Professor of constitutional rights Niki Kaltsogia-Tournaviti encouraged Anastasia to get involved in social justice research, for example, gender and equality. Other professors, like Sakis Karagiorgas and George Contogeorgis, inspired Anastasia to be active at the sociopolitical level, and others, like Demetrios Tsaousis and Nicolaos Konsolas, encouraged her to keep a work-life balance. During her postgraduate studies, one of her professors was Anthony Tritsis, who later became minister of education and the mayor of Athens. He influenced her and involved her in his fight for democracy.

Some of these influential professors went on to be personal friends, some continue to be colleagues, and one became her husband: "Panagiotis Reppas . . . I admired him for his scholarship and for his character in general . . . after the completion of my bachelor's studies [he] became my beloved husband. We share a long-lasting reciprocal admiration, fellow love and two children, Glykeria and Asimakis." Their marriage was a love match and not a match made in the traditional Greek way. Anastasia explained that "it was exceptionally revolutionary for the daughter of a priest to fall in love and bring the groom to the house without the approval of the relatives." However, her parents welcomed her husband into the family.

Early in their marriage Anastasia took on the management of the household and care of the children while her husband studied for his PhD dissertation and had time for writing and building his academic career. But in time Anastasia could count on the support of her husband when it was her turn to study and advance her career, explaining that "in time, of course, it was Panagiotis and the children who had to show tolerance and respect for my choices [to work and study]."

Panteion University was an intellectual community that had a strong influence on those who participated in the political activism against the military dictatorship. "[It] had a glamour and a magic that we admire, even today." In many ways Anastasia was in the right place at the right time. This offered Anastasia not only an opportunity to make a difference, to fight against oppression, but also an opportunity for social mobility, a way out of poverty. She worked in paid employment, she attended all her courses, and she was politically active. Her self-confidence and optimism grew.

Anastasia studied and taught political sciences. She completed two additional undergraduate degrees in public administration and sociology, a master's degree, and finally a PhD. After graduating from Panteion University, Anastasia trained as a high-school teacher at the School of Pedagogical and Technological Education (ASPETE). However, because of the family's difficult financial situation she did not immediately go into teaching (teaching did not pay well), but worked for the Ministry of Industry and Environment until 1983. She then moved into education and taught political sciences in professional-technical lyceums and high schools until 1996. Technical and vocational education in Greece does not enjoy the same status as academic education. However, it was a career that Anastasia found enjoyable and fulfilling. Technical education was the topic she chose for her PhD dissertation.

Apart from her high-school teaching, Anastasia participated in many educational committees to develop educational policy and teacher education. Her activism in the politics of education illustrated her continuing passion for change, for making a difference. She elaborated, "I wrote school books on social and political education, I collaborated with the Pedagogic Institute, I coordinated European programs with schools from five countries, I represented my country in the Council of Europe on subjects of education in citizenship education, and I participated in congresses of Federation of Teachers at Secondary Education."

In 1996 Anastasia became a professor at ASPETE, from where she has recently retired. She found the academic culture at ASPETE very different from what she had experienced at Panteion University. "The remnants of dictatorship in the faculty and institutional structures remained [at ASPETE] from the late 1970s and were there for roughly another thirty years." She found it very hard to adjust to such an authoritarian environment, and so true to form, Anastasia worked to change the culture.

Even though the founder of faculty was a woman, Niki Dedrinou-Antonakaki (in 1959), when she (Niki) retired the administration faculty members were all men, promotion was on seniority and length of service rather than on merit, and the scholarship of highly qualified women faculty was not valued. "We [Anastasia with another female colleague who had two PhDs] were both overqualified . . . the administration and the rest of our colleagues were threatened by us." Unfortunately, the toxic environment drove out her highly qualified colleague. As "she could bear no more the scorn," her colleague is now on faculty at National and Kapodistrian University (usually referred to as University of Athens).

During her tenure at ASPETE, Anastasia managed three outreach branches: one in the island of Crete (southern Greece), one in Ioannina (northwestern Greece), and one in Sapes (northeastern Greece), which is a multicultural village with Muslim minorities. She coordinated pedagogy courses in five undergraduate departments in ASPETE. In 2002 ASPETE increased its status to a university, and Anastasia was very active in the upgrade process. From 2002 to 2004 Anastasia was the only woman on the board of administration, and from 2009 until her retirement she was the head of the pedagogy department. Most recently she has taught in the postgraduate education program and enjoys the friendship and professional work with some ASPETE colleagues who share her vision and mission.

Even though over time the situation did improve for women on the faculty, Anastasia had to work hard to maintain her work/life balance and create a vision for her work. She has especially enjoyed work as a visiting professor at the University of Cyprus and her tutoring at the Open Universities of Greece and Cyprus. She also wrote, "An exceptional source of joy has been working with Angeliki Lazaridou and Linda Lyman, colleagues and friends of mine. They offered me an effective, creative and collaborative research opportunity to study women and educational leadership. I feel gratitude to both my friends for encouraging and inspiring me to work in the international field." This collaboration has resulted in Anastasia presenting at a number of international conferences, including the WLE conferences in Rome, Augsburg, and Volos.

Insights

One of the most powerful insights from Anastasia's narrative is the influence of serendipity or chance on her life. "Chance plays an important role in shaping individual biographies. . . . While many social interactions are routine or planned, unexpected interactions are quite common" (McDonald 2010, 307). A study by Williams, Soeprapto, Like, Touradi, Hess, and Hill (1998) investigated the influence of serendipity/chance on women's career choices. What they found was that chance activities did influence their decisions, depending on the people they were in contact with at the time of the chance event and whether the chance event was earlier or later in their lives. Earlier chance events had more influence. High self-concept was also influential as people with high self-concept are more likely to take advantage of the chance opportunities (Williams et al. 1998).

Anastasia was in the "right" place at the "right" time and met the "right people" who fueled her passion for political social justice action. She was born into a turbulent political time in Greece with Panteion University as a center of the resistance against a military dictatorship. She was there studying political science at a time when the resistance movement was very active, and she met influential professors who were active in the resistance movement. Had she gone to another university or not gone to university, she may not have been involved in political activism in the same way or at all. This is not to deny that Anastasia had agency and could decide how she would engage with those serendipitous occurrences.

A second insight is how poverty can be a motivating force for political action. There is a strong link between social mobility, educational attainment, and employment opportunities (Green, Mason, and Unwin 2011). Anastasia's childhood was loving but economically poor. For a young Greek woman from an economically poor background in the 1970s, educational and professional employment opportunities were very limited. This situation was compounded by the authoritarian military dictatorship. For those fighting against the dictatorship for a freer democratic society, one of the hopes was to improve the opportunities for young women like Anastasia.

Anastasia utilized the academic and political opportunities that Panteion University offered to advance her social mobility and improve her employment prospects. She saw that as her only way, commenting that "[my] passion for attending courses and for all the happenings that I got involved in at the university filled me with self-confidence and optimism for life. I knew very well that I did not have other ways—neither social mobility, nor professional opportunities—beyond my studies."

A third insight is that political activism can occur in both the public and private domains. Anastasia also challenged the cultural norms in her personal life. A personal political act was to choose her husband in a love match without family intervention or negotiations of a dowry. Greece was very culturally conservative when it came to the role of women. Anastasia had been exposed to and involved in exciting political activity at the university. Resisting an authoritarian and brutal dictatorship required courage on the part of activists. It was unlikely, then, that she would accept that her family would choose a husband for her.

Using Power to Make a Difference

Eleven of the WLE women mentioned power in their narratives. Sometimes a reference was to their use of power, sometimes a reference was to the utilization and sharing of power, and sometimes a reference was to the abuse of power by others. Helen Sobehart's narrative titled "Pondering Power—Line or Labyrinth" gives an account of how in her career she first spent time "gaining" power and, having gained it, finds herself reflecting on what do with it and asking herself the question, "Do I really want it?" Helen's story chronicles how she used personal, positional, and relational power to make a difference.

Helen C. Sobehart

 Dr. Helen Sobehart gained her Doctor of Arts (DA) degree from Carnegie-Mellon University in Pittsburgh, Pennsylvania. Helen is graduate education consultant at Point Park University, Pittsburgh. She has been executive director of ASSET, Inc. (Achieving Success in Science through Excellence in Teaching), also based in Pittsburgh. Immediately prior to those positions she served as president of Cardinal Stritch University in Milwaukee, Wisconsin.

In her journey through education to being one of only 25 percent of women who are presidents of universities in the United States, Helen has been a teacher aide, a director for the Pennsylvania education resource system, a classroom teacher and assistant superintendent, a superintendent (at the time one of only 14 percent of women), and a university professor at Duquesne University, where she was associate provost. As she traveled her career journey, Helen learned the importance of having a clear vision, the power of information, the importance of being strong, and how critical it is to look after yourself when you are acting to make a difference.

Catholicism and her Christian faith have been a central part of Helen's personal and professional life. Her career in education has spanned over forty years, much of it in the Catholic education system. Helen was born in the 1940s into a working-class Catholic family in the United States. She wrote,

> I grew up in a three-generation household owned by my grandparents who had emigrated from Croatia. My grandmother was a very stern person who demanded obedience from everyone in the house, even my grandfather who worked as a laborer at the Heinz company. Everyone called him the "gentle giant" because, though a big strong man, he was the kindest person I knew at the time, other than my father. (H. S., e-mail message to author, July 17, 2009)

As a child Helen lived in a working-class neighborhood where her father was the only college-educated person she knew. She was close to her father, who imparted his love of learning to his two daughters. It was from her father that she first began to understand power, she observed. "During our many talks my father would say 'Information really is power.' . . . He passed away when I was twenty-two but his words have guided my practice ever since. It was about learning. . . . It is about wisdom."

Helen achieved very well in school and gained a full-tuition scholarship at an all-girls Catholic high school. However, although achieving high grades was important to Helen, so was helping others. As a result she was also heavily involved in community activities that lowered her grade point average. When Sister, the vice principal, called Helen into her office to reprimand her, Helen talked back and did not let Sister take the power from her. This did not meet with approval, as Helen explains.

> She [Sister] berated me for not maintaining my status as first in the class, and suggested that I give up some of my extracurricular activities. I still vividly remember my heart pounding rapidly as I contemplated what to say. I had been raised to be respectful of, and even compliant to, adults, especially religious figures. A little voice in me said, "Say yes, it's the right thing to do." However, my real voice said, "If being involved with helping others comes at the expense of my being first in the class, so be it. My GPA is something of which my parents and

school can be proud, but my real strength is in helping others." Before I realized it, I was blurting these very words. Sister sat for a moment in amazement, then told me she was disappointed in me and asked me to leave.

Helen reflected on how difficult it is for girls to speak out. As a Catholic girl she had been socialized into how to behave appropriately. She found the explanation in Taylor, Gilligan, and Sullivan's (1995) *Between Voice and Silence: Women and Girls, Race and Relationship* helpful and wished she had understood it earlier. "One of the book's contributing psychologists, Carol Gilligan, describes how adolescent girls, once assured and resilient, sometimes silence or censor themselves in order to be accepted. . . . On the other side of the double-edged sword, when adolescent girls remain outspoken, it is often difficult for others to stay in relationships with them, leaving the girls to be excluded or labeled as troublemakers."

After high school Helen entered college, majoring for her undergraduate liberal arts degree in psychology and sociology. But like many young women of her generation, she dropped out to get married before the completion of her degree. Six months later she was pregnant, and she and her husband had bought a house. She took a job as a teacher's aide so that she could complete her degree over the summers. It was during this time that she realized "what a joy it was to help children learn, especially those for whom it was a challenge. I also powerfully learned, from a male administrator to whom I reported, that educational leadership is about making a positive difference in the lives of children."

Making a difference became the powerful guiding light in Helen's career. Although she thinks she stumbled into teaching and never had a planned career path, she did focus on making a difference and remained focused throughout her career. She prepared herself with credentials and certificates, masters and doctoral degrees. But she did these things because she loved to learn, something she learned from her father. She also wanted to keep her options open as she was facing marital difficulties. "I was not sure if I might have to eventually take care of myself and my children." So Helen was also being practical.

As she threw herself into each teaching position with passion and commitment, an even greater opportunity to make a difference emerged. She took up a staff development position as it "might allow me to influence even more children through the success of their teachers." The formal authority offered through an administrative position in special education showed Helen that as an assistant superintendent she could have an even more powerful impact. Helen understood that as she moved into positions with great authority, she gained greater power to change things and make a difference. She wrote, "I was able to redesign an entire instructional system to meet the needs of all students."

Helen's next career move was to take a superintendent's position so that she could then embed those changes throughout the whole school district. However, sometimes whether or not we make a difference is not readily evident, even to ourselves. Even though Helen has been the recipient of many awards, including the prestigious AASA Effie H. Jones Humanitarian Award that honors leadership in educational equity and excellence, she was questioning whether or not she had made any difference in the school district when two unexpected incidents occurred at a graduation she was attending. They illustrate how Helen had used the power invested in her superintendency to make a difference. Helen shared,

> [L]ike a miraculous gift, two things happened . . . at a reception prior to the graduation ceremony. I was approached by a female senior citizen who had a reputation for being one of the taxpayer naysayers. I expected the worst as she began to speak. She said, "You know, Dr. Sobehart, we haven't always seen eye to eye and you know that. However, I want you to know that even when we disagreed, I have admired and respected the way you have conducted yourself."

This incident reveals the effectiveness of Helen's relational power.

The second incident involved a student who Helen knew only slightly. The student gave Helen a letter to read after the graduation ceremony that came at the end of her public school career as a superintendent. The letter explained how Helen had been a role model, especially for the girls, and how she wished she would be there as a role model for her four younger sisters but understood why Helen needed to move on. Helen shared the ending of the letter. "Finally, she talked about why the male student council president had spoken on my behalf at a public board meeting (a gesture which I had previously assumed was prompted by the high school principal). She ended the letter by saying that students really understood what was going on and what I stood for, saying, 'If someone says it didn't turn out too pretty, remind them that the kids thought it was the prettiest time ever.'"

The above incident reveals that sometimes we make a difference without realizing it; unless someone else points it out, that difference may remain hidden. For Helen this incident underscored the importance of mentoring young women. She wrote, "We are mentoring and modeling all the time, even when we may not be aware. Even more critically, we are unconsciously modeling even in the most difficult situations." The unexpected and positive feedback Helen received from these two women confirmed that she really was making a difference.

Helen decided to move into higher education so that she could work with aspiring and practicing superintendents and influence even more school districts. She became a professor of educational leadership at Duquesne University in Pittsburgh. Hired to direct their doctoral program in educational leadership, Helen then became associate provost. On the wall in her university office, Helen had a large print of Michelangelo's painting of the *Creation of Adam*: "The excerpt shows only the hands of God and Adam in that critical and electric moment just before God's finger touched Adam's to give him life. Attached to the magnificence of that print, in the lower right-hand corner, is a very small pin which states, 'educators touch the future.'" Helen sees this as a powerful analogy for her work.

> Whether or not God closed up that small but incomprehensibly important space between his finger and Adam's made the difference of life to humanity. Whether or not we use the formal and informal skills of our leadership to close up the space of success or failure between ourselves and our students makes an incomprehensible difference in the lives of children—every single one of them.

Helen's success story is also a cautionary tale. As she strove to make a difference she became "Superwoman"; she had forgotten to "breathe" and became seriously ill. She was diagnosed with mononucleosis and hepatitis and was in isolation for three weeks in a hospital. She wanted to die, and she nearly did.

> My doctor and one of the nurses became informal counselors to me. They helped me to want to hang on just long enough, using my children as my motivation, to pursue more in-depth, professional counseling. I began to recover shortly after that. I promised myself that I would never allow myself to become that physically, mentally, or emotionally down again—and I never have. You can't make a difference for anyone if you're dead.

Helen started to "breathe" again and built into her life people and activities that nourished rather than drained. She now tries to live by the mantra—"If it's life enhancing, do more of it. If it's not life enhancing, do less of it. Just breathe."

In 2008 Helen was appointed as president of Cardinal Stritch University, the largest Franciscan University in North America, with 7,500 students. While the people with whom Helen worked at Cardinal Stritch were wonderful, it was not an easy time for Helen and her family. Taking up the appointment at Cardinal Stritch meant a move to Milwaukee. She wrote about that time, "I carry an ambivalent guilt and jealousy that I left not only my loved ones behind (with the exception of Joe my husband), but also left my support system of a few but treasured friends and confidants."

Other personal difficulties arose for Helen and her family, including being badly affected by the collapse of the financial markets in the United States. Her youngest son developed a very serious and rare illness, requiring ongoing and expensive treatment. Due to the recession he had been made redundant (let go) so was unable to afford the medication and a necessary operation.

Helen made the decision to resign from the presidency so that she could support her son through his medical treatment in Pittsburgh.

In the last part of her story, Helen reflects on power in the following words: "Power is not a straight line, nor a career trajectory. It is a labyrinth that takes us back and forth through the full range of human experience. There is not a prize in the middle. It is the experience of the journey, our need as humans to experience the agony and ecstasy and all in between as we try to use it in a useful way."

Helen was the founding chair of WLE and played an organizing role in both the Rome (Italy) and Augsburg (Germany) conferences. Influenced by Hildegard of Bingen, she chose "Sharing the Spirit, Fanning the Flame" as the theme for the first conference. She used the theme to forge the vision of the group and her contacts to bring together both well-established and new women scholars, many from developing economies. We each were drawn to the conference because of a passion for and commitment to leading for social justice. This group continues even though Helen is no longer so actively involved. The WLE group's ongoing existence is a fitting legacy of Helen's lifetime work—using her power and influence to make a difference. A tangible legacy is the book *Women Leading Education Across the Continents*, featuring research presented by the women who attended the first WLE conference in Rome (Sobehart 2009). Helen concludes the book's epilogue by urging readers to "believe that you are the passion that can transform the universe, or at least your piece of it, as a flame transforms ice and turns it into energy" (220).

Insights

Helen's narrative illustrates how formal and informal power can be put in action to make a difference. Her leadership had a strong moral purpose grounded in her Catholic faith. From an early age she clearly understood that she wanted to make a difference and showed a remarkable empathy for the marginalized and the oppressed. Helen understood important things that would help her in her life's work of making a difference. The first was to stay focused on the goal of making a difference; the second was the power of information; and the third was that the power invested in senior positions gave her the authority to act.

Helen suggests that although gaining formal senior positions is important, "[the] goal of making a difference for students must overlay all others, and women may be more adept at this." She cites Hill and Ragland's (1995) comment on why women seek career advancement—"reasons revolve around desires to achieve autonomy and to make a difference." (33). So in that respect, Helen's commitment to make a difference, to social justice leadership, is congruent with the research (Grogan and Shakeshaft 2011) and is particularly congruent with the stories of the other women featured in this book.

Taught by her father that "information really is power," Helen utilized this lesson to empower herself so that she could operate from an informed knowledge base. However, Helen cautions that power acquired through information/knowledge needs to be acquired legitimately. "Learning in the right way for the right reasons . . . a truly learned person attempts to understand through reading, discussion and observation." The information/knowledge Helen acquired through her learning had a twofold outcome. First, it meant she was personally empowered and confident, and second, it enabled her to acquire progressively more senior positions that were invested with the power that enabled her to act to make a difference. Helen's narrative also illustrates how understanding power is essential to activating power to "do good."

Helen's story also conveys how leading to make a difference can be exhausting work and underlines the importance of self-care. Helen worked herself to the point of collapse and near death. The research suggests that women's social justice leadership is imbued with an ethic of care (Strachan 1999). When the ethic of care is coupled with the considerable demands of senior leadership positions, for example, long hours and high stress levels, a woman leader's well-being can suffer. Work/life balance can be difficult to achieve when a leader is very committed to making a difference, letting other people's needs come first. Helen had to learn to "breathe" and to take care of herself.

ACTIONS DEFINE SOCIAL JUSTICE LEADERSHIP: SELECTED SCHOLARSHIP

In the lines that open this chapter, Rapp (2002) reminds us of actions informing our social justice leadership theories. Rapp is not alone in highlighting action as being central to social justice leadership. The literature on social justice leadership points to "change," to "transformation," to "resistance," to "pursuing" social justice, and to "making a difference": all require action. As the saying goes, "If you always do what you have always done you will always get what you have always gotten" (Anon, n.d.).

The literature that helps illuminate the social justice actions of Jane, Anastasia, and Helen points to a strong moral and ethical purpose informed by a belief in fairness and justice. The moral and ethical purpose of Jane's activism was informed by her feminism. Feminism is an "epistemological and political movement" (Blackmore 2009, 73) that is exercised at the organizational and individual levels. Neville and Hamer (2006), in their explanation of why a group of black women feminists became activists, point to two driving forces—difficult personal experiences and the political climate. "Most women activists discuss the role of their life circumstances in shaping their political consciousness and subsequent actions. Growing up black, poor or working class informed a number of women's experiences" (7). Women with wide experiences and backgrounds can be passionate about and committed to taking action.

Making a difference is the underpinning driving force of feminist educational leadership. While not all WLE members publicly identify as feminist—indeed, in some culturally conservative countries it is not safe to do so (Strachan et al. 2010)—the actions of the WLE leaders are feminist in spirit. Although feminism had its roots in challenging the oppression of women and girls, it now has a broader agenda that includes other oppressed and marginalized groups such as indigenous, gay, bisexual, transgender, and special needs peoples (Strachan 1999).

The actions of social justice leadership are carried out in many contexts and on a wide stage within and outside of education. In the school setting, action to improve students' life choices and chances may focus on the academic achievement of students as well as the lives of students beyond the school walls. For example, Shields (2004) exhorts, "I believe firmly that social justice and academic excellence must not be seen as competing goals; but they must go hand in hand. . . . Academic success must be for all students" (9). That is, taking action to improve academic achievement is a social justice action, especially in the lives of students who are not achieving well. Similarly, principals in Theoharis's (2007) study "enacted social justice in their schools by raising student achievement" (232).

Other social justice leaders believe that actions must first address social issues, such as poverty and family violence, that have an impact on achievement. Strachan (1998) shares the story of Jill, a high-school principal in New Zealand. The social justice values of feminism guided the actions she took to support "at-risk" students in her school. She appointed a social worker, a counselor, a youth worker, and two part-time medical practitioners. "Jill believed that unless the school dealt with these issues in young people's lives, then learning would be very difficult" (Strachan 1998, 29).

Social justice leadership is not just confined to changing individual practices and attitudes (Lumby and Coleman 2007). Change at the organizational level is a priority of leaders for social justice, often in a climate of resistance (Theoharis 2007). Another priority of educational leaders for social justice is change on the wider political stage. According to McLaren (1997, cited in Rapp 2002, 227), social justice educational leaders are "dedicated to reconstituting the deep structures of political economy, culture and power." Changes to organizational structures and practices are needed to make a difference (Rapp 2002).

Lumby and Coleman (2007) present three different discourses/frameworks around taking social justice action. They are specifically referring to diversity issues, but their ideas have relevance for the wider social justice stage. The first discourse is linked to "liberal and critical approaches": "liberal approaches focus on equal opportunities . . . respect for the individual" (98). The critical approaches "give us fresh understanding and point to areas of privilege and inequity that might otherwise go unnoticed" (98). They counsel that, although useful, the liberal discourse does not challenge the status quo, and the critical discourse might tell us what is wrong—but not how to fix it.

The next discourse/framework is "legislation." "Legislation regulates issues of equality and discrimination" (Lumby and Coleman 2007, 99). Leaders have to operate within a legal framework and obey the law or suffer the consequences. For example, appointment committees in many countries are not allowed to discriminate on the grounds of gender, race, religion, and other factors. The final discourse/framework is "institutional policies." Policies guide how institutions should operate in respect to meeting their legal obligations, for example, equal opportunities legislation (Lumby and Coleman 2007). It is unlikely that any one approach will in itself be sufficient.

The moral and ethical purposes of Helen's activism were embedded in her strong Catholic faith. The literature suggests that educational leaders for social justice have particular dispositions: "For Catholic school leaders, the language of Catholic social teaching creates a lexicon for the spiritual dimensions of their leadership . . . that are impacted by personal beliefs and meaning" (Scanlan 2011, 310–11).

Power and its place and practice in leadership has been the subject of a great deal of scholarship, particularly as it relates to women and educational leadership. The literature suggests that women use power to make a difference and enable goals to be accomplished by leading "with and through others" (Grogan and Shakeshaft 2011, 6). This indicates that "women conceptualize power differently and are likely to seek to expand everyone's power. This approach has considerable impact on organizational behavior and change" (Grogan and Shakeshaft 2011, 7). In making a difference, Helen was aware of relational power and the importance of using that in moral and ethical ways.

Although the stories in this chapter tell of actions to make a difference by three individual women, history teaches us that collective action can also be a powerful force for change. The moral and ethical purposes of Anastasia's activism were originally, but not solely, informed by the poverty of her childhood and the political climate in Greece during the dictatorship years. Throughout history, oppressive regimes have been a catalyst for resistance: history provides many examples, most recently the 2011 Arab Spring and the overthrow and death of Gadhafi in Libya, as well as other uprisings against dictators.

The three women in this chapter faced resistance to their activism. The scholarship on resistance focuses on how the actions of social justice leaders challenge and are resistant to injustices, such as illustrated in Anastasia's political activism. The focus is also on the resistance of others to actions designed to "make a difference" that will "disrupt traditional norms" (Theoharis 2007,

238). Another focus is the effect that resistance has on the activist. All have relevance for this chapter.

Resistance to change has been well researched. For example, Williamson and Blackburn (2010, abstract) suggest that "no change is successful if the people being asked to change don't see its need." Other change literature focuses on how to overcome resistance (Goldberg and Dent 1999) and, for example, being clear about the goals and objectives of the change (Williamson and Blackburn 2010). However, educational leaders can experience profound consequences from their actions to change practices that are unjust and/or discriminatory. Theoharis's (2007) study of resistance to social justice leadership identified serious physical and emotional consequences that took "a great personal toll" and resulted in "a persistent sense of discouragement" (242).

CONCLUDING THOUGHTS

So how do the stories of Jane Strachan, Anastasia Athanasoula-Reppa, and Helen Sobehart help us to move forward in our understanding and theorizing of how actions define social justice leadership? It is important to acknowledge that culture plays a role in deciding which stories we narrate.

> Each culture contains several options for narrating life, some more dominant and others marginal. When people narrate their identity stories, they use culture as a tool kit (Swidler, 1986), that is, select, mold, and edit cultural meanings into their stories. (Lieblich, Zilber, and Tuval-Mashiach 2008, 614)

The stories Jane, Anastasia, and Helen have shared have been filtered through their own particular cultural lenses, and that filtering impacts what we "see" and interpret as illustrated from their stories.

However, there are givens that seem to operate to some extent across cultures. Without action, there is no social justice leadership; social justice leadership is by definition action. The actions of social justice leaders are strongly informed by the ethical and moral principles of fairness and justice. If these principles are not present, then it is not social justice leadership. Social justice leadership is put in action by people from widely differing backgrounds and in widely differing contexts. No one type of person or one group of people has a stronger claim to social justice leadership than any other person or group of people.

The personal toll of social justice leadership is evident in the stories of the three women featured in this chapter. Jane experienced burnout as a result of her work with abuse victims; Anastasia was discouraged by the patriarchal structures of her academic workplace; and Helen became seriously ill. However, despite the personal toll, they each persisted in their social justice activism. Educational leaders for social justice don't give up.

Helen reminds us about the story of the child on a beach, endlessly throwing starfish back into the sea. "A passerby tries to belittle the youngster by saying, 'Why do you waste your time standing there trying to throw starfish back into the sea when there are so many thousands? You will never be able to save them all, so what difference does it make?' The youngster replies, as she powerfully tosses another starfish into the safety of the water, 'It made a difference to this one!'" The youngster on the beach didn't give up, she wasn't discouraged, and she persisted despite resistance—as did Jane, Anastasia, and Helen.

9

AN INVITATION

Stories differ from advice in that, once you get them, they become a fabric of your whole soul.

—Alice Walker, in an interview about her work in
Common Boundary, 1990

For social justice leaders, the way always leads on because the work is by definition unfinished. There will be twists in the road as new issues arise and claim our attention. Neither the paths nor the outcomes of social justice leadership are predictable, only the need. WLE members are committed to this work as we stated in the opening chapter because we believe as Coleman (2005) does, that "the voices of women and minorities will lead to greater social justice in the vital field of education and an enrichment of the practice and theory of educational leadership" (18). Grogan and Shakeshaft (2011) identify leadership for social justice as an approach to leadership characteristic of large numbers of women leaders. What we do matters locally and globally.

As Jill Blackmore (1999, 5), a member of the WLE group, so clearly articulates, "One is rarely encouraged to ask: leading to what end and for whom—for the national interest, for individual students, for social justice in a democratic society?" We would add "for the world" to the list. Advancing social justice in the world is the underlying purpose we bring to our work. As a human species, across the continents we are faced with multiple adaptive challenges (Heifetz 1994) for which there are no easy answers.

We end not with conclusions as we bring the book to a close, but instead with an invitation to action. We review insights embedded in the chapters, consider the concept of untold stories, highlight what is unique in this book, and invite readers to join in shaping new possibilities for social justice leadership, to consider how defining social justice leadership through actions might fit with existing professional commitments.

SUMMARY OF MAJOR INSIGHTS

Insights exist at several levels. One level is as an ability to perceive something clearly or deeply. A second meaning refers to a penetrating and often sudden understanding, as of a complex situation or problem—those "aha" moments (McLeod 1987). In the "Insights" sections following each woman's story we focused on making observations and interpreting practices that would build understanding of present situations and contribute to new visions of opportunities for social justice leadership. We have emphasized how shaping social justice leadership has the potential to reshape ourselves as well as educational institutions. The practical and conceptual insights developed in each chapter are associated with particular stories and the central themes. Even though we offer major insights chapter by chapter and story by story, they interlace and coexist in many of the individual WLE narratives.

Chapter 2 compared cultural contexts and focused on how our challenges reveal and open the pathways of our lives. The following major insights represent understandings suggested in the five stories, individually and collectively:

- "Embracing difference" may mean confronting and rewriting the cultural script of what is acceptable for women. Embracing difference can lead to personal transformation, a previously unimagined career, and finding a new self.—*Angeliki Lazaridou, Greece*
- "Balancing expectations," particularly if one is a mother, is a concern that persists. Every story touched on this worldwide dilemma of conflicting claims on women's time and energy. Women deserve to have both meaningful work and fulfilling relationships. Somehow we find a way.—*Esther Sui-chu Ho, Hong Kong-China*
- "Finding the way" involves individual life decisions that are influenced by cultural ideas about a woman's place. Finding the way does not require a path, but many times requires a metaphorical and a literal leaving home.—*Linda L. Lyman, United States*
- "Weaving the threads" of a life can twist negative experiences into positive ones. A strengthened fabric supports commitment to living by compassion and other social justice principles. Mentors can make a world of difference by helping girls and women from lower-income families through the passages of accessing education and developing careers.—*Katherine Cumings Mansfield, United States*
- "Pursuing excellence" is not a path reserved for the privileged. Growing up poor need not deter the drive to excel. The powerful influences of family support and intrinsic motivation should never be underestimated.—*Jacqueline Oram-Sterling, Jamaica*

Chapter 3 centers on why women are motivated to undertake social justice leadership, the imperatives for doing so. The three stories featured in the chapter raise our awareness of the unfairness of discrimination, the devastation of sexual violence, and the transformative power of education. Insights into practices of social justice leadership that develop from these factors are described:

- "Discrimination"—Experiencing gender, race, and class-based discrimination can lead to a life's work based on combating and reducing such discrimination. Leaders wounded by discrimination can turn the experience of discrimination into a powerful motivation for doing a world of good.—*Rosangela Malachias, Brazil*
- "Violence"—Undoing the stigma and damage of sexual abuse can take a lifetime. As we shape social justice leadership, preventing sexual abuse must be a priority. Educators should be trained to look for the subtle as well as more obvious signs of abuse and be vigilant in finding help for any child or person so victimized.—*Charol Shakeshaft, United States*
- "Education"—Formal and informal education about injustices when combined with political awareness can lead to powerful advocacy for human rights. A life of privilege does not preclude a lifelong commitment to speaking out about a wide range of social justice issues both local and global.—*Saeeda Shah, Pakistan*

Chapter 4 focuses on values and explores ways to respond through actions to the question "What is leadership *for?*" Values related to the moral purpose of leadership are inherent in social justice leadership. The stories in the chapter feature clusters of values that create larger circles of life and service. Practical insights suggest the importance of clarifying and living one's values.

- "Extending humanitarianism" means serving others in a way that has the ripple effect of opening new possibilities, helping people to possess a larger view of the world, creating openness to change. A passion to heal the world, when combined with active compassion for others, can lead to bold social justice leadership. We work as educators to help others find their gifts.—*Elizabeth C. Reilly, United States*
- New worlds of learning create "expanding circles of concern" and influence. An initial awakening to injustice, strong moral principles, and integrity can lead to prominent organizational leadership roles, with the opportunity to actualize values of caring and justice on a broad scale. Commitment to promoting the rights of others creates a purposeful life.—*Alice Merab Kagoda, Uganda*
- "Developing cosmopolitan consciousness" results from openness to new worldviews, experiences, and ways of thinking. Values evolve as personal

identity develops through turning points, deliberate, purposeful career choices, and chance encounters. Self-transcending values associated with a cosmopolitan perspective include productivity, care, and justice. —*Marianne Coleman, United Kingdom*

Chapter 5 develops a deeper understanding of skillful authentic leadership by examining how such leadership develops, identifying skills of practice, and exploring underlying purpose. Insights for growing in authenticity as a leader include:

- "Growing into authenticity"—Character formation is influenced by others who support and inspire us, as well as by the practice of introspection. Family, community, and mentors can encourage the individual uniqueness that develops into authenticity. In finding one's voice, the capacity for powerful spiritual leadership in the service of social justice is cultivated.—*Sister Hellen Bandiho, Tanzania*
- "Developing *phronesis* (practical wisdom)" includes introspection or knowing oneself, a strong moral inclination, acknowledging people, and working with others toward common goals. This combination of skills and values provides for authentic leadership of learning.—*Pamela Lenz, United States*
- "Leading for *eudaimonia* (well-being)" happens when one becomes more fully conscious of the personal meaning of leading, practices balanced leadership, hears and is influenced by the stories within stories, and engages in stimulating work that leads to attaining wellness or well-being. The work of such a leader is life enhancing for everyone involved. —*Rachel McNae, New Zealand*

Chapter 6 introduces qualities of resilience required by the unfinished risky business of social justice leadership. Multiple insights in the chapter stories are associated with courage, perseverance, and speaking out.

- "Courage" gives a leader the strength to struggle through devastating adversity to the reintegration and growth such experience makes possible. Realistic optimism, strong values, and spiritual grounding lead toward resilient reintegration. Strong, caring mentors are invaluable guides. —*Diane Reed, United States*
- "Perseverance"—Social justice causes and concerns will remain ongoing, we may feel powerless against overwhelming odds, but we persevere anyway knowing that we will be transformed by the struggle.—*Panpim Cheaupalakit, Thailand*

- "Speaking out"—Deep injustices in the educational, economic, and political systems lead us to claim a voice and use it to speak out. We have been too long silenced by the power of discourses in institutions we did not create. We see and advocate for our right to be heard, to have an influence with regard to the larger justice issues of our day as we work to make educational systems more equitable.—*Joyce Wilson-Tagoe, Ghana*

Chapter 7 illustrates three pathways that recurred in the narratives of social justice work in the world: activism, mentoring, and scholarship. A life may involve various interactions among these pathways, but for most of the women one path or another predominated.

- "Activism," informed by strong values, beliefs, feelings, and emotions, is at the heart of social justice work. Key political events can lead one to activism, which may involve the deep emotional work of realizing and overcoming internalized oppression. Activism is transformative social justice work that can transform individuals and society by healing the hurt.—*Vanita Richard, South Africa*
- "Mentoring"—which can be formal or informal—supports women's efforts to advance equality. It is a dyadic form of relational leadership, and a pathway of complexity and power. Mentoring needs of women differ between developed and developing countries. Experiencing the discrimination against women in developing countries can lead a person to a mentoring pathway.—*Jill Sperandio, United Kingdom/United States*
- "Scholarship"—Through education, formal or informal, many women awaken to the reality of oppression and develop feminist perspectives that lead to scholarly research and writing. Such scholarship can focus on women and educational leadership, gender equity, and diversity issues, to name only a few strands. Scholarship that makes discrimination and injustice visible is a powerful form of advocacy for equity.—*Margaret Grogan, United States/Australia*

Chapter 8 focuses on how the featured leaders are defining social justice through their actions. Practical insights from the stories highlight doing feminism, political activism, and using power to make a difference.

- "Doing feminism"—Feminism can be a powerful motivating force for social justice leadership. Feminist leadership builds on a foundation of moral purpose and speaking out to improve the lives of the oppressed and marginalized at both individual and institutional levels. Feminist leadership by women from a wide range of economic levels is manifested in courageous actions to advance justice.—*Jane Strachan, New Zealand*

- "Political activism"—Serendipity or chance can have a determining effect on women's career decisions. Having a high self-concept is also a factor. Political activism can take place in the private sphere as well as in the public domain. Being at the "right" place at the "right" time and meeting the "right" people can motivate commitment to actions of social justice leadership. Poverty can also be a motivating factor.—*Anastasia Athanasoula-Reppa, Greece*
- "Using power to make a difference"—Information gives women power when combined with moral purpose and a passion to eliminate injustice. Power, however, can be a mixed blessing. An ethic of care must include care for oneself, taking time to breathe. Power is a labyrinth . . . with no prize in the middle. The "prize" of power is always the difference we make in the lives of others.—*Helen C. Sobehart, United States*

This summary reviews some of the insights that can be gleaned from the stories. However, the most important insights are those that come to readers engaged in their own reflections.

LISTENING FOR UNTOLD STORIES

Why have we addressed social justice leadership by telling these stories? One answer is Polkinghorne's (1988), that "people conceive of themselves in terms of stories" (105). We are the stories we have to tell. Yet Nigerian novelist Adichie (2009) asks whether any single story is ever the whole story. Her important reminder is that "our lives, our cultures, are composed of many overlapping stories." She warns that if we hear only a single story about another person or country, we risk "a critical misunderstanding." Each featured WLE member composed a narrative of her personal and professional journey in response to an invitation to submit her story "in whatever format and with whatever emphasis made sense and was comfortable for the individual." In doing so, she was asked to respond to the research question developed at the first WLE conference: "How have the lived experiences of conference participants influenced your life and professional/leadership decisions?"

The stories presented in the book have passed through several filters. First, each author shaped what she presented from influences of her life on her professional/leadership decisions. These interpretations were filtered through her cultural eyes, as noted in the previous chapter. Next, as book authors with limited space, we shaped what we presented from each original narrative, inserting a second filter between the actual lived experiences and the reader. Finally, each reader's interpretation of personally meaningful insights from the stories adds a third filter to the layers of meaning.

In a planning session at the 2009 Augsburg conference, many participants brought up and were enthusiastic about including "the stories we cannot tell" in the book. So in addition to the narratives, we invited WLE members to submit for the book those instructive stories they could not tell for whatever reason but that had been critical to their journeys in some way. We suggested short vignettes, promising to report these experiences generally and anonymously and not to circulate them on the listserv. Many indicated that they would write vignettes, but only two persons actually submitted anything in response. Although in any life many stories remain untold and members seemed eager to have such stories in the book, perhaps these are stories we are simply not ready to tell.

Some aspects of personal and professional journeys are too personally sensitive to put in writing. Their telling would cause pain or hurt for someone we know and love. Other things that have happened to us could still have political or other sorts of repercussions, and so we protect ourselves and others by keeping those stories out of our narratives. We bring up "listening for untold stories" in this final chapter as a reminder that any individual's story is more complex than can be captured in words at any point in time, that no one has just a single story. More importantly, moving forward, we have the opportunity to remake ourselves, to continually evolve, to live into new stories.

UNIQUE CONTRIBUTIONS OF THE BOOK

As stated in the opening chapter, the uniqueness of the book comes from its international scope and the power of personal narratives to both inform and inspire. The book reinforces several understandings in the literature about women's leadership and social justice leadership. It is unique in reflecting views of women whose ages range from the thirties to the seventies, representing fourteen different countries, both developed and developing. The book is new in presenting a panorama of social justice leadership practices by women leaders around the globe. It offers not tables and graphs of such practices, but rich narrative detail with the power to inspire. While several scholars have observed that social justice leadership is defined by actions (e.g., Bogotch 2002; Rapp 2002), this is the first book-length treatment of the perspective.

Narratives Are Richly Compelling

In writing this book we have chosen to lead with the stories, using as much language from the original narratives as possible. Hearing people speak in their own voices and cadences is always powerful. As explained in the first chapter, the invitation to submit a narrative was made with minimal specificity, that is, "in whatever format and with whatever emphasis made sense and was comfortable for the individual." This open-ended call encouraged participants to shape their narratives in ways they wanted as opposed to responding to preset questions. This openness contributed complexity to analysis of the narratives but added much richness to what was learned. The images, metaphors, and word pictures of real stories authentically shared can become part of the fabric of your soul in ways that more standardized data cannot. The book does not offer advice; it offers the wisdom of practice through stories.

Perspectives Are Intergenerational and International

The reader can see how the opportunities for women have changed—and not changed—with the successes of the women's movement and the turning of the new century. The book features experiences of women who grew up before maternity leaves and child care were available and women whose careers have benefited from these arrangements. We have presented reflections of women retired and on the brink of retirement as well as women who are just launching or developing their careers while actively parenting children and teenagers.

The WLE members featured are concerned not just with their own communities, but also focus globally wherever they are from in the world. Perhaps this is a reflection of an underlying level of comfort with international settings. It also reflects an understanding of the effects of globalization on our countries and the children and youth of the world. We represent both Western and non-Western countries at various levels of development. Lists of developing countries considered to have a low level of material well-being include Uganda, Tanzania, Ghana, Jamaica, and Pakistan (http://en.wikipedia.org/wiki/Developing_country, accessed 11/11/11). Brazil, South Africa, and Thailand were added to the list of newly industrialized countries (NIC) in 2011. The NIC category is a socioeconomic classification meaning the economy has not yet reached first-world status but has outpaced other developing counterparts (http://en.wikipedia.org/wiki/Newly_industrialized_country, accessed October 27, 2011).

A variety of international experiences reported in stories of seventeen leaders suggests them to be persons with a global view that predates participation in the WLE group. Their experiences range in complexity from international travel to being born in one country yet growing up or choosing to live in another. Still a citizen of the United Kingdom, Jill Sperandio (chapter 7) is now a resident of the United States. Margaret Grogan (chapter 7) has dual citizenship in Australia, where she was born, and the United States, where she now lives. Marianne Coleman (chapter 4) spent her senior year in high school in the United States. A total of seven left their countries to earn doctoral degrees. These include three who earned the degrees in Canada: Angeliki Lazaridou and Esther Sui-chu Ho (chapter 2), and Alice Merab Kagoda (chapter 4). Three others came to the United States: Jacqueline Oram-Sterling (chapter 2), Sister Hellen Bandiho (chapter 5), and Panpim Cheaupalakit (chapter 6). Saeeda Shah (chapter 3) earned her PhD in the United Kingdom.

These prior international experiences and the sharing at WLE conferences of our current research projects have sensitized WLE members to cultural diversity and given us the opportunity to acquire firsthand knowledge of the status of women and girls around the world. Experiences and research in countries other than our own have given us knowledge of the variety of culturally based institutional and educational practices that can contribute to either marginalizing women or supporting them.

Combining Professional and Personal Social Justice Work

During the process of analyzing data for the book, we noticed that some persons commented on social justice work that was not directly related to professional responsibilities. Many of these details have been embedded in the narratives as appropriate. In order to fill out the picture of personal-life social justice endeavors, we sent an e-mail asking participants to look outside their professional commitments and share social justice work from their personal lives. A total of fifteen replied, describing work with causes such as antiracism, domestic violence, supporting immigrants, church outreach projects, interfaith dialogue, advocacy organizations like the American Civil Liberties Union (ACLU), and mentoring—to name only a few.

To give a few examples, Katherine Cumings Mansfield (chapter 2) reported that she tried to live her social justice beliefs on a personal level as well as the professional level. Among other things, she listed activities since the age of sixteen at her church, including visitation of elderly persons and food bank work. Elizabeth Reilly (chapter 4) has been committed to the social cause of protecting women against domestic violence since college. She is a state-certified violence prevention advocate who has worked at women's shelters, run domestic violence support groups, and volunteered on twenty-four-hour hotlines. Anastasia Athanasoula-Reppa (chapter 8) has helped support immigrant women in Greece, especially women from Albania. Saeeda Shah (chapter 3) has worked through UK-based charities to support Asian immigrant communities in the United Kingdom.

Some of those who replied indicated that there was no separation between their personal and professional lives. This fusion contributes to establishing the authenticity of their social justice commitments. For example, Charol Shakeshaft (chapter 3), in addition to antiracism work, added, "I consider my major social justice advocacy work to be my research." Marianne Coleman (chapter 4) wrote, "I am committed to social justice and feel that this principle informs my life." Margaret Grogan (chapter 7) explained, "I don't have much of a personal life at the moment! I do however focus all my energies in my professional life on social justice issues." We suspect that other women who did not reply to the request for more information may fall in this category also—that their personal and professional lives are to a great extent intertwined. The values that incline them to social justice leadership are not values that are turned off when work ends but that permeate their whole lives as they use their skills to make a difference on multiple levels.

Actions Define Social Justice Leadership

We have moved away from theoretical arguments about how to define social justice to instead showing what it looks like in action, letting the actions speak for themselves. How have we viewed the connections between theoretical understandings of social justice leadership and everyday practices? Definitions are not inconsequential. In Lambert's (2003) deceptively simple words, "How we define leadership frames how people will participate in it" (4). We contend that our definitions of social justice leadership both shape and are expressed through our actions. Stories in the book illustrate that we are interested in a wide range of justice issues, including gender, class, race, poverty, ethnicity, religion, sexual orientation, and human rights.

We define social justice leadership actions broadly. Some feel affinity with Rapp's (2002) phrasing that "leaders for social justice . . . resist, dissent, rebel, subvert, possess oppositional imaginations, and are committed to transforming oppressive and exploitative social relations in and out of schools" (226). Others among us are more inclined to quote Noddings (2005), who states that social justice consists of "rights we demand for ourselves that should be offered to others worldwide" (8).

Christie (2010) specifically addresses complexities associated with the right to an education, reminding us of the way still left to travel:

> Since the adoption of the United Nations Universal Declaration on Human Rights (1948), it has become commonplace to talk of education as a basic human right, and to regard it as self-evident that the countries of the world are progressively moving towards this. . . . Yet, whether framed as rights, as goals and targets, or as capabilities, the fact remains that basic education lies beyond the reach of millions of people across the world. (3)

We believe social justice leadership, nevertheless, implies a commitment to rights in spite of the paradox that "rights do not necessarily deliver what they appear to promise" (3). Christie also reinforces how gender still complicates claiming rights, something illustrated over and over again in the WLE stories. She believes that "cultural beliefs and practices may mitigate against rights to equality or protection against discrimination. This is particularly evident in the case of gender" (8).

We acknowledge the difficulty of defining social justice in terms of either equity or equality. Maiztegui-Oñate and Santibáñez-Gruber (2008) cautioned that "when people begin to speak of equity instead of equality, they enter a potential minefield and can find themselves 'under suspicion.' . . . Equity includes, but also transcends, different forms of equality. Equity refers to the concept of justice, which formal equality does not necessarily include" (375). Many of us regard our social justice leadership to be in the service of equity. Ultimately, however, we authors concur with the school of thought represented by Bogotch (2002), who states that "there can be no fixed or predictable meanings of social justice prior to actually engaging in educational leadership practices" (153). We emphasize, as stated in the previous chapter, that our actions are always the real story and the realization of our motivation and values.

NEW POSSIBILITIES

We have metaphorically left home in our public-sphere work to increase gender equity for women in educational leadership. We are about the work of change. As Blackmore (2002) argues, "Women are seen to be more flexible and to cope with change better than their male colleagues. . . . Their power is derived from their difference, their capacities as women to facilitate change" (59). Our previous and current administrative experiences also have given us insights into how to bring about change.

Our marginalized status as outsiders gives us less interest and investment in preserving the status quo. Educational leaders who know how to oppose the status quo can be effective in the ongoing transformation of educational institutions. Having left home and explored new worlds, we are about the redefining of leadership because "past understandings of leadership from a paradigm of power and dominance are not equal to the challenges of today and in fact have contributed to the challenges of today" (Lyman et al. 2005, 143). In their new book about collective leadership, Grogan and Shakeshaft (2011) express clearly that "new directions emerge as outsiders—voices from the margins—make decisions" (3).

The passages of our lives are associated with periods of change. We choose whether that change moves us in a positive direction or stifles growth. Referring to change, Bateson (1989) ends *Composing a Life* with this image: "The compositions we create in these times of change are filled with interlocking messages of our commitments and decisions. Each one is a message of possibility" (241). But how do we move from a message of possibility to the possibility of a more socially just global reality? One answer is that "we must learn to move from a monocentric modernist lens to be able to dance between worlds, to see reality differently, to lead differently. We must move beyond dualistic thinking, one expression of which is gender inequity" (Lyman et al. 2005, 199). We invite readers to respond to the insights of the book by being open to chance and acting courageously for change. We choose to believe that we are the right leaders in the right place at the right time. Courage is perhaps the major virtue, given the difficulty of changing hearts, minds, and behaviors.

We have been composing our lives by varying the pace and tone of the various movements as inspiration, serendipity, and moral purpose call us to new melodies. We can attune our ears to more than one harmony, more than one scale. We can listen for resonant chords. We can create the music of today. We are still lives in process. Just as there are silent, "no applause" separations between movements in symphonies, there are times in our lives when we cannot hear the music, do not know whether we are being heard. We need one another. Consider this book your invitation to join in creating new possibilities. As Grogan and Shakeshaft (2011) emphatically declare, "The new work of organizational leadership is *to form a diverse collective*. This includes hearing ideas from across the globe" (3).

Our decisions as leaders matter to the growth of opportunities for the girls and women of the world to compose their own futures. Our work as leaders in education can increase social justice for all persons who are marginalized by educational institutions. Our passages, commitments, and decisions create messages of possibility. Albeit perhaps unknowingly, we have been on a pilgrimage we are called to continue, making a difference by shaping social justice leadership in places all over the world. Wherever we may arrive, we shift the shape of social justice leadership just by being on the way, together.

AFTERWORD

Embracing the Flower and the Thorn

Though I am privileged to personally know the women whose stories flow through this book, like life-giving blood flows through the heart, having read through them again, I am more convinced than ever that self-narratives uniquely contribute to scholarly understanding. As the authors of chapter 5 observed, our narrators embrace, in one heartbeat, both the flowers and thorns of their lives. My own heart is full of emotions—I am sad, joyful, grateful, and full of renewed energy for the future. Why are these feelings stirred in the soul of a sixty-four-year-old woman who dedicated her own life to these issues yet has learned so much more by reflecting on the lessons these stories teach?

I am *sad* because of the thorns that hurt these pioneers, physically and emotionally, often just because those with power could do so. Though you have read the stories in their entirety, I describe some pieces below, not only as a reminder, but also to illuminate commonalities. Our authors have rightly emphasized that culture and context matter. Yet by collecting some "thorns," masking reference to name or country, one can understand that discrimination transcends lands and time. It will be challenging, I think, to remember each source.

- At age seven, she walked seven miles every day to school to arrive by 7:30 a.m. and then leave at 4:30 p.m. to return home for household chores.
- Being a young mother made her feel alienated from the women's movement since the message said it was impossible to reconcile being a wife with being a real feminist.
- She is aware and happy about her blackness but learned to live in a family, learned to be alone. Most of the black women who have higher education are single. It is not an option. It is their reality.
- Male violence toward women could not be as epidemic as it is without the cooperation of the entire social system—the press, police, courts, legislatures, academia, agencies, and so on.

- Her transparencies to defend her PhD proposal were hidden by her male colleagues the evening before the defense. They did not want to see a woman finishing earlier than them.
- Sometimes she tries so hard to be validated as a talented fisher that the experience of fishing becomes lost in her efforts. She no longer hears the trickle of the stream.
- Despite her own professional success, her family decided she should move to another country where her husband was.
- Her internal assessor rejected parts of her thesis. Though she rewrote and submitted, the thesis vanished for two years, resurfacing after she threatened to sue the university.
- She walked five miles to a prefabricated school containing asbestos. Subconsciously she grew to accept her subordinate position whether she admitted it consciously or not.
- She saw how hard they worked and how they were subject to cultural customs such as genital mutilation, early marriage into polygamist relationships, and domestic violence.
- It is possible for a woman to give too much of herself away and find "herself" lost.
- She became extremely ill physically, trying to balance everything, almost to the point of death, and she didn't care.
- She was sexually abused at the age of three and other times after that by family members and others.

Unfortunately, thorns of discrimination can grow anywhere.

Yet I am *joyful* because these leaders have created living "flowers" from the thorns they were handed. The positive spirit emerges from each page like the fragrance that floats from a garden. Again, here are some examples.

- Her anger served a purpose. It helped her survive an isolated and unsupported childhood. It fueled her commitment to change the world for women and girls.
- Observing her privileged family extend advice and help gave her an understanding of the meaning and importance of knowledge and compassion.
- She hopes that she is a person who leads by listening to others, one who seeks to make a difference in the world by seizing challenge without sacrificing relationships, one who accepts unconditionally.
- It's as if the Divine Seamstress grabbed whatever materials were on hand at the moment, but the quilt is hers. It is the only thing that she truly owns—herself. She uses it for good.

- The more challenges she faced, the more determined she became in her work. Her concern for people and communities found expression in her writing.
- When she became a mother, she quit teaching for a time, working for a church for two years as a women's worker and seeing the reality of discrimination. She works for women's causes.
- She started a scholarship for women who lack the resources to continue their education.
- Though her father was strict, she learned patience and how to talk through a problem and find solutions to it. She uses this in her work for improvement.
- She used scholarship to advance social justice, publishing five books, twenty-five book chapters, and seventeen refereed articles.
- She observed that we are mentoring and modeling all the time, even when we may not be aware. Even in the most difficult situations we touch the future.
- Another key part of her life is being a grandmother and helping to raise grandchildren who, like her two sons, have strong social consciences.
- Like her, the students who fought against unjust government actions went on to be exceptional scientists, journalists, politicians, ambassadors of state, and public servants.
- Early years resembled the halls of hell; the work was daunting. Yet she found a stimulating environment that helped her imagine the art of *possibility*.
- She said that we may not always like nor agree with the questions and the answers and we may not even see them clearly, but we have the opportunity to learn.
- Her requirement to work at home as a child enhanced her self-efficacy.

Fortunately, the fragrance of flowers also travels everywhere.

Hopefully, the small sampling above conveys why I feel *grateful*—grateful that my colleagues chose to write their narratives. The authors of this book have described why "story" is important. It contributes to scholarship, personal growth, awareness, and mentoring. It remains faithful to an original WLE goal—to illuminate the status of women in educational leadership both quantitatively and qualitatively. It paints a picture of what social justice looks like in action, adds to the collective voice we call culture, gives voice to the silenced, passes on meaning, and transcends the spirit. These are valuable reasons. However, a recent news article made clear one of the most important reasons of all—that what has gone before should not be forgotten. Dr. Jackie Blount (1998) laments this when she speaks of the dearth of historical accounts and the loss of some women's history over time.

The news item was about female state legislators who are trying to renew the ratification effort for the Equal Rights Amendment, equity legislation proposed in the United States in the 1980s. I was struck by a quotation from the article, the tone of which the reporter encountered on more than one occasion. "'Our generation is different. . . . It's not really an issue to us on a day to day basis,' said April Thornton, 24, a business major at Broward College in Fort Lauderdale who said she had never heard of the ERA" (Haughney 2011).

This quotation demonstrates the significance of sharing our stories. We see the view of youth who may not yet have witnessed or experienced marginalization. The WLE group intentionally invites young women and men to participate so that they can share with their peers the realities of social justice needs and opportunities. Our commitment comes from the deepest belief that the learning and success of *others* is *our* success.

Moreover, to prevent the loss of women's history, it must be writ large and manifold. The Equal Rights Amendment had vociferous supporters and opponents. Whether it was ultimately the appropriate thing to do is not the concern here. What is a mighty concern is the fact that it was a substantial part of women's history in the United States. That our youth should move forward not knowing of that debate is a dilution of a rich history that calls to serve the future. Similar lapses occur across cultures. Both young women and men must know *all* that has gone before so that they may more conscientiously build the future.

In the end, I overflow with *renewed energy*. As the founding chair of WLE, and semiretired as I write, it would be easy to rest. But how can I in the face of the compelling spirit shared here? How can I not be moved by statements like, "I know envy, I know what it feels like to seek and crave. I know guilt, the weight of a heart, a tear in the eye, a hand in my hand. I know influence, what not to do. I know a shifting identity. I know experience, privilege, pathways, and what opportunity provides or takes away," or "It is in the end—in the bittersweet of looking back—that you can see the true beauty of the journey."

Yet, by our own admission, there are parts of our stories left untold. Even the editor of *Women in Higher Education* wondered about the untold stories behind the decrease of female university presidents in the United States (Wenniger 2010). I am struck by the fact that we are just humans, doing the very best we can, with the flaws and foibles that have faced our ancestors for centuries. The authors proposed reasons for our untold tales earlier in this book. I cannot improve on that list. However, Linda Lyman's poem from chapter 2 perhaps poetically captured the tumultuous spirit that often makes us hesitant to share all aspects of our lives:

Breathless finally
I lay felled by felt needs,

among them
a frantic needing
not to be
at this spot,
making
this choice,
yet knowing
that choice
no longer existed,
had likewise died,
split open in wasting efforts
in waning attempts
to span the opposing worlds
of no longer
and not yet.

Ultimately our stories validate that it is not only all right to exist between the flower and the thorn, between the flame and the light, but it is actually essential to stoke the fire of social justice across time and space. Our work is to decrease the number of thorns that others might face in the future, even as we walk a labyrinth that takes us back and forth through the full range of human experience. It is the journey that transforms the flame into power used for good.

The stories bring me back to the story that inspired our logo and characterizes our ongoing work—and yours if you accept our invitation. In the twelfth century, Hildegard of Bingen in Germany was "given" to the church at the age of twelve. Sent to an anchorage, a one-room cell attached to a church with only a sliding window to receive food; sent with funeral prayers because she was to be dead to the world; sent to communicate for years with only one other human being, an elder nun; sent sickly and prone to "visions" that she dare not share lest she be deemed crazy or a witch; Hildegard felt thorns. Yet she found the strength to nurture seeds that became flowers of influence. She learned all she could at the time, developing skills as a scientist, medical expert, musician, feminist, and powerful advocate for social justice. She gained the respect and confidence of popes and kings even as she railed against injustice in their pulpits and town squares. She did this by eventually writing about both her knowledge and her visions. She believed that her spirit could transcend time and space, not by magic but by music and the word. As an example, the references include a link to her composition, *Vision*. Though the instrumentation is modern, her joyful melody spans a vast expanse of nine hundred years.

Her most well-known vision captures the essence of our work. She wrote in her book, *Scivias* (*Ways of Knowing*), "The woman was in the flame, but not consumed by it. Rather it flowed from her." It described the transcendental energy that these stories convey. We have the power to experience the thorn, the fire, yet use it as a fuel rather than be defeated by it. We know that it can pass through us and be transformed into more powerful energy for good. Our stories confirm this. We will send them through time and space as Hildegard did . . . and I will return to the work of making a positive difference with re-newed vigor.

To my colleagues, my friends, my sisters of WLE, thank you for all that you are and all that we will yet be. To the reader, take strength and guidance from these tales. Believe that you and your story can transform your piece of the universe—then go and do it. Despite thorns and fire, do it anyway. Light, growth, and grateful recipients of social justice await you.

Helen C. Sobehart, WLE Founding Chair

REFERENCES

Acosta-Belen, Edna. 2009. Between the dynamics of the global and the local: Feminist and gender research in Latin America and the Caribbean. In *Global gender research: Transnational perspectives*, ed. Christine Bose and Minjeong Kim, 151–57. New York: Routledge.

Adichie, Chimamanda. 2009. The danger of a single story, YouTube video, 19:17, posted by "TEDtalksDirector," October 7, 2009, http://www.youtube.com/watch?v=D9Ihs241zeg (accessed October 24, 2011).

Ah Nee-Benham, Maenette. 2003. In our mother's voice: A native woman's knowing of leadership. In *Reconsidering feminist research in educational leadership*, ed. Michelle D. Young and Linda Skrla, 223–45. Albany: State University of New York Press.

Ah Nee-Benham, Maenette, and Joanne Cooper. 1998. *Let my spirit soar! Narratives of diverse women in school leadership*. Thousand Oaks, CA: Corwin.

Anyon, Jean. 2005. *Radical possibilities: Public policy, urban education, and a new social movement*. New York: Routledge.

Applebaum, Barbara. 2008. "Doesn't my experience count?" White students, the authority of experience and social justice pedagogy. *Race, Ethnicity & Education* 11 (4) (December): 405–14.

Aristotle. 1908. *Nicomachean ethics*. Trans. William D. Ross. Oxford: Clarendon.

Atlas, Brenda L. H., and Colleen Capper. 2003. *The spirituality of African-American women principals in urban schools: Toward a reconceptualization of Afrocentric feminist epistemology*. Paper presented at the annual meeting of the American Educational Research Association, Chicago, IL, April 21–25.

Avolio, Bruce, and William Gardner. 2005. Authentic leadership development: Getting to the root of positive forms of leadership. *Leadership Quarterly* 16 (3): 315–38.

Baldwin, Julia, Nancy Maldonado, Candace Lacey, and Joan Efinger. 2004. *Resilient women leaders: A qualitative investigation*. Paper presented at the annual meeting of the American Educational Research Association, San Diego, CA, April 12–16. ED500841.

Bandiho, Hellen. 2009. Status of educational leadership and female participation: The case of Tanzania. In *Women leading education across the continents*, ed. Helen Sobehart, 43–48. Lanham, MD: Rowman & Littlefield Education.

Bandura, Albert. 1997. *Self-efficacy: The exercise of control.* New York: Freeman.

Barton, Tracy R. 2006. Feminist leadership: Building nurturing academic communities. *Advancing Women in Leadership Online Journal* 21 (Fall). http://www.advancingwomen.com.ezproxy.waikato.ac.nz/awl/fall2006/barton.htm.

Bateson, Mary Catherine. 1989. *Composing a life.* New York: Grove.

Begley, Paul T. 1996. Cognitive perspectives on values in administration: A quest for coherence and relevance. *Educational Administration Quarterly* 32 (3): 403–26.

——. 1999. Value preferences, ethics and conflicts in school administration. In *Values and educational leadership,* ed. Paul T. Begley, 237–54. Albany: State University of New York Press.

Belenky, Mary, Blythe Clinchy, Nancy Goldberger, and Jill Tarule. 1986. *Women's ways of knowing: The development of self, voice, and mind.* New York: Basic.

Bepko, Claudia, and Jo-Ann Krestan. 1993. *Singing at the top of our lungs: Women, love, and creativity.* New York: HarperCollins.

Biklen, Sari, Catherine Marshall, and Diane Pollard. 2008. Experiencing second-wave feminism in the USA. *Discourse: Studies in the Cultural Politics of Education* 29 (4): 451–69.

Biko, Stephen B. 1978. I write what I like. In *Quotes: Stephen (Steve) Bantu Biko,* ed. Alistair Boddy-Evans. http://africanhistory.about.com/od/bikosteve/p/qts_biko.htm (accessed November 21, 2011).

Bilsky, Wolfgang, and Shalom H. Schwartz. 1994. Values and personality. *European Journal of Personality* 8:163–81.

Birmingham, Carrie. 2004. Phronesis: A model for pedagogical reflection. *Journal of Teacher Education* 55 (4): 313–24.

Blackmore, Jill. 1999. *Troubling women: Feminism, leadership and educational change.* Philadelphia: Open University Press.

——. 2002. Troubling women: The upsides and downsides of leadership and the new managerialism. In *Women and school leadership: International perspectives,* ed. Cecelia Reynolds, 49–70. Albany: State University of New York Press.

——. 2009. Re/positioning women in educational leadership. In *Women leading education across the continents,* ed. Helen C. Sobehart, 73–83. Lanham, MD: Rowman & Littlefield Education.

Blount, Jackie. 1998. *Destined to rule the schools: Women and the superintendency, 1873–1995.* New York: State University of New York Press.

Bogotch, Ira E. 2002. Educational leadership and social justice: Practice into theory. *Journal of School Leadership* 12 (2): 138–56.

Bose, Christine, and Minjeone Kim, eds. 2009. *Global gender research: Transnational perspectives.* New York: Routledge.

Breathnach, Sarah Ban. 1995. *Simple abundance.* New York: Grand Central.

Brooks, Ethel, and Dorothy Hodgson. 2007. "An activist temperament": An interview with Charlotte Bunch. *Women's Studies Quarterly* 35 (3): 60–74.

Brown, Kathleen M. 2004. Leadership for social justice and equity: Weaving a transformative framework and pedagogy. *Educational Administration Quarterly* 40 (1): 79–110.

Cambron-McCabe, Nelda, and Martha McCarthy. 2005. Educating school leaders for social justice. *Educational Policy* 19 (1): 201–22.

Campbell-Stephens, Rosemary. 2009. Investing in diversity: Changing the face (and the heart) of educational leadership. *School Leadership and Management* 29 (3): 321–331.

Capper, Collen C., George Theoharis, and James Sebastian. 2006. Toward a framework for preparing leaders for social justice. *Journal of Educational Administration* (3): 209–24.

Cashman, Kevin. 2003. *Awakening the leader within*. Hoboken, NJ: Wiley.

Chan, Adrienne. 2010. Women at the boundaries. *Forum on Public Policy Online* 2010, no. 2. http://forumonpublicpolicy.com/spring2010.vol2010/womencareers2010. html (accessed August 18, 2011).

Cheaupalakit, Panpim. 2002. The leadership styles of male and female higher education administrators in Thailand. PhD diss., Illinois State University.

——. 2009. *Women in educational leadership in Thailand*. Paper presented at the second conference of Women Leading Education Across the Continents, Augsburg, Germany, September 16–18.

Chesley, Joanne. 2005. Overcoming injustice: A tradition of resilience. *Advancing Women in Leadership Online Journal* 18. http://www.advancingwomen.com/awl/ social_justice1/Chesley.html (accessed July 15, 2011).

Chiu, Ming Ming, and Allan Walker. 2007. Leadership for social justice in Hong Kong schools: Addressing mechanisms of inequality. *Journal of Educational Administration* 45 (6): 724–39. doi:10.1108/09578230710829900.

Christie, Pam. 2010. The complexity of human rights in global times: The case of the right to education in South Africa. *International Journal of Educational Development* 30 (1) (January): 3–11. doi:10.1016/j.ijedudev.2009.06.006.

Christman, Dana, and Rhonda McClellan. 2008. "Living on barbed wire": Resilient women administrators in educational leadership programs. *Educational Administration Quarterly* 44 (1) (December): 3–29. doi:10.1177/0013161X07309744 (accessed July 10, 2011).

Coleman, Marianne. 2005. Gender and secondary school leadership. *International Studies in Educational Administration* 33 (2): 3–20.

——. 2011. *Women at the top: Challenges, choices and change*. Basingstoke: Palgrave Macmillan.

Coleman, Marianne, and Derek Glover. 2010. *Educational leadership and management: Developing insights and skills*. Maidenhead: Open University Press.

Collins, Gail. 2009. *When everything changed: The amazing journey of American women from 1960 to the present*. New York: Little, Brown.

Collins, Patricia Hill. 2000. Gender, black feminism, and black political economy. *Annals of the American Academy of Political and Social Science* 568: 41–53.

Connell, Robert W., Dean Ashenden, Sandra Kessler, and Gary Dowsetts. 1982. *Making the difference: Schools, families and social division*. Sydney, Australia: Allen & Unwin.

Coontz, Stephanie. 2011. *A strange stirring: The feminine mystique and American women at the dawn of the 1960s*. New York: Basic.

Cooper, Joanne E. 1991. Telling our own stories. In *Stories lives tell: Narrative and dialogue in education,* ed. Carol Witherell and Nel Noddings, 96–112. New York: Teachers College Press.

Cooper, Joanne, and Jane Strachan. 2006. Welcome ground for women faculty in academe: An international perspective. *Advancing Women in Leadership Online Journal.* http://www.advancingwomen.com/awl/summer2006/Cooper_Strachan.html (accessed November 21, 2011).

Coutu, Diane. 2002. HBR at large: How resilience works. *Harvard Business Review* 80 (5): 46–49.

Covey, Stephen, and Rebecca Merrill. 2006. *The speed of trust: The one thing that changes everything.* New York: Free Press.

Crossley, Michael, and Peter Jarvis. 2001. Context matters. *Comparative Education* (4) (November): 405–8.

Dantley, Michael E. 2005. The power of critical spirituality to act and to reform. *Journal of School Leadership* 15:500–518.

——. 2010. Successful leadership in urban schools: Principals and critical spirituality, a new approach to reform. *Journal of Negro Education* 79 (3): 214–19.

Dantley, Michael E., and Linda C. Tillman. 2005. Social justice and moral/transformative leadership. In *Leadership for social justice: Making it happen,* ed. Catherine Marshall and Maricela Oliva, 16–30. Boston: Pearson.

Day, Christopher. 2004. The passion of successful leadership. *School Leadership and Management* 24 (4): 425–37.

Delpit, Lisa. 1995. *Other people's children: Cultural conflicts in the classroom.* New York: Free Press.

Dodson, Mick. 1993. *Annual report of the Aboriginal and Torres Strait Islander Social Justice Commission.* http://www.austlii.edu.au/au/other/IndigLRes/1993/3/index.html (accessed September 15, 2010).

Donnell, Kelly, Li-Ling Yang, Annie Winfield, Alan Canestrari, Bruce Marlowe, and Mieko Kamii. 2008. Conversations about social justice. *Encounter* (4): 37–39.

Downie, Andrew, and Marion Lloyd. 2010. At Brazil's universities, affirmative action faces crucial tests. *Chronicle of Higher Education International* (August 1). http://chronicle.com/article/At-Brazils-Universities/123720/ (accessed September 21, 2010).

Elie, Paul. 2003. *The life you save may be your own.* New York: Farrar, Straus & Giroux.

Emmons, Robert A. 1999. *The psychology of ultimate concerns: Motivation and spirituality in personality.* New York: Guilford.

Enomoto, Ernestine K., Mary E. Gardiner, and Margaret Grogan. 2000. Notes to Athene. *Urban Education* 35 (5) (December): 567–83. doi:10.1177/0042085900355007.

Enslin, Penny, and Shirley Pendlebury. 1998. Transforming education in South Africa? *Cambridge Journal of Education* 28 (3) (November): 261.

Erickson, Rebecca J. 1994. Our society, our selves: Becoming authentic in an inauthentic world. *Advanced Development Journal* 6:27–39.

——. 1995. The importance of authenticity for self and society. *Symbolic Interaction* 18 (2): 121–44.

Erikson, Erik. 1950. *Childhood and society.* New York: Horton.

——. 1956. The problem of ego identity. *Journal of the American Psychoanalytic Association* 4:56–121.

Eudaimonia. n.d. Wikipedia. http://en.wikipedia.org/wiki/Eudaimonia (accessed November 21, 2011).

Evers, Colin W., and Gabriele Lakomski. 1996. Science in educational administration: A postpositivist conception. *Educational Administration Quarterly* 32 (3): 344–65.

Fischer, Ronald, and Peter B. Smith. 2006. Who cares about social justice? The moderating effect of values on the link between organisational justice and work behavior. *Applied Psychology: An International Review* 55 (4): 541–62.

Fitzgerald, Tanya, and Jane Wilkinson. 2010. *Travelling towards a mirage? Gender, leadership and higher education.* Mt Gravatt, Australia: Post Pressed.

Flyvbjerg, Bent. 2006. Making organizational research matter: Power, values, and phronesis. In *The Sage handbook of organization studies,* ed. Stewart Clegg, Cynthia Hardy, Thomas Lawrence, and Walter Nord, 370–87. Thousand Oaks, CA: Sage.

Foskett, Nicholas, and Jacky Lumby. 2003. *Leading and managing education: International dimensions.* London: Paul Chapman.

Freire, Paolo. [1970] 2002. *Pedagogy of the oppressed.* 30th anniversary ed. New York: Continuum.

French, Marilyn. 1992. *The war against women.* New York: Ballantine.

Fris, Joe, and Angeliki Lazaridou. 2006. An additional way of thinking about organizational life and leadership: The quantum perspective. *Canadian Journal of Educational Administration and Policy* 48 (January): 1–29. http://umanitoba.ca/publications/cjeap/articles/fris.html (accessed September 10, 2011).

Fu Jun. 1995. Personal communication with author, later published in Chinese as The problems that Chinese women are faced with, in *Women's Studies,* Vol. 5, Ginling College, Beijing.

Fua, Seu'ula J. 2007. Looking towards the source—Social justice and leadership conceptualizations from Tonga. *Journal of Educational Administration* 45 (6): 672–83.

Fullan, Michael. 2003. *The moral imperative of school leadership.* Thousand Oaks, CA: Corwin.

Furman, Gail. 2003. The 2002 UCEA presidential address. *UCEA Review* 45 (1): 1–6.

Gardiner, Mary E., Ernestine Enomoto, and Margaret Grogan. 2000. *Coloring outside the lines: Mentoring women into school leadership.* Albany: State University of New York Press.

Gardner, Howard. 1995. *Leading minds: An anatomy of leadership.* New York: Basic.

——. 1999. *The disciplined mind: What all students should understand.* New York: Simon & Schuster.

Gardner, William, Bruce Avolio, Fred Luthans, Douglas May, and Fred Walumbwa. 2005. Can you see the real me? A self-based model of authentic leader and follower development. *Leadership Quarterly* 16:343–72.

George, William. 2003. *Authentic leadership: Rediscovering the secrets to creating lasting value.* San Francisco: Jossey-Bass.

Gewal, Jyoti. 2008. Theorizing activism, activizing theory: Feminist academics in Indian Punjabi society. *NWSA Journal* 20 (1): 161–84.

Gilligan, Carol. 1982. *In a different voice: Psychological theory and women's development.* Cambridge, MA: Harvard University Press.

Goldberg, Susan G., and Eric B. Dent. 1999. Challenging resistance to change. *Journal of Applied Behavioral Science* 35 (1): 25–41.

Goldfarb, Katie P., and Jaime Grinberg. 2002. Leadership for social justice: Authentic participation in the case of a community center in Caracas, Venezuela. *Journal of School Leadership* 12:157–73.

Goleman, Daniel. 2006. *Social intelligence: The new science of human relationships.* New York: Bantam.

Goodman, Diane J. 2001. *Promoting diversity and social justice: Educating people from privileged groups.* Thousand Oaks, CA: Sage.

Green, Andy, Geoff Mason, and Lorna Unwin. 2011. Education and inequality: Introduction. *National Institute Economic Review* 215 (1): R1–R5.

Grobler, Bennie, Kholeka Moloi, Coert Loock, Tom Bisschoff, and Raj Mestry. 2006. Creating a school environment for the effective management of cultural diversity. *Educational Management, Administration and Leadership* 34 (4): 449–72.

Grogan, Margaret. 1996. *Voices of women aspiring to the superintendency.* Albany: State University of New York Press.

——. 2004. Keeping a critical, postmodern eye on educational leadership in the United States: In appreciation of Bill Foster. *Educational Administration Quarterly* 40 (2): 222–39.

Grogan, Margaret, and Charol Shakeshaft. 2011. *Women and educational leadership.* San Francisco: Jossey-Bass.

Guth, Ruth, and Fran Wright. 2009. Women in the higher education sector. *Industrial Law Journal* 38 (1): 139–42.

Harber, Clive, and Lynn Davies. 1997. *School management and effectiveness in developing countries.* London: Cassell.

Harder, Arlene. 2009. The developmental stages of Erik Erikson. http://www.scribd.com/doc/24976266/The-Developmental-Stages-of-Erik-Erikson (retrieved November 21, 2011).

Harris, Alma. 2002. *School improvement: What's in it for schools?* New York: Routledge.

Hart, Jeni. 2005. Activism amongst feminist academics: Professionalized activism and activist professionals. *Advancing Women in Leadership Online Journal* 18. http://www.advancingwomen.com/awl/social_justice1/Hart.html (accessed November 21, 2011).

Haughney, Kathleen. 2011. The ERA: Still a cause for some South Florida women, forgotten history for others. *Sun Sentinel*, September 27. http://articles.sun-sentinel.com/2011-09-27/news/fl-female-lawmakers-still--want-era-20110926_1_broward-college-women-gender (accessed November 30, 2011).

Heifetz, Ronald A. 1994. *Leadership without easy answers.* Cambridge, MA: Harvard University Press.

Helle, Anita P. 1991. Reading women's autobiographies. In *Stories lives tell: Narrative and dialogue in education*, ed. Carol Witherell and Nel Noddings, 48–66. New York: Teachers College Press.

Henderson, Nan, and Mike Milstein. 2002. *Resiliency in schools: Making it happen for students and educators.* Updated ed. Thousand Oaks, CA: Corwin.

Hildegard of Bingen. 1990. *Scivias*. Trans. Columba Hart and Jane Bishop. Introduction by Barbara J. Newman. Preface by Caroline Walker Bynum. New York: Paulist Press.

———. 1994. Vision, YouTube video, 3:38, posted by "Orome 73," September 18, 2009, http://www.youtube.com/watch?v=M48_LZUpo0Q&feature=related.

Hill, Marie, and Joyce Ragland. 1995. *Women as educational leaders: Opening windows, pushing ceilings*. Thousand Oaks, CA: Corwin.

Hills, Michael D. 2002. Kluckhohn and Strodtbeck's values orientation theory. In *Online readings in psychology and culture*, ed. W. J. Lonner, D. L. Dinnel, S. A. Hayes, and D. N. Sattler. Bellingham, WA: Center for Cross-Cultural Research, Western Washington University. http://www.wwu.edu/~culture (accessed November 21, 2011).

Ho, Sui-chu. 2005. *Can basic education system in Hong Kong be equal and excellent: Results from PISA 2000*. Occasional paper, PISA series, no. 57 (in English). Chinese University of Hong Kong.

Hodgkinson, Christopher. 1991a. *Educational leadership: The moral art*. Albany: State University of New York Press.

———. 1991b. *Towards a philosophy of administration*. Oxford: Basil Blackwell.

Hofstede, Geert. 1980. *Culture's consequences: International differences in work-related values*. Beverly Hills, CA: Sage.

———. 2001. *Culture's consequences: Comparing values, behaviors, institutions, and organizations across nations*. Beverly Hills, CA: Sage.

Hofstede, Geert, and M. H. Bond. 1984. Hofstede's culture dimensions: An independent validation using Rokeach's value survey. *Journal of Cross-Cultural Psychology* 15 (4): 417–433.

Howell, Jane, and Bruce Avolio. 1992. The ethics of charismatic leadership: Submission or liberation? *Academy of Management Executive* 6:43–54.

Hoy, Wayne K., C. Tarter, and A. Hoy. 2006. Academic optimism of schools: A force for student achievement. *American Educational Research Journal* 43 (3): 425–46.

Hoyle, Rick H., Michael Kernis, Mark Leary, and Mark Baldwin. 1999. *Selfhood: Identity, esteem, regulation*. Boulder, CO: Westview.

Huberman, Michael. 1995. Working with life history narratives. In *Narrative in teaching, learning, and research*, ed. Hunter McEwan and Kieran Egan, 127–65. New York: Teachers College Press.

Humanitarianism. n.d. Answers.com. http://www.answers.com/topic/humanitarianism#cite_ref-7 (accessed November 21, 2011).

Ilies, Remus, Frederick Morgeson, and Jennifer Nahrgang. 2005. Authentic leadership and eudaemonic well-being: Understanding leader-follower outcomes. *Leadership Quarterly* 16 (3): 373–94.

Integrity. n.d. The Teal Trust. http://www.teal.org.uk/dl/integrity.htm (accessed November 21, 2011).

Jamieson, Kathleen Hall. 1995. *Beyond the double bind: Women and leadership*. New York: Oxford University Press.

Jansen, Jonathan David. 1998. Curriculum reform in South Africa: A critical analysis of outcomes-based education [1]. *Cambridge Journal of Education* 28 (3) (November): 321.

——. 2006. Leading against the grain: The politics and emotions of leading for social justice in South Africa. *Leadership and Policy in Schools* 5 (1): 37–51. doi:10.1080/15700760500484027.

Johnson, Karen A. 2009. Gender and race: Exploring Anna Julia Cooper's thoughts for socially just educational opportunities. *Philosophia Africana* 12 (1) (March): 67–82.

Kagoda, Alice M., and Jill Sperandio. 2009. Ugandan women: Moving beyond historical and cultural understandings of educational leadership. In *Women leading education across the continents*, ed. Helen C. Sobehart, 49–56. Lanham, MD: Rowman & Littlefield Education.

Kaparou, Maria, and Tony Bush. 2007. Invisible barriers: The career progress of women secondary school principals in Greece. *Compare* 27 (2): 221–37. Accessed August 20, 2011. doi:10.1080/03057920601165587.

Karaiskaki, T. 2006. Commentary: A gloomy future for Greek women. *Kathimerini* (English edition), May 21–22.

Kelly, Rita M., Jane Bayes, Mary Hawkesworth, and Brigitte Young, eds. 2001. *Gender, globalization, and democratization*. Lanham, MD: Rowman & Littlefield.

Kernis, Michael. 2003. Toward a conceptualization of optimal self-esteem. *Psychological Inquiry* 14 (1): 1–26.

Keyes, Corey, Dov Shmotkin, and Carol Ryff. 2002. Optimizing well-being: The empirical encounter of two traditions. *Journal of Personality and Social Psychology* 82 (6): 1007–22.

Kim, Minjeong, and Christine Bose. 2009. Introduction to gender research in Asia and the Middle East. In *Global gender research: Transnational perspectives*, ed. Christine Bose and Minjeong Kim, 67–72. New York: Routledge.

Kleinerman, Kay. 2010. Singing for leadership: Fostering the development of female leaders through voice. *Advancing Women in Leadership Online Journal* 30 (4): 1–23. http://www.advancingwomen.com/awl/2010/KayKleinerman.pdf (accessed August 18, 2011).

Kluckhöhn, Florence R., and Fred L. Strodtbeck. 1961. *Variations in value orientations*. Evanston, IL: Row, Peterson.

Kristoff, Nicholas D., and Sheryl WuDunn. 2009a. Why women's rights are the cause of our time. *New York Times Magazine*, August 23, 28–39.

——. 2009b. *Half the sky: Turning oppression into opportunity for women worldwide*. New York: Vintage.

Lakoff, George, and Mark Johnson. 1980. *Metaphors we live by*. Chicago: University of Chicago Press.

Lambert, Linda. 2003. *Leadership capacity for lasting school improvement*. Alexandria, VA: ASCD.

Lambert, Linda, and Mary Gardner. 2009. *Women's ways of leading*. Indianapolis: Dog Ear Publishing.

Larson, Colleen L., and Teboho Moja. 2010. Individual transformation for global impact. In *Bridge leadership: Connecting educational leadership and social justice to improve schools*, ed. Autumn K. Tooms and Christa Boske, 173–206. Charlotte, NC: Information Age.

Larson, Colleen L., and Khaula Murtadha. 2002. Leadership for social justice. In *The educational leadership challenge: Redefining leadership for the 21st century*, ed. Joseph Murphy, 134–61. Chicago: National Society for the Study of Education.

Lave, Jean, and Etienne Wenger. 1991. *Situated learning: Legitimate peripheral participation.* Cambridge: Cambridge University Press.

Lawrence-Lightfoot, Sara, and Jessica H. Davis. 1997. *The art and science of portraiture.* San Francisco: Jossey-Bass.

Lazaridou, Angeliki, ed. 2004. *Contemporary issues on educational administration and policy: An introduction.* Athens, Greece: Athens Institute for Education and Research.

——. 2007. Values in principals' thinking when solving problems. *International Journal of Leadership in Education* 10 (4): 339–56.

Lee, Sharon Shockley, and Kelly McKerrow. 2005. Advancing social justice: Women's work. *Advancing Women in Leadership Online Journal* 19. http://www.advancingwomen.com/awl/fall2005/preface.html (accessed November 21, 2011).

Leithwood, Kenneth, Paul Begley, and J. Bradley Cousins. 1994. *Developing expert leadership for future schools.* New York: Routledge.

Leithwood, Kenneth, and Doris Jantzi. 1990. Transformational leadership: How principals can help reform school cultures. *School Effectiveness and School Improvement* 1 (4): 259–80.

Leithwood, Kenneth, K. Louis, S. Anderson, and K. Wahlstrom. 2004. *How leadership influences student learning.* New York: Wallace Foundation.

Leithwood, Kenneth, Blair Mascall, and Tiiu Strauss. 2009. *Distributed leadership according to the evidence.* New York: Routledge.

Lieblich, Amia, Tammar Zilber, and Rivka Tuval-Mashiach. 2008. Narrating human actions: The subjective experience of agency, structure, communion, and serendipity. *Qualitative Inquiry* 14 (4): 613–31.

Lumby, Jacky. 2009. Disappearing gender: Choices in identity. In *Women leading education across the continents*, ed. Helen C. Sobehart, 29–38. Lanham, MD: Rowman & Littlefield Education.

Lumby, Jacky, with Marianne Coleman. 2007. *Leadership and diversity: Challenging theory and practice in education.* London: Sage.

Lundin, Stephen C., Harry Paul, and John Christensen. 2000. *Fish! A remarkable way to boost morale and improve results.* New York: Hyperion.

Luthans, Fred, and Bruce Avolio. 2003. Authentic leadership: A positive developmental approach. In *Positive organizational scholarship*, ed. Kim Cameron, Jand Dutton, and Robert Quinn, 241–61. San Francisco: Barrett-Koehler.

Luthans, Fred, Carolyn Youssef, and Bruce Avolio. 2007. *Psychological capital: Developing the human competitive edge.* Oxford: Oxford University Press.

Lyman, Linda L., Dianne Ashby, and Jenny S. Tripses. 2005. *Leaders who dare: Pushing the boundaries.* Lanham, MD: Rowman & Littlefield Education.

Lyman, Linda L., and Dianne C. Gardner. 2008. Enhancing leadership education: Insights from a seminar evaluation. *Journal of Research on Leadership Education* 3 (1). http://222.ucea.org/JRLE/issue.php (accessed November 21, 2011).

Lyman, Linda L., Angeliki Lazaridou, and Anastasia Athanasoula-Reppa. 2009. Leadership, change, and gender: Reflections of Greek and U.S. women leaders. In *Women leading education across the continents*, ed. Helen C. Sobehart, 115–27. Lanham, MD: Rowman & Littlefield Education.

Lyman, Linda L., and Christine J. Villani. 2004. *Best leadership practices for high-poverty schools*. Lanham, MD: Rowman & Littlefield Education.

MacBeath, John. 2005. Leadership as distributed: A matter of practice. *School Leadership and Management* 25 (4): 349–66.

Macha, Hildegard, Claudia Fahrenwald, and Quirin J. Bauer, eds. 2011. *Gender and education—Towards new strategies of leadership and power*. Berlin, Stuttgart: Holtzbrinck Verlagsgruppe.

Magee, Ann. 2001. Women. *Asia Pacific Viewpoint* 42 (1): 35.

Mahtani, Shalini. 2005. *Women leaders in Hong Kong: Insights into their workplace experiences*. Hong Kong: Community Business Limited.

Maizetegui-Oñate, Concepción, and Rosa Santibáñez-Gruber. 2008. Introduction: Access to education and equity in plural societies. *Intercultural Education* 19 (5) (October): 373–81. doi:10.1080/14675980802531432.

Marshall, Catherine. 2004. Social justice challenges to educational administration: Introduction to a special issue. *Educational Administration Quarterly* 40 (1): 5–15.

Marshall, Catherine, and Michael Ward. 2004. "Yes, but . . .": Education leaders discuss social justice. *Journal of School Leadership* 13: 530–63.

May, Douglas, Timothy Hodges, Adrian Chan, and Bruce Avolio. 2003. Developing the moral component of authentic leadership. *Organizational Dynamics* 32 (3): 247–51.

McDonald, Steve. 2010. Right place, right time: Serendipity and informal job matching. *Socio-Economic Review* 8:307–31.

McKenzie, Kathryn B., Dana E. Christman, Frank Hernandez, Elsy Fierro, Colleen A. Capper, Michael Dantley, Maria L. Gonzalez, Nelda Cambron-McCabe, and James J. Scheurich. 2008. From the field: A proposal for educating leaders for social justice. *Educational Administration Quarterly* 44 (1): 111–38.

McLeod, William T., ed. 1987. *The new Collins dictionary and thesaurus*. London: Collins.

McPherson, Marlene. 2006. A Sterling performance. *Jamaica Gleaner*, January 22. http://www.jamaica-gleaner.com/gleaner/20060122/out/out2.html (accessed September 21, 2011).

Mercer, Ramona, Elizabeth Nichols, and Glen Doyle. 1989. *Transitions in a woman's life: Major life events in developmental context*. New York: Springer.

Milstein, Mike, and Doris Annie Henry. 2008. *Leadership for resilient schools and communities*. 2nd ed. Thousand Oaks, CA: Corwin.

Mohanty, Chandra T. 2003. *Feminism without borders*. Durham: Duke University Press.

Moments of peace for the evening. 2005. Bloomington, MN: Bethany House.

Müller, Christine. 2003. Knowledge between globalization and localization: The dynamics of female spaces in Ghana. *Current Sociology* 51 (3/4): 329–46. www.sagepublications.com. doi:0011-3921(200305/07)51:3/4;329-346;032652 (accessed July 10, 2011).

Murtadha-Watts, Khaula. 1999. Spirited sisters: Spirituality and the activism of African American women in educational leadership. In *School leadership: Expanding horizons of the mind and spirit*, ed. Leslie T. Fenwick, 155–67. Proceedings of the National Council for Professors of Educational Administration. Lancaster, PA: Technomic.

Neville, Helen, and Jennifer Hamer. 2006. Revolutionary black women's activism: Experience and transformation. *Black Scholar* 36 (1): 2.

Noddings, Nel. 2005. Global citizenship: Promises and problems. In *Educating citizens for global awareness*, ed. Nel Noddings, 1–21. New York: Teachers College Press.

Nussbaum, Martha C. 2004. Women's education: A global challenge. *Signs: Journal of Women in Culture and Society* 29 (2): 325–55.

Online Entymology Dictionary. www.etymonline.com/index.php?term=courage (accessed August 31, 2011).

Oram-Sterling, Jacqueline. 2009. The Joan Wint story: Biography of a principal whose leadership for social justice transformed a rural Jamaican high school. PhD diss., Illinois State University.

Patterson, Jerry, George Goens, and Diane Reed. 2008. Joy & resilience: Strange bedfellows. *School Administrator* 65 (11): 28–29. http://www.aasa.org/schooladministrator article.aspx?id=3828 (accessed July 10, 2011).

——. 2009. *Resilient leadership for turbulent times: A guide to thriving in the face of adversity*. Lanham, MD: Rowman & Littlefield Education.

Peterson, Christopher, Nansook Park, and Martin Seligman. 2005. Orientations to happiness and life satisfaction: The full life versus the empty life. *Journal of Happiness Studies* 6 (1): 25–41.

Peterson, Christopher, and Martin Seligman. 2004. *Character strengths and virtues: A handbook and classification*. Oxford: Oxford University Press.

Peterson, V. Spike, and Anne Sisson Runyan. 1999. *Global gender issues*. Boulder, CO: Westview.

Phendla, Thidziambi. 2004. "Musadzi u fara lufhanga nga hu fhiraho"–Life stories of black women leaders in South Africa. *Perspectives in Education* 22 (1): 51–63.

——. 2009. Women on the rise: Women navigating across social, political, economic and cultural arenas to claim their stake in educational leadership positions in South Africa. In *Women leading education across the continents*, ed. Helen C. Sobehart, 57–64. Lanham, MD: Rowman & Littlefield Education.

Phronesis. n.d. Wikipedia. http://en.wikipedia.org/wiki/Phronesis (accessed November 21, 2011).

Pinker, Steven. 2008. The moral instinct. *New York Times Magazine*, January 13. http://www.nytimes.com/2008/01/13/magazine/13Psychology-t.html?e (accessed September 20, 2010).

Polkinghorne, Donald E. 1988. *Narrative knowing and the social sciences*. Albany: State University of New York Press.

Rapp, Dana. 2002. Social justice and the importance of rebellious, oppositional imaginations. *Journal of School Leadership* 12 (May): 226–45.

Reed, Diane, and Jerry Patterson. 2007. Voices of resilience from successful female superintendents. *Journal of Women in Educational Leadership* 5 (2): 89–100.

Reynolds, Cecilia. 2002. *Women and school leadership: International perspectives*. Albany: State University of New York Press.

Ribeiro, Gustavo Lins. 2005. What is cosmopolitanism? *Vibrant* 2 (1/2): 19–26. http://www.vibrant.org.br/english/articles/2005.htm (accessed November 10, 2011).

Richardson, Glenn. 2002. The metatheory of resilience and resiliency. *Journal of Clinical Psychology* 58 (3): 307–21. doi:10.1002/jclp.10020 (accessed July 12, 2011).

Rokeach, Milton. 1979. *Understanding human values: Individual and societal.* New York: Free Press.

Rost, Joseph C. 1993. *Leadership for the twenty-first century.* Westport: Praeger.

Ryan, William. 1971. *Blaming the victim.* New York: Vintage.

Ryff, Carol, and Corey Keyes. 1995. The structure of psychological well-being revisited. *Journal of Personality and Social Psychology* 69 (4): 719–27.

Sanga, Kabini, and Cherie Chu, eds. 2009. *Living and leaving a legacy of hope: Stories by new generation Pacific leaders.* Wellington, New Zealand: Victoria University.

Scanlan, Martin. 2011. How principals cultivate a culture of critical spirituality. *International Journal of Leadership in Education* 14 (3): 293–315. doi:10.1080/13603124.2011.560283.

Schein, Virginia. 2007. Women in management: Reflections and projections. *Women in Management Review* 22 (1): 6–18.

Scheurich, James J., and Kathryn B. McKenzie. 2006. The continuing struggle for social justice: 2006 politics of education association yearbook. *Educational Policy* 20 (1): 8–12.

Schwartz, Shalom H. 1992. Universals on the content and structure of values: Theoretical advances and empirical tests in 20 countries. *Advances in Experimental Social Psychology* 25:1–65.

———. 1994. Are there universal aspects in the structure and contents of human values? *Journal of Social Issues* 4:19–45.

Senge, Peter M. 1990. *The fifth discipline.* New York: Currency Doubleday.

Sergiovanni, Thomas J. 1992. *Moral leadership: Getting to the heart of school improvement.* San Francisco: Jossey-Bass.

Shah, Saeeda. 2009. Women and educational leadership in a Muslim society: A study of women college heads in Pakistan. In *Women leading education across the continents,* ed. Helen C. Sobehart, 128–42. Lanham, MD: Rowman & Littlefield Education.

Shakeshaft, Charol. 1987. *Women in educational administration.* Newbury Park: Sage.

———. 1999. The struggle to create a more gender-inclusive profession. In *Handbook of research on educational administration,* ed. Joseph Murphy and Karen S. Louis, 99–118. San Francisco: Jossey-Bass.

Shamir, Boas, and Galit Eilam. 2005. What's your story?: A life-stories approach to authentic leadership development. *Leadership Quarterly* 16 (1): 395–417.

Sheehy, Gail. 1995. *New passages: Mapping your life across time.* New York: Random House.

Shields, Carolyn M. 2004. Good intentions are not enough: Leadership for social justice and academic excellence. *New Zealand Journal of Educational Leadership* 19:7–20.

———. 2009a. Leading justly in a complex world. In *Bridge leadership: Connecting educational leadership and social justice to improve schools,* ed. Autumn K. Tooms and Christa Boske, 125–48. Charlotte, NC: Information Age.

——. 2009b. Transformative leadership: A call for difficult dialogue and courageous action in racialised contexts. *International Studies in Educational Administration* 37 (3) (October): 53–68.

Shoho, Alan, Betty Merchant, and Catherine Lugg. 2005. Social justice: Seeking a common language. In *The Sage handbook of educational leadership*, ed. Fenwick English, 47–67. Thousand Oaks, CA: Sage.

Skrla, Linda, Kathryn B. McKenzie, and James J. Scheurich. 2007. Concluding reflections on "Leadership for learning in the context of social justice: An international perspective." *Journal of Educational Administration* 45 (6): 782–87.

Smith, Joan K. 1979. *Ella Flagg Young: Portrait of a leader.* Ames: Educational Studies Press and the Iowa University Research Foundation.

Sobehart, Helen C., ed. 2009. *Women leading education across the continents.* Lanham, MD: Rowman & Littlefield Education.

Sosik, John. 2005. The role of personal values in the charismatic leadership of corporate managers: A model and preliminary field study. *Leadership Quarterly* 16 (2): 221–44.

Sperandio, Jill. 2010. Modeling cultural context for aspiring women educational leaders. *Journal of Educational Administration* 48 (6): 716–26. doi:10.1108/09578231011079575.

Still, Leonie. 2006. Gender, leadership and communication. In *Gender and communication at work*, ed. Mary Barrett and Marilyn Davidson. Aldershot: Ashgate.

Strachan, Jane. 1993. The man in the literature. *Delta* 47:18–21.

——. 1998. Feminist leadership: Leading for social justice. *Waikato Journal of Education* 4:27–44.

——. 1999. Feminist educational leadership: Locating the concepts in practice. *Gender and Education* 11 (3): 309–22.

——. 2005. Working out of my comfort zone: Experiences of developing national women's policy in Vanuatu. *Delta* 57 (1–2): 47–66.

Strachan, Jane, Shalom Akao, Bessie Kilavanwa, and Daisy Warsal. 2010. You have to be a servant of all: Melanesian women's educational leadership experiences. *School Leadership and Management* 30 (1): 65–76.

Strachan, Jane, Rachel Saunders, Liku Jimmy, and Grayleen Lapi. 2007. Ni Vanuatu women and educational leadership development. *New Zealand Journal of Educational Leadership* 22 (2): 37–48.

Taylor, Jill, Carol Gilligan, and Amy Sullivan. 1995. *Between voice and silence: Women and girls, race and relationship.* Cambridge, MA: Harvard University Press.

Terry, Robert W. 1993. *Authentic leadership: Courage in action.* San Francisco: Jossey-Bass.

Theoharis, George. 2007. Social justice educational leaders and resistance: Toward a theory of social justice leadership. *Educational Administration Quarterly* 43 (2): 221–58.

——. 2008. Woven in deeply: Identity and leadership of urban social justice principals. *Education and Urban Society* 41 (3): 3–25.

Tripp, Aili Mari. 2001. The politics of autonomy and cooptation in Africa: The case of the Ugandan women's movement. *Journal of Modern African Studies* 39 (1): 101–28.

Trowbridge, Richard. 2005. The scientific approach of wisdom. PhD diss., Union Institute and University.

Unterhalter, Elaine. 1998. Economic rationality or social justice? Gender, the national qualifications framework and educational reform in South Africa. *Cambridge Journal of Education* 28 (3) (November): 351.

——. 2008. Cosmopolitanism, global social justice and gender equality in education. *Compare* 38 (5): 539–53.

Vaillant, George E. 2002. *Aging well.* Boston: Little, Brown.

Van Hoose, Sandra. 2008. Twisted paths and spiritual geography: Of places, passages, and pilgrimage. Lecture, University of Saint Mary Delta Epsilon Sigma, Leavenworth, KS, March 13, 2008.

Walker, Alice, and Anne Simpkinson. 1990. A self of one's own. *Common Boundary,* March–April, 14–20. Quoted in Jean Shinoda Bolen, *Crossing to Avalon: A woman's midlife pilgrimage* (San Francisco: HarperCollins, 1994), vii.

Walumbwa, Fred, Bruce Avolio, William Gardner, Tara Wernsing, and Suzanne Peterson. 2008. Authentic development and validation of a theory-based measure. *Journal of Management* 34 (1): 89–126.

Welty, Eudora. 1998. *One writer's beginnings.* Cambridge, MA: Harvard University Press.

Wenniger, Mary Dee. 2010. Why have the women presidents gone? *Women in Higher Education* 19 (2) (February): 28.

Whyte, David. 2001. *Crossing the unknown sea: Work as a pilgrimage of identity.* New York: Riverhead.

Williams, Elizabeth, Elvie Soeprapto, Kathy Like, Pegah Touradi, Shirley Hess, and Clara Hill. 1998. Perceptions of serendipity: Career paths of prominent academic women in counseling psychology. *Journal of Counseling Psychology* 45 (4): 379–89.

Williamson, Ronald, and Barbara Blackburn. 2010. Dealing with resistance to change. *Principal Leadership* 10 (7): 73–75.

Wilson, Marie. 2004. *Closing the leadership gap: Why women can and must help rule the world.* New York: Viking.

Witherell, Carol, and Nel Noddings. 1991. *Stories lives tell: Narrative and dialogue in education.* New York: Teachers College Press.

Xin, Zhou, and Liang Hongyi. 2000. Initial analysis of the factors enabling women teachers in higher education to become talented. *Chinese Education & Society* 33 (4): 47–52.

Young, Michelle D. 2003. Considering (irreconcilable?) contradictions in cross-group feminist research. In *Reconsidering feminist research in educational leadership,* ed. Michelle D. Young and Linda Skrla, 35–79. Albany: State University of New York Press.

Zagzebski, Linda. 1996. *Virtues of the mind: An inquiry into the nature of virtue and the ethical foundations of knowledge.* Cambridge: Cambridge University Press.

Zembylas, Michalinos. 2010. The emotional aspects of leadership for social justice: Implications for leadership preparation programs. *Journal of Educational Administration* 48 (5): 611–25. doi:10.1108/09578231011067767.

INDEX

ABOUT THE AUTHORS

Linda L. Lyman is a professor in the Department of Educational Administration and Foundations at Illinois State University. She has a BA in English from Northwestern University, an MAT from Harvard University, and a PhD in administration, curriculum, and instruction from the University of Nebraska, Lincoln. In 2005 she spent six months in Greece as a Fulbright Scholar, where she taught about women's leadership in American culture at Aristotle University in Thessaloniki. Her scholarship and publications, including three previous books, focus on educational leadership with an emphasis on issues of gender, caring, poverty, women, and social justice.

Jane Strachan recently retired from her position as an associate professor at the University of Waikato in Hamilton, New Zealand. Her teaching and research interests focused on educational leadership, social justice, gender, women, policy development, and Pacific education. For ten years she lived and worked in Vanuatu and the Solomon Islands, assisting the government with education and women's human rights policy development, teacher education, and research. She has published widely on these subjects.

Angeliki Lazadirou is a lecturer (on tenure track) at the University of Thessaly, Greece. She has a BEd and an after-degree diploma in special education–early intervention from the University of Athens, and an MEd in early childhood/special education and PhD in educational administration and leadership, both from the University of Alberta, Canada. Her teaching and research interests focus on school administration and leadership, particularly on issues of effectiveness, ethics and values, gender, women, and learning communities.

CPSIA information can be obtained at www.ICGtesting.com
Printed in the USA
BVOW022241210512

290767BV00003B/1/P